# Caribbean REEF LIFE
## of The Bay Islands, Honduras

All material © Mickey Charteris, 2012

## REFERENCES & SUGGESTED READINGS:

Alevizon, W.S. *Caribbean Reef Ecology*. Gulf Publishing Company, Houston (1994)
Humann, P., DeLoach, N. *Reef Coral Identification*. New World Publications, Jacksonville, Florida (2004)
Humann, P., DeLoach, N. *Reef Creature Identification*. New World Publications, Jacksonville, Florida (2004)
Humann, P., DeLoach, N. *Reef Fish Identification*. New World Publications, Jacksonville, Florida (2004)
Kaplan, E.H. *A Field Guide to Coral Reefs: Caribbean and Florida*. Houghton Mifflin Harcourt, Boston, MA (1999)
Littler, D.S., Littler, M.M. *Caribbean Reef Plants*. Offshore Graphics, Nittany, Florida (2000)
Rohwer, F. *Coral Reefs in the Microbial Seas*. Plaid Press, Basalt, Colorado (2010)
Snyderman, M., Wiseman, C. *Guide to Marine Life: Caribbean-Bahamas-Florida*. Aqua Quest Publications, Locust Valley, NY. (1996)
Sefton, N., Webster, S.K. *Caribbean Reef Invertebrates*. Sea Challengers, Monterrey, California (1986)
Valdez, A., Hamman, J., Behrens, D.W., DuPont, A. *Caribbean Sea Slugs*. Sea Challengers Natural History Books, Washington, DC (2006)

## USEFUL ONLINE RESOURCES:

www.algaebase.org : A comprehensive resource for marine plant identification.
www.coris.noaa.gov : NOAA's coral reef information system.
www.discoverlife.org : A broad-range species identification web site.
www.fishbase.org : The most comprehensive, worldwide fish identification resource.
www.jaxshells.org : A great resource for shellfish identification.
www.nudipixel.net : A searchable database of nudibranchs and flatworms.
www.reefguide.org : Florent's Guide to the Florida, Bahamas and Caribbean Reefs.
www.species-identification.org : A broad-range marine species identification web site.
www.spongeguide.com : A definitive and searchable sponge identification resource.
www.stri.si.edu : The Smithsonian Tropical Research Institute web site.
www.theissresearch.org : An organization of independent scientists and taxonomists.
www.worldwideconchology.com : A useful reference for mollusc identification.

## SCIENTIFIC ACKNOWLEDGMENTS:

I would like to thank the following scientists and experts in marine taxonomy for their time and patience in looking over some of my photographs:
**Dr Marymegan Daly**, University of Kansas. **Dr Sammy DeGrave**, Oxford Museum of Natural History. **Dr Gordon Hendler**, Natural History Museum of Los Angeles. **Mr Paul Kersten**, Netherlands. **Dr Harry Lee**, Jacksonville, Florida. **Dr Steven E McMurray**, University of North Carolina Wilmington. **Dr Ross Robertson**, Smithsonian Tropical Research Institute, Panamá. **Dr Nadya Sanamyan**, Pacific Institute of Geography, Kamchatka, Russia. **Dr James C Tyler**, Smithsonian Museum of Natural History. **Dr Michael Vecchione**, Smithsonian Museum of Natural History. **Dr Benjamin Victor**, Ocean Science Foundation. **Dr Mary Wicksten**, Texas A&M University. **Dr Sven Zea**, University of Colombia.
Special thanks go to Elizabeth Walters and Miriam Ree Hanson for all their hard work in editing and proof-reading the first edition.

PLEASE NOTE THAT ALL ERRORS IN IDENTIFICATION AND SPECIES DESCRIPTIONS ARE THE AUTHOR'S OWN.

## ABOUT THIS BOOK:

For each species in this book, I have included both the accepted common name, and the scientific name in Latin. Most taxonomists and scientists shun the use of common names, but I believe it makes the reef more accessible to the average diver, for whom this book is written. Some species had no generally accepted common name, and I have taken the liberty of assigning one. Where the exact species could not be described from photographs, only the family name or the accepted genus is given.

## NOTES ON SPECIES IDENTIFICATION:

Species identification can be very difficult, if not impossible, from photographs. Marine taxonomy is still evolving, with new discoveries and reclassifications being published every month. While many common reef species will be genetically similar throughout the Caribbean, regional differences can abound for many others. Taxonomists were often surprised to find certain species had been seen in the Bay Islands, and the true range of these species is now being investigated. The author was fortunate enough to discover a few new species while compiling the book.

The Swimming Crinoid Shrimp (p. 177) pictured below was found to be new to science, and has been officially named. The new blennies are localized genetic variations of known species, confirmed using DNA analysis. Until they are officially named in the scientific literature, their Latin names will be followed by the abbreviation "*sp.*"

*Periclimenes rincewindi*

*Emblemaria vitta sp.*

*Starksia nanodes sp.*

The new trend of using DNA to describe species is now leading to some interesting, if confusing, results. The Banded Pipefish (p. 239) and the Harlequin Pipefish (p. 241) are now the same species, despite their difference in appearance. The Punk Blenny is now known to be the true Secretary Blenny (p. 214), while the macro favorite we have always called the Secretary Blenny is now known to be a variety of the Spinyhead Blenny (p. 215). This 2nd edition has attempted to keep up with these new changes.

It's heartening to realize that we have not yet learned all there is to know about the creatures that we see on every dive. It is also saddening, however, as coral reefs in the Caribbean are dying off from pollution and human development. We may never get to understand everything we see underwater; animals that have spent millennia evolving to live in threatened habitats, in places that we have only recently begun to visit.

## PHOTO CREDITS:

All photographs in this book were taken by Mickey Charteris, except: Balloonfish inflated: Ken Wallace, Conch harvest: Chris Benson, Lagoon: Brandon Rundquist, Manta Ray: Irma Korb, The Thing: Alex Harper- Brown, Whale Shark mouth: Caroline Power, Hammerhead: Martin Cabrera Deheza.

All the photos in this book were taken on the reefs surrounding Roatan, except for the Yellow Stingray (p. 321) and Colin's Cleaning Goby (p. 201), which were taken off Cayos Cochinos. All photographs were taken using Canon G-series cameras, in standard Canon underwater housings.

🤿 The full story of a Caribbean reef actually begins on land, with an amazingly adaptable group of trees known as mangroves. They live half in the ocean and half on land, with a root system that keeps them alive in this harsh, salty environment. Each type of mangrove is modified to deal with salt in different ways. Black Mangroves have tiny tubes extending up from the water to take in oxygen, similar to a snorkel. White Mangroves can literally drink up the seawater, with the excess salt being excreted from tiny glands under the leaves. In this way, 99 percent of the salt is removed.

Mangroves are essential to Caribbean coasts because these naturally flexible trees break up the storm surge that would otherwise hit the coasts. More importantly, they also protect the reef from the land. The roots act as natural sediment traps, keeping the silt and run-off from settling on delicate corals.

Traditionally, the slow-growing mangroves have been cut for charcoal, but today it is for tourism. Countless acres of this important habitat are now being cut down to make way for holiday homes and resorts. By cutting down the mangroves trees we are seriously limiting the diversity on coral reefs just beyond the shore. A mangrove forest is like a nursery for the reef; the trees are an essential part of the life cycle of many fishes. For some species there can be up to 25 times more fish in areas next to mangrove forests. A good example is the huge Rainbow Parrotfish (p. 278). Studies show that where deforestation of mangroves has taken place, the population of this fish can die out completely.

# MANGROVES : MARINE PLANTS

### RED MANGROVES
*(Rhizophora mangle)*
Long prop roots, with reddish bark, growing into the water. Small, blunt leaves with a shiny green color.

### WHITE MANGROVES
*(Laguncularia racemosa)*
Grows furthest from the water's edge. Pale bark and lighter green leaves that are rounded at both ends.

### BLACK MANGROVES
*(Avicennia germinans)*
Largest of the mangroves trees. Darker bark on the trunks. Short roots grow up around the tree.

### BUTTONWOOD
*(Conocarpus erectus)*
Shorter, bushier mangrove with dark brown or black bark. Long leaves and collections of reddish berries.

The brackish waters of the mangrove forest are essential feeding and nursing grounds for many species: not only fish, but also lobsters, crabs, urchins, sea turtles and more. By keeping silty, nutrient rich waters close to shore, mangroves make sure the waters around coral reefs are clear. This allows the most important element for coral growth to get through to the reef: sunlight. Coral reefs and the mangroves are two environments that exist side by side, each dependent on the other.

 Beds of Turtle Grass play an important role in a coral reef's complex ecosystem. They form the primary food source for many animals, even larger ones like the Green Sea Turtle (p. 325) and the Manatee (p. 327). Like most plants, Turtle Grass relies on sunlight for photosynthesis, absorbing carbon dioxide and producing oxygen.
Lagoons are like the lungs of a reef ecosystem. On a hot day swimmers can even see tiny streams of bubbles coming up from the grasses. In this way the water near a coral reef is kept well oxygenated. Despite being underwater, Turtle Grass is actually a flowering plant. Tiny, pale flowers can be seen near the base of the plant in the spring.

In many areas of the Caribbean, the green expanse of the lagoon occupies a far greater area than the reef itself. It is an important spawning area and nursery. Many juveniles make their home in the safety of the lagoon before moving out into deeper water. Often overlooked on the way out to a dive site, beds of seagrass can hold some of the greatest finds, from turtles and rays to dolphins.

# LAGOONS : MARINE PLANTS

### TURTLE GRASS
*(Thalassia testudinum)*
2 ft max. Flat green leaves, about 0.5 in wide, with
rounded tips. Often covered in sediment and algae.

The extensive root system of a seagrass bed holds the sand in place and allows sediments and nutrients to be stored at the base of the reef system. In the relatively nutrient-poor waters of a coral reef, this reserve of shelter and nutrients is essential to all Caribbean reef life.

### MIDRIB SEAGRASS
*(Halophila baillonis)*
2 in max. Flat, green leaves with smooth edges
and an elongated, oval shape. Grows on runners.

### MANATEE GRASS
*(Syringodium filiforme)*
18 in max. Thin, green, tubular leaves growing
in clumps, often among rubble and Turtle Grass.

## FUZZY CAULERPA
*(Caulerpa verticillata)*
10 in max. Grows on long runners with delicate
spiral patterns of light green with pale centers.

Marine plants are some of the most important organisms on Earth. Firstly, there are the algae that we can't even see: the tiny, free-floating phytoplankton. They produce 70 to 80 percent of all the oxygen we breathe. Then there are the tiny algae that live inside the flesh of the corals themselves, the zooxanthellae. These use sunlight to photosynthesize food for the corals, and without them the reef could not grow. Finally, there are the large plants that a diver can actually see: the macroalgae. These are essential for a reef ecosystem; just like on land, they form the base of the food chain. They absorb nutrients from the water and store them in their tissues, making them available to all the higher life forms on a reef, from crabs and lobsters to the fishes themselves.

The balance between the plants and the corals on any given reef is a delicate one that has taken countless generations to perfect. Schools of herbivores, like the parrotfish and the Blue Tang, keep the algae levels in check by constantly traveling and grazing on the plants. Without this steady pruning the algae would soon overgrow the coral and no sunlight would get to the polyps, starving them of food. Smaller fishes eat the algae, get eaten by larger fishes, and so on; herbivores greatly outnumber carnivores on a reef. At the base of all this activity is a tiny plant cell, silently working in the sunlight to feed both itself and the reef.

# GREEN ALGAE : MARINE PLANTS

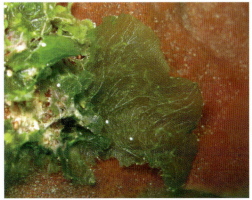

### PAPYRUS PRINT ALGA
*(Anadyomene stellata)*
4 in max. Very thin, green, rounded blades with distinctive lighter veins running towards the edges.

### FRAGILE FEATHER ALGA
*(Bryopsis pennata)*
0.75 in max. Small clusters of feather-shaped leaves, growing outwards. Light green with white stalks.

### SHINY SEA GRASS
*(Gracilaria tikvahiae)*
8 in max. Dense clusters of thin, shiny filaments of dark green, growing outwards from the center.

### FLESHY TWIG ALGA
*(Codium repens)*
1 in max. Fleshy, branching, dark green leaf-shapes growing in a thick tangle. Two-lobed branchlets.

### GREEN NET ALGA
*(Microdictyon boergesenii)*
A fine network of thin tubular threads that can cover many square feet of reef. Pale to dark green.

### FLAT GREEN FEATHER ALGA
*(Caulerpa mexicana)*
8 in max. Flat, dark green, feather-shaped leaves growing upwards from thin runners on the sand.

### ELONGATED SEA PEARLS
*(Valonia macrophysa)*
0.75 in max. A spreading mat of pale green, rounded or oval bubbles. They have a distinctive silvery sheen.

Each Sea Pearl is actually a single plant cell, one of the largest single cells on Earth. It is filled with water and attached to the reef by tiny, hair-like filaments. They can often be seen rolling around after a storm. It is sometimes covered with a thin layer of Lavender Crust Alga (p. 23).

### CREEPING BUBBLE ALGA
*(Valonia utricularis)*
1 in max. Clumps of dark green, rounded or oval bubble shapes, growing outwards from runners.

### SEA PEARL
*(Ventricaria ventricosa)*
2 in max. Large, dark green bubbles with a silvery sheen. Solitary or in small groupings.

# GREEN ALGAE : MARINE PLANTS

### MERMAID'S FAN
*(Udotea sp.)*
8 in max. Broad, fan-shaped blades on a single stalk, with distinctive radial lines from stalk to blade ends.

### SAUCER BLADE ALGA
*(Avrainvillea asarifolia)*
6 in max. Broad, fan-shaped blades with smooth surfaces. Bottom turns upward to attach to the stalk.

### PADDLE BLADE ALGA
*(Avrainvillea longicaulis)*
4 in max. Paddle-shaped blade on a short stalk. Smooth sides. Narrower than other Blade Algae.

### RUFFLED BLADE ALGA
*(Udotea flabellum)*
6 in max. Narrow fan shape from a single stalk. Thick-bodied, dark green with pale edges on the blade.

### GREEN BUBBLE WEED
*(Dictyosphaeria cavernosa)*
8 in max. Light green, bulbous shapes with small, rounded cells giving it a cobbled texture.

### DEAD MAN'S FINGERS
*(Codium isthmocladum)*
8 in max. A bushy growth of rounded branches, covered in fine green hairs. Usually found in the shallows.

**GREEN MERMAID'S WINEGLASS**
*(Acetabularia calyculus)*
1.5 in max. Dark green cup shape on long, slender stalk.
Rounded ridges radiate from the center.

The stem and cup of each of these tiny plants is calcified like the Halimeda species and, in their small way, they add material each year to the sand patches and beaches of the Caribbean. Amazingly, each of the small cups is formed by one single plant cell.

**WHITE MERMAID'S WINEGLASS**
*(Acetabularia crenulata)*
1.5 in max. Round, white cup shape on a long,
white stalk. Rounded ridges radiate from the center.

**PALE MERMAID'S WINEGLASS**
*(Acetabularia schenckii)*
1.5 in max. Pale green cup, often with hints of white.
The cup is deeper, often growing in clusters.

# GREEN ALGAE : MARINE PLANTS

### LEAFY ROLLED BLADE ALGA
*(Padina boergesenii)*
6 in max. Large clumps of leafy blades with rounded edges. Banded in shades of brown, green or blue.

### FUZZY TIP ALGA
*(Neomeris annulata)*
1.5 in max. Short, cylindrical stalks growing from the reef, singly or in small groups. The tips are fuzzy.

### SAWBLADE ALGA
*(Caulerpa serrulata)*
2 in leaves max. Narrow, green leaves with serrated edges, growing in dense clumps from green runners.

### SERRATED ALGA
*(Caulerpa webbiana)*
1 in leaves max. Dense, bright green clumps of short stalks with lateral branches forming serrated edges.

### GREEN FEATHER ALGA
*(Caulerpa sertularioides)*
8 in max. Tall, erect, feather-shaped leaves of light green, growing from runners along the sea bed.

### GREEN GRAPE ALGA
*(Caulerpa racemosa)*
4 in max. Clumps of tiny, green ball shapes, growing from pointed runners like clusters of grapes.

## LARGE LEAF HANGING VINE
*(Halimeda copiosa)*
2 ft max. Long chains of green, rectangular segments,
joined down the middle by a single stalk.

> Algae in the Halimeda family are some of the most common on the reef. They will absorb calcium carbonate from the water and use it to make a skeleton, or framework, around which the algae can grow. Eventually this material will go back into the reef ecosystem as sand.

## SMALL LEAF HANGING VINE
*(Halimeda goreaui)*
1 ft max. Short chains of smaller, rectangular
segments joined down the middle by a single stalk.

## CRYPTIC ALGA
*(Halimeda cryptica)*
10 in max. Bushy clumps of thin, fan-shaped
leaves with distinctly pointed, three-lobed blades.

# GREEN ALGAE : MARINE PLANTS

### STALKED LETTUCE LEAF ALGA
*(Halimeda tuna)*
10 in max. Rounded, thin, fan-shaped blades, growing outward in a single plane. Green to yellowish.

### THREE LOBED ALGA
*(Halimeda optunia triloba)*
10 in max. Widely-separated, flattened, dark green, spade-shaped leaves growing on a common stalk.

### JOINTED STALK ALGA
*(Halimeda monile)*
6 in max. Tall bunches of segmented stalks growing upwards from a common base. Found in the shallows.

### THREE FINGER LEAF ALGA
*(Halimeda incrassata)*
10 in max. Chains of thin, dark green, distinctively three-lobed, leaf-like segments growing upwards.

### CACTUS TREE ALGA
*(Caulerpa cupressoides)*
10 in max. Short, bushy shape of upright branches from a single stalk, with small, irregular branchlets.

### GREEN HELMET ALGA
*(Caulerpa nummularia)*
0.75 in max. Small clusters of thin stalks growing upward from the reef, with swollen, rounded tips.

## WATERCRESS ALGA
*(Halimeda opuntia)*
8 in max. Dense clumps of rounded, three-lobed leaf shapes. Dark green to yellowish green.

> Just like plants on land, marine plants need lots of sunlight in order to grow. Algae will often branch out and grow in dense clusters of stalks, spreading out to expose the most surface area as possible to the sunlight. Underwater, this can lead to some unique plant shapes.

## MERMAID'S TEACUP
*(Udotea cyathiformis)*
6 in max. Thin, ragged-edged cup of light green. It attaches to the reef by a thin stalk. Often in groups.

## RAGGED MERMAID'S TEACUP
*(Udotea sp.)*
4 in max. Concentric arrangement of ragged cup-shaped leaves, growing upwards from a thin stalk.

# GREEN ALGAE : MARINE PLANTS

### NEPTUNE'S SHAVING BRUSH
*(Penicillus capitatus)*
6 in max. Tufts of green, bristle-like branches from a common stalk. White skeletal material on the surface.

### PINECONE ALGA
*(Rhipocephalus phoenix)*
6 in max. Thin, plate-like leaves grow upwards in a concentric or spiral pattern. Pointed at the tip.

### ELONGATE PINECONE ALGA
*(Rhipocephalus brevifolius)*
5 in max. Short, dense leaves grow from a central stalk. The general shape is thinner and more elongated.

### RAGGED PINECONE ALGA
*(Rhipocephalus longifolius)*
5 in max. Leaves grow upwards from central stalk. Leaves are not as dense and end in a blunt tip.

### BRISTLE BALL BRUSH
*(Penicillus dumetosus)*
6 in max. A rounded ball of tightly packed filaments on top of a thin, green stalk. Usually a darker green.

### FLAT TOPPED BRISTLE BRUSH
*(Penicillus pyriformis)*
5 in max. Inverted cone shape on a long stalk. Tightly packed filaments that end in a flat top.

## SMOOTH STRAP ALGA
*(Dictyota dichotoma)*
8 in max. Bushy clumps of branching leaves in a tangled mass. Light brown to green.

Some of the fastest-growing algae, and the most harmful to the reef, are the Brown Algae. In areas where there is too much coastal development, the levels of nutrients and nitrates in the water from human run-off are unnaturally high. Algae thrives under these conditions and will soon smother the lagoons and shallow reefs, blocking sunlight from getting to the corals. Algae blooms are a common part of the life cycle of a reef, usually in the late summer when there are longer days and warmer waters. Corals can recover. But given too much opportunity, algae will quickly upset the balance of a healthy reef.

Some Brown Algae will have small, gas-filled sacs attached to their stalks. This allows the plants to float up toward the surface to get at more sunlight. Others, like the Sargassum Alga, will be detached from the reef completely and can be found floating on the surface, often in huge tangled mats. As they get blown across the reef, usually in winter, they can add to the diversity of a reef because of the countless juvenile fishes and crustaceans that have hitched a lift.

# BROWN ALGAE : MARINE PLANTS

### SARGASSUM SEAWEED
*(Sargassum fluitans)*
1.5 ft max. Dense floats of individual plants with tiny gas-filled sacs. It can cover large areas of the surface.

### SARGASSUM ALGA
*(Sargassum sp.)*
5 ft max. A collective name for several species of plants with tiny, gas-filled sacs keeping them upright.

### WESTERN TUBULAR ALGA
*(Cladosiphon occidentalis)*
4 in max. Dense clusters of long, tube-shaped stalks with hairy filaments. Slimy to the touch.

### WHITE VEINED SARGASSUM
*(Sargassum hystrix)*
16 in max. Elongated, oval leaves with a whitish central vein. Olive to light brown. Grows in clusters.

### NOTCHED BLADE ALGA
*(Dictyota crenulata)*
1.5 in max. Pale brown, twin-lobed blades growing in small clusters. Tips of blades are edged in light brown.

### BRANCHING WHITE ALGA
*(Danonema farinosum)*
3 in max. Tangles of white to light brown, highly branched stalks. Slimy to the touch.

### YELLOW BLADE ALGA
*(Dictyota bartayresiana)*
1 in max. Small, yellow, twin-lobed blades edged in green.
Distinct wavy patterns on the leaves.

Brown Algae have many commercial uses for humans. Elements from these plants are used in many products we use every day, from toothpaste to ice cream. Chemicals isolated from these fast-growing plants have also been important in the development of many new medicinal drugs.

### ENCRUSTING FAN LEAF ALGA
*(Lobophora variegata)*
6 in max. Thin, fan-shaped blades in shades of green to light brown, often overlapping.

### LEAFY FLAT BLADE ALGA
*(Stypopodium zonale)*
6 in max. Fan-shaped blades in shades of green to brown with pale green bands.

# BROWN ALGAE : MARINE PLANTS

### MUCOSA WHITE ALGA
*(Mucosa sp.)*
12 in max. Tangles of thin, slimy, white branchlets.
Often covers a large area of the shallows.

### SAUCER LEAF ALGA
*(Turbinaria tricostata)*
16 in max. Clumps of triangular, cone-shaped
structures on a short central stalk. Light brown to tan.

### SPROUTING BLADE ALGA
*(Dictyota humifusa)*
2 in max. Flat, deep purple to blue blades, often with
a network pattern of holes in the middle of the blade.

### FLOWER BLADE ALGA
*(Dictyota menstrualis)*
1 in max. Dense clusters of dark brown, twin-lobed
blades edged in yellow with yellow speckles.

### WHITE SCROLL ALGA
*(Padina pavonica)*
6 in max. Rounded, spiralling, leafy blades growing
in dense clumps. Concentrically banded in white.

### BLUE BANDED ALGA
*(Taonia sp.)*
4 in max. A rounded, flat-leaf alga with pale
filamentous edges. Banded in bright green or blue.

## CRUSTOSE CORALLINE ALGA
*(Peyssonnelia sp.)*
18 in max. A collective name for all encrusting, rounded plates of red algae. Outer edges often overlap.

Red Algae is often overlooked in a reef ecosystem, but without it a reef would crumble apart with the first storm. If stony corals are the building blocks of the reef, then red algae is the cement that binds it all together. It grows with little sunlight and, as such, can get down into the crevices below the coral heads. It spreads between the corals and binds them together, as can be seen in the cross section of the fragile Yellow Pencil Coral (p. 59) on the right. In the shallows, Reef Cement (p. 23) binds together acres of storm-vulnerable reef top. It is fed upon by parrotfish, sea urchins and other reef inhabitants.

The red color in these algae comes from additional protein pigments in the plant, and it allows them to grow at greater depths than green or brown algae. It also allows them to grow in caves and recesses where there is little light, even in the daytime. They can completely cover the walls of caves and canyons on the reef. The coralline (or coral-like) algae absorbs calcium carbonate directly from the seawater, using it to make rigid and inflexible skeletons.

# RED ALGAE : MARINE PLANTS

### MATTE RED CRUST ALGA
*(Peyssonnelia inamoena)*
3 ft colony max. Mottled red and orange encrusting alga, forming a rough fan-shape.

### BURGUNDY CRUST ALGA
*(Peyssonnelia sp.)*
3 ft colony max. Deep red encrusting alga. Outer edges may not touch the substrate, often overlapping.

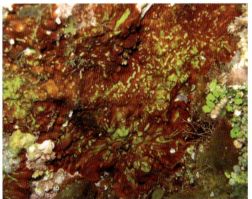

### RED-ORANGE CRUST ALGA
*(Peyssonnelia boergesenii)*
18 in max. Orange to orange-red encrusting alga with faint, concentric bands of broken lines.

### MOTTLED CRUST ALGA
*(Peyssonnelia stoechas)*
18 in max. The base color is more orange, with red spots in a concentric pattern. On shallower reefs.

### LAVENDER CRUST ALGA
*(Titanoderma sp.)*
2 in max. A thin layer of encrusting red alga growing on other algae species such as Sea Pearls (p. 10).

### REEF CEMENT
*(Porolithon pachydermum)*
A pale pink to gray crust of thin alga that takes on the shape of the underlying reef, holding it in place.

**FRAGILE BRANCHING ALGA**
*(Tricleocarpa fragilis)*
1 ft max. Long, fleshy, branching stalks in pale to dark pink. The colony narrows towards the stem.

The compounds found in red algae have been used for thousands of years to make medicines for boosting the immune system. They are rich in minerals taken directly from the seawater. Red Algae contains twenty times the amount of minerals that can be found in similar, land-based algae.

**MUCOSA PINK ALGA**
*(Liagora dendroidea)*
10 in max. Tangled mats of very fine, branching stalks. Shades of pink and gray. Can cover a large area.

**GOLDEN FUZZBALL ALGA**
*(Meristiella schrammii)*
6 in max. Deep yellow clusters of finely divided branchlets from a common stem. Found in shallows.

# RED ALGAE : MARINE PLANTS

### BULBOUS ALGA
*(Predea feldmanni)*
3 in max. Small clumps of bulbous, smooth-walled, red alga with slightly lobed, pale pink endings.

### PINK TANGLED ALGA
*(Gracilaria blodgettii)*
8 in max. Dense clusters of long, tapering, rounded branches. Color varies from gray to pinkish.

### CRYPTIC BLADE ALGA
*(Cryptonemia crenulata)*
4 in max. Elongated, deep red leaves growing in clusters. The edges are rough and crenulated.

### PEACOCK ALGA
*(Martensia pavonia)*
2 in max. Flattened blades of red to pink alga with a distinctive network of holes and frills on the outside.

### STRIVING RED ALGA
*(Ceramium nitens)*
2 ft max. Dense tangles of fine, hair-like branches. Uniform reddish-orange in color.

### RED FILAMENT ALGA
*(Wurdemannia miniata)*
12 in max. Tangled mass of deep red, very fine, hair-like filaments with repeated branchings.

### TUBULAR THICKET ALGA
*(Galaxaura rugosa)*
1 in max. A squat, rugged, branching alga found in the shallows. Covered in fine, fuzzy filaments.

> 🥽 Red Algae gets its color from different pigments than their green or brown cousins. The most important is called phycoerythrin. This pigment absorbs blue light and reflects the red light back out. This allows red algae to thrive on deeper reefs and inside caves.

### MAROON HAIR ALGA
*(Pterocladiella capillacea)*
4 in max. Rounded, deep red stalks with numerous tapering branches. Grows from runners on the bottom.

### ENCRUSTING FUZZ ALGA
*(Spermothamnion gymnocarpum)*
2 ft colony max. Thin, reddish-brown mats of fine, hair-like filaments, overgrowing the substrate.

# RED ALGAE : MARINE PLANTS

### FUZZY THICKET ALGA
*(Galaxaura subverticillata)*
1 in max. Small tufts of short, branching tubes that split at the ends. Often found on live sponges and corals.

### PINK BUSH ALGA
*(Wrangelia penicillata)*
8 in max. Tall, bushy, pink plant with pale branches and light pink branchlets, alternating on either side.

### PURPLE BUSH ALGA
*(Ochtodes secundiramea)*
4 in max. Dense clusters of deep purple, slightly flattened branches, tapering at the tips. Fleshy texture.

### FUZZY BUSH ALGA
*(Aglaothamnion herveyi)*
6 in max. Clumps of fine, brownish stalks with numerous hair-like filaments, denser toward the base.

### PINK FUZZ ALGA
*(Dudresnaya crassa)*
3 in max. Small clumps of long, fine, hair-like filaments. Red to purple with white speckling.

### FUZZ BALL ALGA
*(Symploca sp.)*
6 in max. A very dense ball of fine, hair-like filaments. Can roll about on the reef. Dark red to burgundy.

### FLAT TWIG ALGA
*(Amphiroa tribulus)*
4 in max. Randomly branched, segmented alga with flattened segments. Pink to reddish with white tips.

> 🥽 Some Red Algae are soft and slimy, waving in the currents and rough waters as they grow. Others have a skeleton of calcium carbonate, absorbed directly from the seawater. It is stored in the plant's cell walls, giving strength to the structure as it branches out and grows.

### PINK SEGMENTED ALGA
*(Jania adherens)*
2 in max. Small tangled clumps of very fine, branching stalks. Shades of pink, with white joints.

### HANCOCK'S TWIG ALGA
*(Amphiroa hancockii)*
4 in max. A more flattened variety of Twig Alga, often in lavender to gray. Thick joints between the segments.

# RED ALGAE : MARINE PLANTS

### TUBULAR PINK ALGA
*(Solieria filiformis)*
10 in max. Rounded, semi-transparent tubes of pale red branches, growing in tangled clumps.

### BRAZILIAN TWIG ALGA
*(Amphiroa brasiliana)*
6 in max. Tangled clusters of thin, tan to gold branches that divide near the tips. Found in shallow water.

### Y TWIG ALGA
*(Amphiroa rigida)*
2 in max. Thin, branched, pink, segmented alga. Pale pink to white in color. Grows in dense clumps.

### DELICATE TWIG ALGA
*(Amphiroa fragilissima)*
2 in max. Dense clusters of extremely fine, pale pink to white stalks with branched ends, tipped in white.

### PINK BRANCHLET ALGA
*(Haliptilon cubense)*
5 in max. Dense clusters of long, pink stalks with numerous, short, pink branchlets tipped in white.

### WHITE TUBULAR THICKET ALGA
*(Galaxaura sp.)*
6 in max. Cylindrical, hollow-looking, branching, pink alga with the appearance of tiny holes on the tips.

Sponges are some of the most vibrant and noticeable creatures to be found on a coral reef. Each sponge is actually an individual animal, connected to the reef and constantly growing. They feed by slowly filtering the nutrients out of seawater. All sponges are covered with tiny incurrent pores that suck water in, and large excurrent pores that send it on its way. Sponges are so successful that they have been around for over 500 million years.

They are both food and shelter for many fish species, and can be found in all reef environments, from the shallowest lagoons to the deepest walls.

Sponges are beautiful animals in their own right, but looking closer, such as inside the tube and barrel sponges, a diver can find a variety of animals taking shelter. Sponges can also be used by ambush predators, as places to lie in wait, or by nocturnal species waiting for nightfall.

# SPONGES

  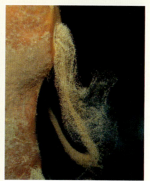

Divers can sometimes see long, stringy mats of eggs around sponges. Sponges can be hermaphrodites, meaning that each individual produces both sperm (center) and eggs (right) when it comes time to reproduce. Each species has its own specific day of the year when it does this, usually in the spring. Encountering countless millions of fertilized eggs on the reef on the same day overwhelms predators, and the chances for survival are higher.

Some sponges will release fertilized eggs, while others will allow their eggs to hatch first. Once fertilized, the eggs will join the plankton, floating in the open ocean for weeks. They are distributed by ocean currents and may eventually settle on a reef hundreds, or even thousands of miles away. While still in this early stage, most will be able to move about using tiny, whip-like appendages called flagellae. Once they land, the larvae can even crawl across the reef for short distances, until they find the most advantageous spot to take root and grow into mature sponges themselves.

Some sponges are also able to reproduce by budding. When a piece of a sponge breaks off, it can float to another location and, once it lands on the reef again, begin to grow into a new colony. The cellular structure of a sponge is very simple. In fact, if a sponge were to be cut up and pressed through a piece of cloth, it could start to reassemble itself on the other side into a new shape.

There are about 180 different species of sponges found in the Caribbean, and because of their highly variable shapes and colors, it can be difficult to tell them apart. For the purposes of this book they have been divided into the following groups, based on their general shape:

Encrusting Shapes

Rope Shapes

Ball Shapes

Vase Shapes

Tube Shapes

Barrel Shapes

### PEACH ENCRUSTING SPONGE
*(Clatharia sp.)*
10 in max. Thin-walled sponge in shades of pink to orange. Large excurrent pores with radiating veins.

> Divers and underwater photographers will often be tempted to put a hand onto the reef to stabilize themselves. If they touch an encrusting sponge, however, the pigments can stain the diver's skin for days, not to mention causing unnecessary damage to the sponge itself.

### ORANGE LUMPY ENCRUSTING SPONGE
*(Ulosa ruetzleri)*
12 in max. Encrusting sponges with rough-textured walls. Excurrent pores do not protrude outwards.

### NETTED ORANGE SPONGE
*(Myrmekioderma sp.)*
18 in max. Light orange, encrusting sponge overlaid with a reticulated network of darker orange.

# ENCRUSTING SPONGES : SPONGES

### PINK AND RED ENCRUSTING SPONGE
*(Spirastrella coccinea)*
3 ft max. Pink with tiny red speckles. Excurrent pores are lighter and protrude out from the body.

### WHITE VEINED ENCRUSTING SPONGE
*(Clatharia sp.)*
10 in max. Thin-walled sponge, white with hints of blue. Large excurrent pores with radiating veins.

### ORANGE ENCRUSTING SPONGE
*(Rhaphidophlus venosus)*
12 in max. Thin-walled, deep orange with protruding excurrent pores. Radiating veins intersect each other.

### MELTED SPONGE
*(Oscarella sp.)*
10 in max. Bright yellow to orange. Surface appears as melting blobs with excurrent pores at the tips.

### RED ENCRUSTING SPONGE
*(Monanchora barbadensis)*
10 in max. Thin-walled sponge in shades of pink to red. Large excurrent pores with darker radiating veins.

### YELLOW ENCRUSTING SPONGE
*(Monanchora barbadensis)*
A rare yellow variety of M. barbadensis. Radiating veins are thicker and the excurrent pores are larger.

## LUMPY OVERGROWING SPONGE
*(Holopsamma helwigi)*
16 in max. Pink to orange encrusting sponge, often forming dangling ropes with large excurrent pores.

Encrusting sponges can be found in all marine environments, from the shallow lagoons to the deep walls and under ledges. Spreading rapidly, these thin-walled sponges can grow over exposed limestone, living coral heads or even other, larger sponges.

ENCRUSTING ELEPHANT EAR SPONGE
*(Agelas sventres)*
12 in max. Lumpy orange sponge with smooth walls. The excurrent pores are elongated and clustered.

BROWN VARIABLE SPONGE
*(Anthosigmella varians)*
18 in max. Tan or brown with large, pale excurrent pores. Encrusts or forms rounded ball shapes.

# ENCRUSTING SPONGES : SPONGES

### RED SIEVE ENCRUSTING SPONGE
*(Phorbas amaranthus)*
18 in max. Deep red encrusting sponge with densely packed, rounded incurrent pores.

### ORANGE SIEVE ENCRUSTING SPONGE
*(Diplastrella sp.)*
18 in max. Light orange sponge with darker clumps of incurrent pores surrounding large excurrent pores.

### CORAL ENCRUSTING SPONGE
*(Cliona langae)*
36 in max. Very thin walled, reddish-brown sponge with small excurrent pores. Bores into coral heads.

### STAR ENCRUSTING SPONGE
*(Halisarca sp.)*
10 in max. Thin-walled sponge with tiny, pale excurrent pores surrounded by star-shaped lines.

### WHITE ICING SPONGE
*(Mycale laevis)*
18 in max. Less common, white variety of the Mycale sponge, usually found growing under flat corals.

### ORANGE ICING SPONGE
*(Mycale laevis)*
18 in max. Usually grows underneath flat corals. Uniform orange color with large excurrent pores.

## ELEPHANT EAR SPONGE
*(Agelas clathrodes)*
6 ft max. Massive, rounded sheet of orange sponge with a pitted surface. More common on deeper reefs.

> Many sponges can sting bare skin and may even cause tetanus, so divers should take care around them. After a sting, the pain, a rash and numbness can last for days. Treatment is vinegar or alcohol to neutralize the poisons. A hydrocortisone cream will take away some of the sting.

## BROWN OCTOPUS SPONGE
*(Ectyoplasia ferox)*
16 in max. Interconnected mass of small, brown, tube-shaped sponges with pale excurrent pores.

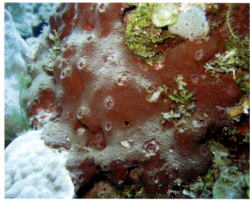

## BROWN OCTOPUS SPONGE (VARIETY)
*(Ectyoplasia ferox)*
A flattened, encrusting variety of E. ferox. Dark red with a pitted surface and scattered excurrent pores.

# ENCRUSTING SPONGES : SPONGES

### DARK VOLCANO SPONGE
*(Calyx podatypa)*
3 ft max. Dark red sponge with pointed tips towards the excurrent pores. Soft and easily broken.

### GOLDEN ENCRUSTING SPONGE
*(Ptilocaulis sp.)*
15 in max. Interconnected mass of large, scattered excurrent pores. Colors run from white to golden.

### FIRE SPONGE
*(Tedania ignis)*
12 in max. Orange to red, with a few, large excurrent pores. Found in the shallows. Can sting bare skin.

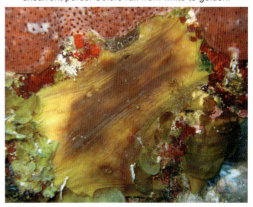

### VISCOUS SPONGE
*(Plakortis angulospiculatus)*
12 in max. A brown to yellow sheet of encrusting sponge, seeming to stretch across the substrate.

### RED ENCRUSTING TUBE SPONGE
*(Aiolochroia Crassa)*
12 in max. Short, bulbous, red sponges connected to a common body. Uniform red in color.

### PINK ENCRUSTING TUBE SPONGE
*(Aiolochroia sp.)*
12 in max. Thin, pink tube sponges connected to a common body. Usually found under ledges.

### CRYPTIC SPONGE
*(Leucandra aspera)*
12 in max. Short tubes, usually upside-down in clusters under ledges. White to pale pastel colors.

> 😎 Many sponges will actually grow into the limestone of the coral, rather than growing out away from it. They secrete chemicals that will kill existing coral heads and allow them to burrow into the substrate of the reef. Their excurrent pores can go down many inches below the top of the reef.

### WHITE CALCAREOUS SPONGE
*(Calcarea sp.)*
4 in max. Small, white, interconnected tubes with a visible skeletal structure. Found under ledges.

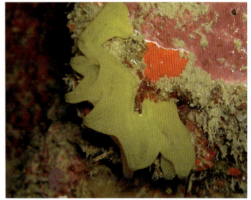

### YELLOW CALCAREOUS SPONGE
*(Clathrina canariensis)*
4 in max. Bright yellow, interconnected tubes with a visible skeletal structure. Found under ledges.

# ENCRUSTING SPONGES : SPONGES

### STRIATED SPONGE (VARIETY)
*(Smenospongia aurea)*
A rope-like, encrusting variety of S. aurea found in deeper water. Lavender to purple with large pores.

### STRIATED SPONGE
*(Smenospongia aurea)*
8 in max. Gray to light brown with a netted surface. Excurrent pores are on top of short, pointed tubes.

### VARIABLE BORING SPONGE (VARIETY)
*(Siphonodictyon coralliphagum)*
4 in max. Clusters of short white spikes found under ledges. No visible excurrent pores.

### VARIABLE BORING SPONGE
*(Siphonodictyon coralliphagum)*
4 in max. Short, pointed sponge growing above and into coral heads. Single excurrent pores.

### RED BORING SPONGE
*(Cliona delitrix)*
12 in max. Red to orange crust over coral heads. Large excurrent pores down into the main body.

### RED BORING SPONGE (VARIETY)
*(Cliona delitrix)*
Instead of encrusting over coral heads, this variety eats down into the coral by secreting acids.

## SCATTERED PORE ROPE SPONGE
*(Aplysina fulva)*
8 ft max. Rounded ropes in orange, green or brown.
Excurrent pores are randomly placed along the sides.

Rope Sponges are difficult to identify because of the various color and growth patterns within each species, depending on depth, currents and the available nutrients. It is the arrangement of the excurrent pores (random, in a row or paired) that gives a hint to the different species of Rope Sponge.

## SCATTERED PORE ROPE SPONGE
*(Aplysina fulva)*
A light green variety of A. fulva. The pores are still randomly scattered across the surface.

## HORNED ROPE SPONGE
*(Agelas cervicornis)*
2 ft max. Slightly flattened, tan to brown ropes with larger excurrent pores. Rarely with branching tips.

# ROPE SPONGES : SPONGES

### ROUNDED ROPE SPONGE
*(Agelas sceptrum)*
4 ft max. Lumpy, tan to brown sponge with lighter excurrent pores. This is an uncommon rope variety.

### ERECT ROPE SPONGE
*(Amphimedon compressa)*
4 ft max. Shorter, bright red ropes, usually standing straight up. Sometimes branching and connected.

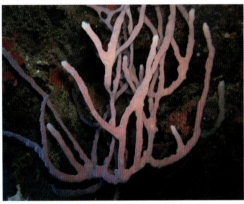

### LAVENDER ROPE SPONGE
*(Niphates erecta)*
6 ft max. Light purple ropes, usually short and unbranching, with a porous, rough-textured surface.

### GREEN FINGER SPONGE
*(Iotrochota birotulata)*
3 ft max. Dark green ropes with pale highlights, rarely branching. Excurrent pores are large, with pale rims.

### ROW PORE ROPE SPONGE
*(Aplysina cauliformis)*
8 ft max. Thin ropes, often branching and tangled. Excurrent pores in uniform rows along the sides.

### THIN ROPE SPONGE
*(Rhaphidophlus juniperinus)*
6 ft max. A fine network of tangled ropes. Tan to reddish brown. Usually found on deeper reefs.

### ORANGE BRANCHING SPONGE
*(Ptilocaulis sp.)*
1 ft max. Uniform orange tangle of short ropes with
a rough texture. Grows in clumps from a common stem.

> Rope Sponges are usually found on walls and deeper reefs, and a dive light is often needed to appreciate the vibrant colors of these sponges. Their tangled shapes make them an ideal place to search for smaller, hidden animals like shrimps or decorator crabs (p. 187).

### RED BRANCHING SPONGE
*(Ptilocaulis sp.)*
1 ft max. Orange to red tangle of short ropes with
a rough texture, branching from a common stem.

### WALPER'S ROPE SPONGE
*(Ptilocaulis walpersi)*
1 ft max. Dark red tangle of short ropes with a
rough texture. Grows in clumps from a common stem.

# ROPE SPONGES : SPONGES

### RETICULATED ROPE SPONGE
*(Dragmacidon reticulata)*
12 in max. Bright red, wedge-shaped sponge.
The body is flattened with few excurrent pores.

### RED STALAGMITE SPONGE
*(Oceanapia stalagmitica)*
6 in max. Thin, dark red stalks growing in clumps.
Smooth texture with no visible excurrent pores.

### YELLOW STRING SPONGE
*(Halichondria lutea)*
6 in stalks max. Thin, orange stalks with tapered
ends, growing in clumps from a buried base.

### BURIED SPONGE
*(Oceanapia peltata)*
7 in stalks max. White, ragged stalks growing in
clumps of three or four. The body is buried in sand.

### ENCRUSTING STRING SPONGE
*(Ulosa funicularis)*
8 in max. Olive green, encrusting mat with elongated,
thin, stringy filaments. Often covers other sponges.

### CIRCULAR COLUMN SPONGE
*(Topsentia ophiraphidites)*
18 in max. Tall, erect spines growing from
a common, circular base. Dark red to brown in color.

## SPINY BALL SPONGE
*(Leucetta barbata)*
0.75 in max. Tiny white ball with thin transparent spines covering the body. Found on deeper reefs.

> The Spiny Ball Sponge is the smallest of the sponges to be found on the reef, about the size of a small fingernail. They are protected by hair-thin needles sticking out in all directions. Look for them at greater depths, often growing on Black Corals (p. 78) and Elephant Ear Sponges (p. 36).

## ORANGE BALL SPONGE
*(Cinachyra sp)*
10 in max. Rounded, dark orange ball with numerous lighter excurrent pores. Often found under ledges.

## CONVOLUTED ORANGE SPONGE
*(Myrmekioderma styx)*
3 ft max. Dark orange sponge with a pattern of lighter valleys and excurrent pores. Found under ledges.

# BALL SPONGES : SPONGES

### BROWN VARIABLE SPONGE
*(Anthosigmella varians)*
18 in max. Rounded, tan-colored ball shape with pale, protruding excurrent pores.

### STINKER SPONGE
*(Ircinia felix)*
12 in max. Rounded, gray ball with an hexagonal design of spikes. Pores scattered around the body.

### BLACK BALL SPONGE (VARIETY)
*(Ircinia strobilina)*
Under ledges and in deeper water, the Black Ball Sponge will have fewer pigments, appearing white.

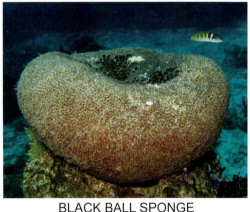

### BLACK BALL SPONGE
*(Ircinia strobilina)*
18 in max. Rounded, brown ball with a spiny texture. Excurrent pores in two or more separate clusters.

### PERNUCLEATA SPONGE
*(Aaptos pernucleata)*
12 in max. Smooth, black, rounded shape with no markings. Excurrent pores are randomly distributed.

### CONVOLUTED BALL SPONGE
*(Aplysina sp.)*
A squat, ball-shaped growth pattern of the Convoluted Barrel Sponge. Found under ledges.

**AZURE VASE SPONGE**
*(Callyspongia plicifera)*
2 ft max. Bright blue vase shape with highly ruffled walls.
Often grows in groups. May fluoresce at depth.

Sponges get their shape and rigidity from microscopic, glass-like fibers in their bodies called spicules. These are woven together to create a framework around which the animal can grow. It also allows them to be flexible in currents and surge, in much the same way that fiberglass does. Their color and variety comes from specialized pigments. The bright pigments of the Azure Vase Sponge can fluoresce (below left). In another example of symbiosis on a coral reef, the skeleton of the Rigid Vase Sponge (below right) is actually made up of living plant tissues (Dictya sp.). The plant is embedded into the walls of the sponge to support it. This small sponge is half plant and half animal.

# VASE SPONGES : SPONGES

### STRAWBERRY VASE SPONGE (VARIETY)
(Mycale laxissima)
In shallower water the pigments of the Strawberry Vase Sponge are paler, giving it an orange color.

### STRAWBERRY VASE SPONGE
(Mycale laxissima)
12 in max. Deep red vase shapes with rough textured walls, often in groups. They appear black at depth.

### BRANCHING VASE SPONGE (VARIETY)
(Callyspongia vaginalis)
Although normally in a vase shape, C. vaginalis can form tubes, similar to Branching Tube Sponges.

### BRANCHING VASE SPONGE
(Callyspongia vaginalis)
3 ft max. Thin, gray-walled vase shape with a spiky texture on the outside and a smooth texture inside.

### RIGID VASE SPONGES
(Dysidea janiae)
2 in max. Short, rounded tubes with a netted pattern of filaments on the outside. Lavender to brown color.

### PINK VASE SPONGE
(Niphates digitalis)
12 in max. Thin, pink, rough-walled vase shape with an almost transparent rim of growth around the top.

## BRANCHING TUBE SPONGE
*(Pseudoceratina crassa)*
18 in max. Thick-walled tubes, often growing in clusters. The shape and color are highly variable.

A good example of the variability of sponges, the Branching Tube Sponge can take on many different colors and even growth patterns. It is found on all kinds of terrain and at all diving depths, often making positive identification of this species difficult for divers.

# TUBE SPONGES : SPONGES

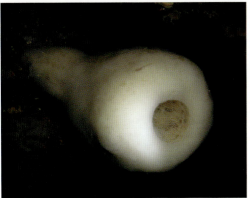

### IVORY TUBE SPONGE
*(Aplysina bathyphila)*
18 in max. Very thick-walled, white sponge with rounded edges. Found in caves and under ledges.

### BROWN CLUSTERED TUBE SPONGE
*(Agelas wiedenmyeri)*
6 in max. Smooth-walled, reddish-brown tube sponge with distinctively pinched excurrent pores.

### BROWN TUBE SPONGE
*(Agelas conifera)*
3 ft max. Smooth-walled, tan to brown tubes with rounded ends. They are often interconnected.

### BROWN TUBE SPONGE (VARIETY)
*(Agelas conifera)*
A short, clustered variety of A. conifera. Found in deeper water, under ledges with little current.

### MINIATURE TUBE SPONGES
*(Hyatella cavernosa)*
1 in max. Small, lavender tube shapes growing from a common base, usually covered in algae.

### GRAY AMPHORA
*(Hyrtios sp.)*
12 in max. Rounded, gray body with small spikes and a protruding excurrent pore. The inside is black.

## STOVE PIPE SPONGE
*(Aplysina archeri)*
7 ft max. Long, rough-textured, thick-walled tubes.
Flexible enough to sway in currents. The color is variable.

Stove-Pipe Sponges are usually found on deeper reefs or under overhangs where there is less water movement, allowing these flexible sponges to reach great lengths. They are attached to the reef by a holdfast that must take the weight of the entire sponge. By looking closely at the large excurrent pore at the end, a diver can see how much water is being processed. This steady stream of filtered water continues day and night; thousands of gallons a day can pass through the filtering walls of Stove Pipe Sponges. In areas with a healthy sponge population, nearly a quarter of all the reef's water can be filtered out by its resident sponges.

# TUBE SPONGES : SPONGES

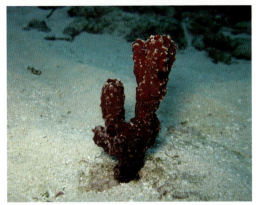

### RED TUBE SPONGE
*(Pandaros acanthifolium)*
12 in max. Short, rough-textured, deep red sponge with scattered excurrent pores. Often found on sand.

### PITTED TUBE SPONGE
*(Verongula rigida)*
8 in max. Short, tube shaped variety of V. rigida, with a rough network pattern on the sides.

### PITTED SPONGE
*(Verongula rigida)*
14 in max. Tan to light brown, bulbous sponge with randomly scattered, pale to yellow excurrent pores.

### YELLOW TUBE SPONGE
*(Aplysina fistularis)*
4 ft max. Thick-walled, yellow tubes often growing in clusters. Fine, yellow filaments extend from the walls.

### FLATTENED TUBE SPONGE
*(Plakinastrella onkodes)*
10 in max. Tan body with a mottled brown surface. The excurrent pore and the inside is a lighter brown.

### CONVOLUTED TUBE SPONGE
*(Aplysina lacunosa)*
3 ft max. Elongated, tube-shaped variety of A. lacunosa that is found in calmer waters, under ledges.

👁 Giant Barrel Sponges have earned the nickname "The Redwoods of the Caribbean" because of their great size and age. Some are estimated to be 2000 years old! Almost six feet tall, and six feet in diameter, the sponge on the left could easily be over 800 years old. In fact, when Columbus was first "discovering" the Caribbean, this sponge could already have been attached to this exact spot on the reef, and growing happily. Divers should take care when moving around these giants. Despite their size they are very fragile, especially around the rim where most of the new growth takes place.

👁 Sponges are very delicate animals and can easily be crushed or broken apart by the careless dropping of an anchor, destroying hundreds of years of growth in seconds. Even a dragging fishing line can slice through a large sponge, often killing it. Because they are filter feeders, a sponge will suffer quickly from any pollutants or contaminants in the seawater. They are like the canary in the coal mine, warning us of dangerous water quality on our reefs.

# BARREL SPONGES : SPONGES

### GIANT BARREL SPONGE
*(Xestospongia muta )*
6 ft max. Massive red to brown barrel shape with a wide, central excurrent pore. Sometimes in groups.

### NETTED BARREL SPONGE
*(Verongula gigantea)*
5 ft max. Yellow to dark green barrel shape with a rubbery, netted texture. The inside is the same color.

### ROUGH TUBE SPONGE
*(Oceanapia bartschi)*
4 ft max. Rounded barrel or tube shape with a knobby texture and a thin, protruding excurrent pore.

### LEATHERY BARREL SPONGE
*(Geodia neptuni)*
3 ft max. Thick-walled barrel shape with a pitted texture. Often broken open and fed upon by turtles.

### LEATHERY BARREL SPONGE (VARIETY)
*(Geodia neptuni)*
In deeper water and under dark ledges, the Leathery Barrel Sponge becomes more bulbous and rounded.

### ORANGE BARREL SPONGE
*(Agelas citrina)*
3 ft max. On exposed reefs, A. citrina takes on a thick-walled, barrel shape. (Compare p. 36).

### RETICULATED BARREL SPONGE
*(Verongula reiswigi)*
4 ft max. Yellow to green, squat barrel shape.
The walls are thick with a bulbous, lumpy texture.

For most sponges, the growth shape depends largely on the local environment. Factors such as currents and depth can change the shape of a sponge dramatically. In deeper water, away from storm surge and surface currents, they are free to take on larger and more bizarre shapes.

### BROWN BOWL SPONGE
*(Cribrochalina vasculum)*
3 ft max. A dark brown to red, smooth-walled bowl shape with tiny, almost invisible, excurrent pores.

### BROWN BOWL SPONGE (VARIETY)
*(Cribrochalina vasculum)*
On deeper reefs this sponge will give up its bowl shape to become large, thin-walled and flattened.

# BARREL SPONGES : SPONGES

### YELLOW BARREL SPONGE
*(Verongula reiswigi)*
A smooth-walled variety of the Reticulated Barrel Sponge, found in shallower waters with more current.

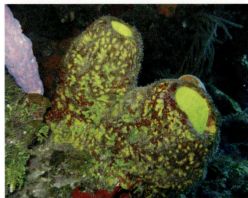

### CONVOLUTED BARREL SPONGE
*(Aplysina lacunosa)*
3 ft max. Thick yellow walls with a lumpy texture. The inside is always bright yellow with green highlights.

### MAROON BARREL SPONGE (VARIETY)
*(Xestospongia rosariensis)*
On shallower reefs the Maroon Barrel Sponge will form elongated tubes or other random shapes.

### MAROON BARREL SPONGE
*(Xestospongia rosariensis)*
4 ft max. Dark brown to reddish, elongated barrel shape with flared ends. Often grows in loose clusters.

### TOUCH-ME-NOT SPONGE
*(Neofibularia nolitangere)*
5 ft max. Dark brown to maroon, thick-walled, squat barrel shape. Toxic, causes itching in divers.

### LOGGERHEAD SPONGE
*(Spheciospongia vesparium)*
5 ft max. Rounded, brown ball with a rough texture. Excurrent pores are all found in a central depression.

🔷 Corals form the building blocks of a reef ecosystem. They offer both food and shelter for countless animals that call a reef home. Each coral is made up of a collection of tiny animals called polyps, growing together in different shapes, depending on their species. Each polyp has a central mouth for eating and expelling waste, surrounded by a ring of tentacles. These tentacles are armed with tiny stinging cells called nematocysts that can stun their prey, even tiny fishes, and move it into the mouth. In this way they are similar to jellyfish, but the sting is so mild it can rarely be felt by divers. As a coral grows it lays down a thin skeleton of calcium carbonate. Decade after decade, as the coral continues to grow, the skeleton is repeatedly laid down until a coral reef is born.

Corals are some of the simplest and also the oldest forms of life on Earth. Some coral reefs alive today actually started growing over 50 million years ago. They are wildly diverse ecosystems. While coral reefs cover only 0.2 percent of the ocean, they contain over 25 percent of all marine species.

Corals themselves are almost translucent animals, in the same general family as the jellyfish. It is only the resident alga that gives each species of coral its unique and vibrant colors.

# CORALS

Corals are largely nocturnal animals that remain closed up during the day, looking more like colorful stones. It is at night that divers can truly appreciate that these are active animals. Corals will open up their bodies and begin an evening of quietly feeding on the plankton floating over the reef. Close inspection reveals countless tentacles, moving about and grabbing tiny bits of food.

Living within the tissues of each coral polyp there is a collection of plant cells called zooxanthellae, which live in a symbiotic relationship with the coral. Most of a coral's food is produced by these plants. During daylight hours, when the coral is retracted into its skeleton, the algae provides food and oxygen through photosynthesis and removes the animal's waste products. In return, it gets a safe place to live within the stinging tentacles. When the coral is under stress from pollution, or higher sea temperatures, the coral can expel the algae within its tissues, called coral bleaching (p. 91). After the stresses have passed, the algae can be reabsorbed into the flesh and growth can continue.

Highly sensitive ecosystems, coral reefs are under threat from pollution, coastal development and rising sea temperatures. An estimated 25 percent of the world's reefs have already disappeared.

For the purposes of identification, the corals in this book have been roughly separated by both shape and species type into the following general categories:

Branching Corals | Massive Corals | Flat Corals

Solitary Corals | Black Corals | Soft Corals

57

## PILLAR CORAL
*(Dendrogyra cylindrus)*
10 ft max. Light brown to yellow, rounded spires growing from a common base. Small, dense tentacles.

Pillar Corals are usually found in the shallows, growing up toward the surface. As storms and hurricanes blow across the coral reefs of the Caribbean, these tall, fragile-looking corals seem to be at a disadvantage, and they do fall down quite often. But they have actually turned this to their advantage. When a pillar falls over it begins to grow again, sprouting new pillars along the top. In this way it can spread out and grow, covering more area on the reef. With competition for reef-space at a premium in the sunlit shallows, this species has turned its fragility into an asset.

While most corals keep their tentacles safely tucked away during the daytime, the Pillar Coral keeps its short tentacles out most of the time, giving it a texture like a plush carpet. It needs as much sunlight as it can get in order to survive and grow. The crevices between the pillars, especially towards the base, are a good place to look for nocturnal animals, like eels, hiding in the daytime.

# BRANCHING CORALS : CORALS

### YELLOW PENCIL CORAL
*(Madracis mirabilis)*
4 ft max. Dense clumps of short, yellow, pencil-sized branches. Polyps remain extended during the day.

### EIGHT RAY FINGER CORAL
*(Madracis formosa)*
5 ft max. Light orange to tan, rounded branches with double tips. Mouths of polyps are yellow.

### BRANCHED FINGER CORAL
*(Porites furcata)*
4 ft max. Branches split into two rounded lobes on a longer stalk. Polyps often randomly retracted.

### CLUB TIPPED FINGER CORAL
*(Porites porites)*
4 ft max. Grows on deeper reefs in mounds. Branches end in thick, wide lobes. Polyps often randomly retracted.

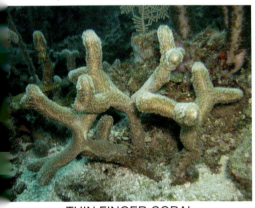

### THIN FINGER CORAL
*(Porites divaricata)*
1 ft max. Tan to light brown. Long, thin stalks growing in smaller colonies. Usually on shallower reefs.

### ROSE LACE CORAL
*(Stylaster roseus)*
4 in max. Tiny, fan-shaped colonies in pink to bright purple. Found under ledges and in crevices.

Staghorn Coral gets its name from its many sharp, dividing branches, like a stag's horns. It is always found in shallow areas and is very fragile. Pieces that are broken off can tumble across the reef floor for long distances and still be able to grow into new colonies. Under the right conditions, with clear water, far from the land's run-off and with lots of sunlight, Staghorn Coral can dominate the landscape for acres, stretching unbroken for as far as the eye can see. Staghorn is the fastest growing coral in the Caribbean and can grow as much as 8 inches every year. Despite its abundance in certain areas, it is very sensitive to pollution and is now under threat. It has been placed on the CITES Endangered Species List.

Some of the most common branching corals are the Fire Corals. They are found in the shallows, close to the sunlight, where they grow rapidly and can even take over and encrust other corals. They are not a true reef-building coral, but a hydrocoral: in the same family as the jellyfish and the stinging anemones.
Their name comes from the intense sting they can cause if touched. Fire Corals are covered with countless tiny spines. If stung, never wash the area in fresh water, as this will only make it worse. Wash the affected area in vinegar to neutralize the poisons.

# BRANCHING CORALS : CORALS

### FUSED STAGHORN CORAL
*(Acropora prolifera)*
4 ft max. Rounded branches end in a flattened array of smaller branchlets that are each tipped in white.

### ELKHORN CORAL
*(Acropora palmata)*
12 ft max. Brown to yellow, flattened branches grow from a sturdy base. Whitish tips to the branches.

### BLADE FIRE CORAL
*(Millepora complanata)*
18 in max. Tan to yellow, flattened blades with large pores. Covered in fine white spines.

### STAGHORN CORAL
*(Acropora cervicornis)*
8 ft max. Light brown, branching tubes of coral with pointed tips. Grows in dense thickets.

### BOX FIRE CORAL
*(Millepora squarrosa)*
18 in max. Thick-walled colonies with pale tips. Appear as hexagonal or box-like shapes viewed from above.

### BRANCHING FIRE CORAL
*(Millepora alcicornis)*
18 in max. Often encrusts living reef and continues to form branching fan shapes. Tan to yellow.

Lettuce Corals are some of the most abundant corals in the Caribbean, and they can be found in the widest variety of reef habitats, from close to the surface to well below safe diving depths. They are fast-growing and unusually resistant to the stresses that put other corals at risk. They often cover wide expanses of the reef, especially in the shallows where they can get a lot of sunlight. They are an ideal place for other animals to make homes and to lay eggs. There has been some debate as to whether there are different species or just one (Agaricia agaricites) that has taken on different growth patterns. They will be represented here according to their appearance on the reef.

**LETTUCE CORAL**
*(Agaricia sp.)*
3 ft max. Flattened branches of green to yellow coral plates, forming a rounded, lettuce-shaped dome.

**THIN LEAF LETTUCE CORAL**
*(Agaricia tenuifolia)*
12 ft colony max. Thin, vertical sheets of lettuce coral with polyps on both sides. Brown to bright yellow.

# LETTUCE CORALS : CORALS

**PURPLE LETTUCE CORAL**
*(Agaricia purpurea)*
3 ft max. Lettuce coral with long, parallel rows of ridges and valleys. Brown to yellow or purplish.

**SCALED LETTUCE CORAL**
*(Agaricia danai)*
3 ft max. Lettuce coral growing in thick-walled, vertical plates with polyps on both sides.

**KEELED LETTUCE CORAL**
*(Agaricia carinata)*
3 ft max. Lettuce coral forming an irregular mound with numerous, blunt protrusions.

**ENCRUSTING LETTUCE CORAL**
*(Agaricia agaricites)*
3 ft max. An encrusting form of Lettuce Coral with a reticulated pattern of ridges on the surface.

**SUNRAY LETTUCE CORAL**
*(Helioceris cucullata)*
10 in max. Thin lines (septa) run toward the edges. Sharp ridges with pale polyps on the steeper side.

**LOW RELIEF LETTUCE CORAL**
*(Agaricia humilis)*
5 in max. Flattened plate of dense polyps with a reticulated pattern. Often with green in the valleys.

👓 Brain Corals get their name from their convoluted rows of polyps and their generally rounded shapes. They can grow to over six feet and may live to be very old. One Caribbean brain coral gave scientists a 500-year cross-section of climate conditions. All brain coral species can take on the typical rounded shape, so identification needs to be done by looking at the shape of the ridges. Clockwise from the right: Knobby, Boulder, Symmetrical and Grooved.

👓 These distinctive coral heads are good places for fish like Neon Gobies (p. 201) to set up their cleaning stations. The deep grooves of the brain coral provide a perfect place for these tiny fishes to hide during the night, or to rest between cleaning jobs. Larger fish can often be seen circling around brain corals, waiting for their turn to come in and get cleaned.

# BRAIN CORALS : CORALS

### SYMMETRICAL BRAIN CORAL
*(Diploria strigosa)*
6 ft max. Dome-shaped colonies of convoluted ridges. The tops of the ridges are smooth.

### BOULDER BRAIN CORAL
*(Colpophyllia natans)*
8 ft max. Dome-shaped colonies with interconnected ridges. Grooves run along the tops of ridges.

### KNOBBY BRAIN CORAL
*(Diploria clivosa)*
4 ft max. Rounded dome of coral ridges with irregular, knobby protrusions. No grooves on ridges.

### GROOVED BRAIN CORAL
*(Diploria labyrinthiformis)*
4 ft max. Domed colonies with interconnected ridges, separated by wide, flattened grooves.

### BRAZILIAN ROSE CORAL
*(Meandrina forma brasilliensis)*
3 ft max. Often confused for a Brain Coral. A rounded Maze Coral with no central valley (compare p. 73).

### GOLFBALL CORAL
*(Favia fragum)*
2 in max. Small colonies of more elongated polyps. Yellow to brown. Usually found at shallower depths.

👓 The names of the Flower Corals can be deceiving. The Spiny Flower Coral (pictured above) is actually more rounded and fleshy, and the Smooth Flower Coral is more pointed. The names come from the shape of the skeletons growing under the actual polyps.

Flower Corals grow on shallow reefs and along walls where there is more current to bring in nutrients. They are a relatively fast-growing coral and will often overhang the reef, making good places for fish to take shelter. Colonies can grow to over 8 ft wide and the tops can provide safe shelter for juveniles. Once the coral grows too far out, pieces will break off and fall down the wall, where they may take root and begin to grow as a new colony.

👓 Corals reproduce by spawning; releasing countless millions of sperm and eggs into the water at the same time. Eggs are fertilized as they drift away, perhaps to land on a suitable patch of reef to begin a new colony. For each species, this only happens for a short period, on only one night of the year, usually after a full moon in late summer.

# FLOWER CORALS : CORALS

**ELONGATED FLOWER CORAL**
*(Eusmilia flabellata)*
A rare variety of E. fastigiata with a highly elongated and thin-walled skeletal structure.

**SMOOTH FLOWER CORAL**
*(Eusmilia fastigiata)*
4 ft max. Bunches of widely-spaced polyps on long stalks spreading outward. Yellow to light brown.

**SPINY FLOWER CORAL (VARIETY)**
*(Mussa angulosa)*
Spiny Flower Coral is sometimes seen in bright green or even blue and may fluoresce on deeper reefs.

**SPINY FLOWER CORAL**
*(Mussa angulosa)*
3 ft max. Large fleshy polyps with a rough texture, tightly packed in a dome shape. Usually reddish gray.

**MUSTARD HILL CORAL (VARIETY)**
*(Porites astreoides)*
2 ft max. A gray to light brown variety of P. astreoides, in rounded domes or plates, often in deeper water.

**MUSTARD HILL CORAL**
*(Porites astreoides)*
2 ft max. The most common variety of P. astreoides, forming irregular, lumpy mounds in the shallows.

## GREAT STAR CORAL
*(Montastraea cavernosa)*
8 ft max. Massive rounded domes of large, rounded polyps, tightly packed together. Color highly variable.

Star Corals get their name from the tiny lines radiating out from the mouth of each polyp. The Great Star Coral comes in a variety of colors, usually depending on the type of symbiotic algae (zooxanthellae) inside its flesh. The deeper colonies tend to attract an algae that is redder in color, so that it can make more use of the darker conditions, while up in the shallows a green algae can absorb more sunlight. Sometimes two different colors can be seen sharing the same coral head, or even the same individual coral polyp.

# STAR CORALS : CORALS

### LESSER STARLET CORAL
(*Siderastrea radians*)
12 in max. Flat, encrusting plates of tightly-packed corallites that appear pinched. Tan to gray.

### MASSIVE STARLET CORAL
(*Siderastrea siderea*)
6 ft max. Massive domes of uniform brown to yellow. Corallites are evenly sized and symmetrically round.

### BLUSHING STAR CORAL
(*Stephanocoenia intersepta*)
2.5 ft max. Rounded domes of yellow to light brown. Polyps retract quickly, hence the "blushing".

### ROUGH STAR CORAL
(*Isophyllastrea rigida*)
8 in max. Oval-shaped dome of densely-packed, fleshy polyps. A thin line separates each polyp.

### DIFFUSE IVORY TREE CORAL
(*Oculina diffusa*)
15 in max. Star-shaped polyps on long, branching arms. Polyps are raised away from the main stems.

### TEN RAY STAR CORAL
(*Madracis decactis*)
6 in max. Short, bulbous mounds of brown coral, with ten radiating lines extending from each coral polyp.

**MOUNTAINOUS STAR CORAL**
*(Montastraea faveolata)*
8 ft max. Very large colonies with one or more
rounded tips, often growing close to the surface.

Star Corals get their name from the appearance of their individual polyps. Each has a star-shaped opening around which the short tentacles protrude. Members of the Montastraea family were once thought to be a single species with varying growth shapes.

**LOBED STAR CORAL**
*(Montastraea annularis)*
10 ft max. Collections of rounded, light brown
coral heads. Only the tops have living polyps.

**BOULDER STAR CORAL**
*(Montastraea franksi)*
8 ft max. Grows in irregular, lumpy mound shapes in
shades of green to brown, often with white patches.

## STAR CORALS : CORALS

### BOULDER STAR CORAL (VARIETY)
*(Montastraea franksi)*
A deeper variety of Montastraea that spreads out into plates to catch more available sunlight.

### ENCRUSTING STAR CORAL
*(Madracis pharensis)*
6 in max. Thin layer of encrusting, star-shaped polyps. Green to reddish. Found under ledges.

### BLUE CRUST CORAL
*(Porites branneri)*
6 in max. Encrusting coral with pitted corallites that appear blue to purple in natural light.

### ELLIPTICAL STAR CORAL
*(Dichocoenia stokesi)*
15 in max. Domes or rounded plates of densely packed corallites that are elongated. Tan to brown.

### ELLIPTICAL STAR CORAL (VARIETY)
*(Dichocoenia stokesi)*
On deeper reefs the Elliptical Star Coral spreads out into a plate to catch more of the available sunlight.

### SMOOTH STAR CORAL
*(Solenastrea bournoni)*
18 in max. Rounded domes with slight, irregular lumps. Tan to yellow, with darker brown polyps.

Some cactus corals are fluorescent, reflecting light in different wavelengths. This usually occurs in deeper water. They will look normal under lighted conditions, but on their own they will stand out with a bright green or reddish glow. The protein responsible is thought to be acting as a kind of sunscreen to protect the colony from coral bleaching.

**ROUGH CACTUS CORAL**
*(Mycetophyllia ferox)*
24 in max. Ridges border the plates and run toward the center. Valleys have white clusters of polyps.

**LOWRIDGE CACTUS CORAL**
*(Mycetophyllia danaana)*
16 in max. Ridges border the plates and run toward and through the center. Often in contrasting colors.

# CACTUS CORALS : CORALS

### MAZE CORAL
*(Meandrina meandrites)*
3 ft max. Maze Coral is shown here because it can be confused with Cactus Corals. (Compare p. 65).

### KNOBBY CACTUS CORAL
*(Mycetophyllia aliciae)*
18 in max. Ridges border the plates, are light in color and broken into smaller, independent ridges.

### BUTTERPRINT ROSE CORAL
*(Meandrina forma danae)*
6 in max. Oval-shaped colony with a deep central valley and branched ends. Tan to yellow.

### RIDGED CACTUS CORAL
*(Mycetophyllia lamarckiana)*
12 in max. Ridges border the plates in a scalloped pattern and do not join. Often in contrasting colors.

### ROSE CORAL
*(Manicina areolata)*
6 in max. Oval-shaped colony, light to dark brown, with a long central valley and short side-valleys.

### SINUOUS CACTUS CORAL
*(Isophyllia sinuosa)*
8 in max. Small dome-shaped colonies with steep sided ridges. A thin white line runs along the ridges.

🤿 All corals need sunlight in order to grow. But the power of the sun's rays is absorbed by the seawater, and the amount of light available down on deeper reefs changes the way that corals grow. In order to make the most of the available sunlight, Plate Corals spread themselves out and form large, thin, fragile plates with their polyps facing upwards on the top. Often overlapping each other in an attempt to catch sunlight, the deeper the coral is, the more it tends to form itself into spiral shapes.

🤿 Identifying the true Plate Corals can be difficult, as there are some species of shallow-water coral that will also try to compete for limited sunlight in the deep by spreading out into thinner, plate-like shapes. Shapes can become so similar at depth that one has to look at the individual polyps for identification. Below are deeper examples of Mustard Hill, Lettuce and Star Corals.

# PLATE CORALS : CORALS

### GRAHAM'S SHEET CORAL
*(Agaricia grahamae)*
6 ft max. Large plates, often in fan shapes. Distinctive tiny, dark, pitted polyps nestled in low valleys.

### SCROLL CORAL
*(Agaricia undata)*
6 ft max. Large plates, often curving upwards. Tiny polyps only on the steep sides of concentric ridges.

### SCROLL CORAL (VARIETY)
*(Agaricia undata)*
Sometimes in deeper water the symbiotic algae in the coral will be green. Often with wide brown edges.

### LAMARCK'S SHEET CORAL
*(Agaricia lamarcki)*
6 ft max. Large plates, often in swirls. Distinctive tiny, white, star-shaped polyps nestled in low valleys.

### FRAGILE SAUCER CORAL
*(Agaricia fragilis)*
6 in max. Small, thin, saucer-shaped plates. Ridges and valleys form concentric circles. Brown to green.

### HONEYCOMB PLATE CORAL
*(Porites colonensis)*
18 in max. Flattened gray to brown plate with no ridges and a white border. Bright white polyps

### SPECKLED CUP CORAL
*(Rhizosmilia maculata)*
0.5 in max. Circular polyp with a deep central pit.
12 large septa and numerous smaller septa. Speckled.

Cup Corals can be found under ledges and overhangs, as well as deep within cave systems, where they need little sunlight in order to thrive. Most are no larger than a thumbnail, and they tend to grow in clusters of the same species. The rim is divided by rounded blades called septa.

### ARTICHOKE CORAL
*(Scolymia cubensis)*
4 in max. Large, fleshy polyp with raised, radiating lines from a flattened center. Gray, green or brown.

### ATLANTIC MUSHROOM CORAL
*(Scolymia lacera)*
6 in max. Largest single polyp. Fleshy ring with a concave central pit. Rough textured. Green to brown.

# CUP CORALS : CORALS

### BAROQUE CAVE CORAL
*(Thalamophyllia riisei)*
0.5 in max. Long, pink polyps with tall septa and deep central pits. Clustered on deeper reefs.

### ORANGE CUP CORAL
*(Tubastraea coccinea)*
12 in colony max. Orange to red corals with yellow tentacles. Grow in clusters from a common base.

### ORANGE SOLITARY CORAL
*(Rhizopsammia goesi)*
0.5 in max. Bright pink to orange. Six thick, primary septa and six smaller secondary septa.

### LESSER SPECKLED CUP CORAL
*(Colangia immersa)*
0.5 in max. Circular to oval polyp with few speckles. Brown patches. Deep central pit has a lighter color.

### TWO TONE CUP CORAL
*(Phacelocyathus flos)*
0.5 in max. Circular to oval polyp. The outer septa are reddish-brown and the central pit is white.

### BUTTON CUP CORAL
*(Coenocyathus caribbeana)*
0.5 in max. Solitary, thick-walled polyp with 12 rounded septa. Pale ring around the central pit.

## BUSHY BLACK CORAL
*(Antipathes n. sp.)*
15 ft max. Large bushy colonies of branching stalks,
getting lighter toward the ends. Tentacles are whitish.

Black Coral is not actually black, but usually appears as a delicate, white, bushy structure. They are found under dark ledges or on deeper reefs, usually near the limit of recreational diving. Their name comes from the base, or steadfast, that holds the coral to the reef. It has been collected for centuries for use as jewelry. In many parts of the Caribbean this rare and slow-growing coral is endangered, and the trade is outlawed, though harvesting continues.

Do not buy Black Coral jewelry. It looks much better on the reef than it does on you!

Look closer into the branches of Black Corals to find a number of animals that choose to call this rare and beautiful coral home. The Black Coral Shrimp (p. 176) is found nowhere else. It is also a good hiding place for juvenile fishes like the Trumpetfish (p. 306) and some of the Decorator Crabs (p. 187).

## BLACK CORALS : CORALS

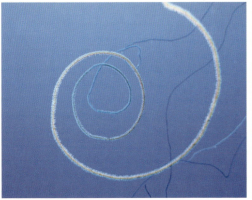

### WIRE CORAL
*(Cirrhipathes leutkeni)*
14 ft max. Single thin, dark stalk that often coils and spirals. Tentacles are white to transparent.

### FEATHER BLACK CORAL
*(Antipathes pennacea)*
5 ft max. Darker branches with lateral branchlets in a single plane, resembling a leaf or a broad feather.

### GRAY SEA FAN BLACK CORAL
*(Antipathes atlantica)*
4 ft max. Gray to light green fan shape with numerous tiny branchlets in a single plane.

### ORANGE SEAFAN BLACK CORAL
*(Antipathes gracilis)*
4 ft max. Bright orange to brown fan shape with numerous tiny branchlets in a single plane.

### SCRAGGLY BLACK CORAL
*(Antipathes sp.)*
12 in max. Rigid, dark branches from a common stalk in a loose bush. Tentacles are white to transparent.

### HAIRNET BLACK CORAL
*(Antipathes lenta)*
10 in max. Tiny gray to brown branchlets form a thick, tangled mass. Tentacles are white to transparent.

Soft Corals are bushy structures that are often mistaken for marine plants. They are actually animal colonies, made up of thousands of tiny coral polyps that share a common stalk. A strong holdfast keeps them in place and allows them to grow away from the reef, out into the water column. Here the polyps can feed on more of the tiny bits of plankton passing by in the current.

Look closely into the branches of the soft corals themselves. They play host to many creatures, feeding and taking shelter from their predators. There are many species of shrimps, crabs and even smaller fishes that have evolved to hide in these micro-environments.

## SOFT CORALS : CORALS

**RIGID RED TELESTO**
*(Stereotelesto corallina)*
10 in max. Red stalks covered with alternating white polyps. Each stalk is tipped with a single polyp.

**WHITE TELESTO**
*(Carijoa riisei)*
10 in max. Pink to white stalks covered with alternating white polyps. Each stalk is tipped with a single polyp.

**CORKY SEA FINGERS (VARIETY)**
*(Briareum asbestinum)*
1 ft max. Encrusting variety of B. asbestinum, forming a dense clump of purple ball shapes.

**CORKY SEA FINGERS**
*(Briareum asbestinum)*
2 ft max. Colony of single, unbranched purple rods with dense, brown polyps. Grows in clusters.

**RED POLYP OCTOCORAL**
*(Swiftia exserta)*
18 in max. Bushy colony of long, red polyps on thin, red branches. Found under deeper ledges.

**ENCRUSTING GORGONIAN**
*(Erythropodium caribaeorum)*
3 ft max. Encrusting layer of fleshy brown with fine, hair-like polyps. Often retracted during the day.

## COMMON SEA FAN
*(Gorgonia ventalina)*
6 ft max. Huge fans growing in a single plane.
Yellow to light brown with purple holdfasts and veins.

> Seafans that grow in the shallows have very strong holdfasts that keep them anchored to the reef floor, while their bodies are flexible enough to sway back and forth in even the strongest waves and storms. This movement also helps them to feed, bringing them into contact with more plankton.

## VENUS SEA FAN
*(Gorgonia flabellum)*
4 ft max. Large, fan-shaped colonies with numerous small, flat branchlets growing outward from the sides.

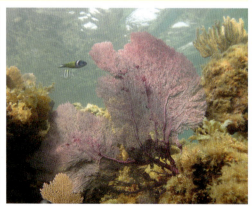

## COMMON SEA FAN (VARIETY)
*(Gorgonia ventalina)*
In shallow waters the Common Sea Fan can be a bright purple, because of different zooxanthellae.

# SEA FANS : CORALS

### SPINY SEA FAN
*(Muricea muricata)*
2 ft max. Dense, branching rods in a fan shape. Retracted polyps have a spiny aperture.

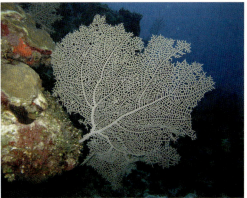

### WIDE MESH SEA FAN
*(Gorgonia mariae)*
14 in max. Smaller, gray to yellow fans with larger spaces between the branches. Polyps in two rows.

### LONG SPINE SEA FAN
*(Muricea pinnata)*
6 ft max. Highly branched, gray to yellow fan shape. Retracted polyps have a spiny aperture.

### GOLDEN SEA SPRAY
*(Heterogorgia uatumani)*
12 in max. Thick, light brown to yellow branches form a fan shape, with bright yellow polyps.

### ORANGE DEEPWATER FAN
*(Nicella goreaui)*
18 in max. Bright orange to red fans with distinctive white polyps. Found under ledges and overhangs.

### DEEPWATER SEA FAN
*(Iciligorgia schrammi)*
5 ft max. Large, reddish fans with widely-spaced branches and lighter polyps. Found on deeper walls.

### COLORFUL SEA ROD
*(Diodogorgia nodulifera)*
12 in max. Bright red fan with white to transparent polyps with yellow bases. Found under ledges.

> Sea Rods live mainly in shallow waters, though larger colonies, up to 7 ft tall, can be found at depth. Their color can vary, depending on whether their tentacles are open and feeding or retracted. Most are yellow or brown, but on deeper reefs and under dark ledges, they can be very colorful.

### BLACK SEA ROD
*(Plexaura homomalla)*
2 ft max. Large, bushy colonies of branching black rods with brown polyps. Common in the shallows.

### BLACK SEA ROD (VARIETY)
*(Plexaura homomalla)*
With the lighter polyps retracted, the rod appears darker with slight bumps around the polyp openings.

# SEA RODS : CORALS

### SWOLLEN KNOB CANDELABRUM
*(Eunicea mammosa)*
1.5 ft max. Light yellow to brown rods branching in a fan shape. Densely-packed polyps on longer stalks.

### DOUGHNUT SEA ROD
*(Eunicea fusca)*
1.5 ft max. Short, bushy colonies with gray stalks and yellow polyps with rounded, raised apertures.

### KNOBBY SEA RODS (VARIETY)
*(Eunicea sp.)*
Knobby Sea Rods come in many colors, from purple to tan, most noticeable when polyps are retracted.

### KNOBBY SEA RODS
*(Eunicea sp.)*
3 ft max. Light brown to yellow rods branching in a single plane. Retracted, it has a knobby surface.

### POROUS SEA RODS
*(Pseudoplexaura sp.)*
7 ft max. Rounded colony of thin rods branching from a single holdfast. Polyps have oval apertures.

### POROUS SEA RODS (VARIETY)
*(Pseudoplexaura sp.)*
With polyps retracted (left side) the oval apertures can be seen. Color varies from gray to purple.

### DELICATE SPINY SEA ROD
*(Muricea laxa)*
2 ft max. Pale, slender rods branch out into a
bushy shape. Retracted polyps have a spiny aperture.

> 👓 Sea Rods provide an excellent shelter for many juvenile fish species that can hide among the stalks, such as the Slender Filefish (p. 257). Sometimes butterflyfish (p. 250) and certain nudibranch species (p. 145) can be found feeding on the fleshy polyps.

### DELICATE SPINY SEA ROD (VARIETY)
*(Muricea laxa)*
Delicate Spiny Sea Rods can appear quiet different
with the polyps retracted. Stems are tan to purple.

### SHELF KNOB SEA ROD
*(Eunicea succinea)*
2 ft max. Yellow to brown fan or bush shape.
The base of each polyp forms a shelf-like projection.

# SEA RODS : CORALS

### SLIT-PORE SEA ROD
(Plexaurella sp.)
4 ft max. Thick, rounded rods, rarely branching.
Retracted polyps have a flat, slit-like aperture.

### GIANT SLIT PORE SEA RODS
(Plexaurella nutans)
7 ft max. Thick, tall, rounded rods with swollen tips.
Retracted polyps have a rounded, slit-like aperture.

### ORANGE SPINY SEA RODS
(Muricea elongata)
1.5 ft max. Bushy colonies branching in all directions.
Yellow to light brown with bright white polyps.

### BENT SEA ROD
(Plexaura flexuosa)
16 in max. Rounded, light brown branches grow
in fan shapes. Polyps are paler than the branches.

### ROUGH SEA PLUME
(Muriceopsis flavida)
2.5 ft max. Numerous, short, purple branches
from main stalks. Polyps are randomly distributed.

### SLIMY SEA PLUME
(Pseudopterogorgia americana)
3.5 ft max. Bushy yellow plume with purple
main branches. Long, feather-like branchlets.

## BUSHY SEA WHIP
*(Nicella schmitti)*
2 ft max. A single stalk branches and re-branches to form a fan shape. Bright red with white polyps.

Sea Whips are often mistaken for Black Corals (p. 78) because they can also be found at greater depths and the tentacles of each individual coral polyp are white in color, just like true Black Corals. Sea Whips are also commonly found growing under ledges and overhangs.

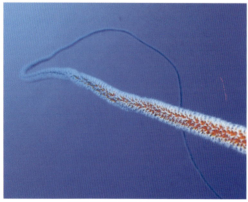

## DEVIL'S SEA WHIP
*(Ellisella barbadensis)*
8 ft max. Long, whip-like, red to orange stalk tapering slightly towards the tip. Dense white polyps.

## GROOVED BLADE SEA WHIP
*(Pterogorgia guadalupensis)*
2 ft max. Flattened, purple branches in fan or bush shapes. White polyps extend from grooves on edges.

# SEA WHIPS : CORALS

### BIPINNATE SEA PLUME (VARIETY)
*(Pseudopterogorgia bipinnata)*
Occasionally the branches of the Bipinnate Sea Plume will be bright yellow or even white.

### BIPINNATE SEA PLUME
*(Pseudopterogorgia bipinnata)*
2 ft max. Single plane of widely-spaced branches with paired branchlets. Most commonly purple.

### SEA PLUMES
*(Pseudopterogorgia sp.)*
7 ft max. Tall, unbranched, delicate stalks in gray or purple with fine branchlets. Polyps are brown to gray.

### YELLOW SEA WHIP
*(Pterogorgia citrina)*
14 in max. Short, yellow, bushy colonies of flattened branches. White polyps on all branch edges.

### ANGULAR SEA WHIP
*(Pterogorgia anceps)*
2 ft max. Bushy, branching colony with each branch having an "X" or "Y" shape in cross section.

### LONG SEA WHIPS
*(Ellisella elongata)*
5 ft max. Dozens of thin, red stalks branching out from a single base. Tiny, dense white polyps.

In the last 10 years there has been a dramatic upsurge in the number of diseases that are threatening coral reefs throughout the Caribbean. The bacteria that cause these diseases are naturally occurring elements of a reef ecosystem and coral reefs can usually recover from small outbreaks. Too many nutrients in the seawater will allow the harmful bacteria to thrive, causing outbreaks of diseases that the reef cannot recover from. Reefs actually grow best in relatively nutrient-poor water, where more sunlight can make it down through the water column to the corals. Clear water is vital to coral reef health.

As the Caribbean becomes more crowded, run-off from coastal development upsets a fine balance that has taken millennia to reach. A recent introduction of land-based pollutants and human sewage is allowing microbial diseases, once held in check, to flourish and spread at an alarming rate.

Algae grows much faster than corals, and if an infected coral head suddenly dies, the algae will soon take over. The plants will grow faster than they can be eaten by the local herbivores, leading to what is known as an algae bloom: a reef covered with a smothering layer of green that no light can penetrate.

Animals that need the coral for food and shelter die off and the larger fish on the top of the food chain are finally unable to live. Too many nutrients in the water means coral diseases, algae growth, and eventually a barren, silent reef.

# CORAL DISEASES : CORALS

### BLACK BAND DISEASE
First discovered in the 1970's in Belize and Florida, this disease is now found throughout the Caribbean. It appears as a thin line of black cyanobacteria that spreads across a living coral head, "consuming" the flesh of the coral as it moves, leaving the white skeleton exposed. This skeleton is soon covered with opportunistic algae that destroy any chance of the colony regrowing. It spreads quickly, up to an inch a day, so a coral head that took decades to grow can die off in just a few weeks.

### WHITE BAND DISEASE
This disease was first spotted in St. Croix in 1977 and is also now found throughout the Caribbean. It attacks mainly Acropora species like Staghorn and Elkhorn Corals (p. 61) and there are areas where the populations of these important reef-building corals have been completely wiped out. The disease begins at the base of a coral head and works it's way towards the tips, with living tissue falling dead off the coral head. Its spread throughout the Caribbean is linked to increased human development and activity.

### WHITE PLAGUE
White Plague is a coral disease that appears similar to White Band Disease, but affects a greater number of coral species. It begins at the base of a coral head and spreads upward and outward in an arc. It can devour as much as 1 inch of living coral in a day. The large plate coral shown on the left was completely dead within a week of this photograph being taken. The primary cause of this disease has been attributed to poor water quality and pollutants from human sources, such as chemical run-off and sewage.

### WHITE BLOTCH DISEASE
Affecting Star Corals (genus Montastraea, p. 68) and Brain Corals (p. 65) this disease is spreading rapidly. It was first detected in Florida in 1994 and has already spread to cover the whole of the Caribbean. Fortunately this disease is one of the slowest to advance, killing about 1 inch every month. Once the disease sets in, however, algae soon grows over the exposed coral skeleton and the coral's fate is usually sealed. The causes and mechanisms of this disease are still largely unknown.

### CORAL BLEACHING
Coral Bleaching occurs when a coral expels the symbiotic algae that gives it its color. This happens due to stresses in the environment such as higher temperatures and salinity due to global warming or El Niño weather patterns. The white of the underlying skeleton can be seen through the transparent flesh of the coral. If conditions become favorable again, the corals can reabsorb the symbiotic algae and continue to grow. However, while it is in this bleached, dormant phase the coral is vulnerable to the diseases listed above.

## AGUA VIVA JELLY
*(Olindias sambaquiensis)*
2 in max. Rounded dome is wider than it is tall.
Both short primary and long secondary tentacles.

Jellyfish, some of the oldest and simplest forms of life, have been around for over 650 million years, long before the time of the dinosaurs. They are about 95% water and have a very simple nervous system, used for detecting light, orientation and salinity. They can actively hunt plankton and small pelagic fishes, using stinging cells on their tentacles called nematocysts. The prey is pulled up into the main body for digestion. Some fish have adapted to live among these tentacles without getting stung, catching a safe ride throughout the world's oceans.

The sting of some jellyfish can be quite painful to divers. The best thing to do is scrape off any remaining tentacles from the skin with a razor blade or other flat object. Do not rub the area or apply fresh water, this will only cause more nematocysts to activate. Hot water or vinegar will neutralize some of the sting.

The Thimble Jelly (on the right) can gather in groups of millions of individuals. This is called a bloom, and usually occurs in late summer when nutrient levels in the ocean are high. The blooms can be so dense as to blot out the sun!

# JELLYFISHES : INVERTEBRATES

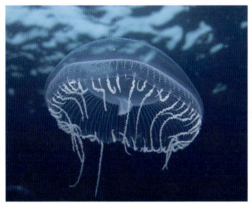

### JELLY HYDROMEDUSA
*(Aequorea aequorea)*
4 in max. Transparent dome. Thicker tentacles attach to the dome and also appear to continue into it.

### CLUB HYDROMEDUSA
*(Orchistoma pileus)*
1 in max. Transparent dome. Long thin tentacles have a club-shaped bulge where they attach.

### THIMBLE JELLY
*(Linuche unguiculata)*
0.75 in max. Thimble-shaped dome is transparent on top and brown below. Only a few, short tentacles.

### CLINGING JELLYFISH
*(Gonionemus vertens)*
2 in max. Clear bell with dozens of orange tentacles with rounded tips for holding onto the reef.

### UPSIDEDOWN JELLY
*(Cassiopea frondosa)*
8 in max. Flattened bell with short, bunched tentacles above. Swims upside down in the shallows.

### MANGROVE UPSIDEDOWN JELLY
*(Cassiopea xamachana)*
12 in max. Flattened bell with long branching tentacles. Swims upside down in the shallows.

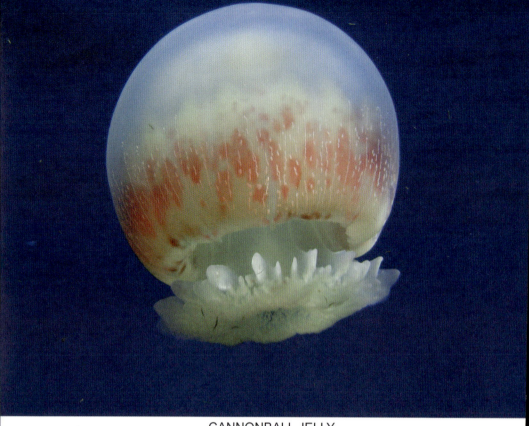

### CANNONBALL JELLY
*(Stomolophus meleagris)*
8 in max. Large round dome with short skirt of tentacles below. Red, yellow or blue markings around the rim.

> 🤿 Jellyfish can have large, rounded domes that use a jet-like motion to propel them through the water to hunt for food. Others, like the Comb Jellies, have no stinging tentacles and comb-like rows of cilia rippling along their bodies, allowing them to move slowly through the water column.

### MOON JELLY
*(Aurelia aurita)*
16 in max. Large, whitish dome with a four-leaf clover pattern inside. Numerous thin tentacles.

### MARBLE JELLY
*(Lychnorhiza sp.)*
6 in max. White, rounded dome with black marbled markings. Shorter clusters of white tentacles.

# COMB JELLIES : INVERTEBRATES

### SEA WALNUT
*(Mnemiopsis mccraydyi)*
4 in max. Transparent body, sometimes with brown or green blotches inside. Small warty lumps.

### SPOTWING COMB JELLY
*(Ocyropsis maculata)*
4 in max. Transparent, flattened body with four distinctive brown to black spots on the wings.

### WARTY COMB JELLY
*(Leocothea multicornis)*
8 in max. The largest Comb Jelly. Transparent, with distinctively long spikes along the body.

### WINGED COMB JELLY
*(Ocyropsis crystallina)*
3.5 in max. Transparent body, somewhat flattened, with four distinctive wings. No other markings.

### FLATTENED HELMET COMB JELLY
*(Beroe ovata)*
6 in max. Flat transparent body with wide lines. Straight edge on one side, rounded on the other.

### SLENDER COMB JELLY
*(Beroe gracilis)*
5 ft max. Long, slender body with faint muscular lines inside. Fluorescence along the outer edges.

## RED SPOTTED SIPHONOPHORE
*(Forskalia edwardsi)*
3 in max. Transparent bell with tiny red spots.
Thin tentacles with purple spots can reach up to 12 in.

Siphonophores, including the Portuguese Man-of-War, are not true jellyfish, but can deliver a painful sting to divers. They often have pink or purple spots or tentacles, which makes them easier to see. They should be given a wide berth, some of their tentacles can be up to 30 feet long.

## SEA GOOSEBERRY
*(Euplakamis sp.)*
0.5 in max. Tiny, transparent, oval shape with reddish tints. Two long, thin tentacles extend outwards.

## WARTY JELLYFISH
*(Pelagia noctiluca)*
4 in max. The bell has a rough texture with tiny purple spots. Color ranges from pink to transparent.

# SIPHONOPHORES : INVERTEBRATES

### PORTUGUESE MAN-OF-WAR
*(Physalia physalis)*
6 in max. Pale purple, gas-filled float with a pinched edge at the top. Purple tentacles can reach 30 ft.

### PAIRED BELL SIPHONOPHORE
*(Agalma okeni)*
3 in max. Transparent body with bell-shaped sides. Thin tentacles can reach up to one foot in length.

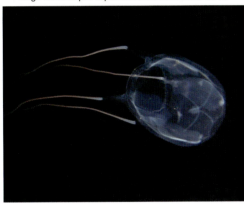

### SEAWASP
*(Carybdea alata)*
3.5 in max. Transparent to purplish dome with four long, thin tentacles. Sting causes intense pain.

### FLOATING SIPHONOPHORE
*(Rhizophysa spp.)*
2 in max. A small bubble of air in the main body. Tentacles have purple spots and can reach 30 feet.

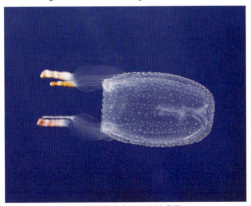

### WARTY SEAWASP
*(Carybdea marsupialis)*
3.5 in max. A shorter dome with tiny bumps that also contain nematocysts. Four retractable, purple tentacles.

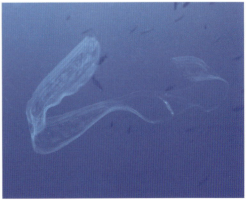

### VENUS' SEA GIRDLE
*(Cestum veneris)*
5 ft max. Transparent, ribbon-like body with a thin central band. Lower edge may show fluorescence.

Tunicates are often overlooked on the reef. These simple animals resemble sponges, as they have large openings for expelling water. Unlike sponges, they have bands of muscles around the body that allow them to quickly open and close these siphons for protection. Tunicates are filter feeders, constantly sucking in water through smaller incurrent siphons around their body, and filtering out tiny, even microscopic, plankton as food before sending the water out through larger excurrent siphons. Usually quite small, they also are some of the most colorful animals on the reef.

There are three main types of tunicates: larger tube-shaped animals where both siphons are visible, flattened colonies of encrusting animals with visible excurrent siphons, and the transparent, free-floating Pelagic Tunicates that can be found drifting onto reefs from the open ocean.

Tube-Shaped Tunicate

Encrusting Tunicate

Pelagic Tunicate

# TUNICATES : INVERTEBRATES

### REEF TUNICATE
*(Rhopalaea abdominalis)*
1.5 in max. Smooth, rounded body with large incurrent and excurrent siphons. Purple to brown.

### GREEN TUBE TUNICATE
*(Ascidia sydneiensis)*
5 in max. Single, green to yellow tube extending from the reef. Single, large siphon at the tip.

### PAINTED TUNICATES
*(Clavelina picta)*
0.75 in max. Transparent body with purple circles "painted" around the siphons. Often grows in clusters.

### BULB TUNICATES
*(Clavelina sp.)*
This term describes the many species of tunicate with this general shape. Often with yellow markings.

### YELLOW BULB TUNICATES
*(Clavelina sp.)*
0.5 max. Found under ledges and overhangs in dense clusters. Faint yellow lines inside the body.

### GIANT TUNICATE
*(Polycarpa spongiabilis)*
5 in max. Large, globular body, often encrusted in algae. The siphons have long, inward-facing spines.

## STRAWBERRY TUNICATE
*(Eudistoma sp.)*
1.5 in max. Tiny individuals bunched together in a bulb and attached to a central stalk. Their color varies greatly.

Strawberry Tunicates are often found growing upside-down under ledges and in crevices in the reef. Despite their name they are not always red, but often purple, orange or even white in color. Sometimes they grow singly and sometimes in patches of up to a few dozen individuals.

## BLACK CONDOMINIUM TUNICATE
*(Eudistoma obscuratum)*
4 in max. Tiny individuals joined in a common black tunic. Each siphon is outlined with thin white lines.

## WHITE CONDOMINIUM TUNICATE
*(Eudistoma sp.)*
4 in max. Numerous individuals can be seen by their paired siphons, all encased in a common, pale tunic.

# TUNICATES : INVERTEBRATES

**BLACK OVERGROWING TUNICATE**
*(Didemnum vanderhorsti)*
4 in colony max. Made up of tiny individuals with
fine white markings in a common, swollen, black tunic.

**WHITE SPECK TUNICATE**
*(Didemnum conchyliatum)*
2 in colony max. Tiny, with shared excurrent
siphons. Grows under ledges in small clusters.

**ROW ENCRUSTING TUNICATES**
*(Botrylloides sp.)*
0.5 in max. Collective name for growth in rows.
Pale incurrent siphons, larger, dark excurrent siphons.

**FLAT TUNICATE**
*(Botrylloides nigrum)*
0.25 in max. Long colonies of rusty and yellow to
orange individuals, sharing a larger excurrent siphon.

**GEOMETRIC ENCRUSTING TUNICATE**
*(Botryllus sp.)*
0.25 in max. Collective name for shapes with small
incurrent siphons and a shared excurrent siphon.

**GEOMETRIC ENCRUSTING TUNICATE**
*(Botryllus sp.)*
There are dozens of species in this group. All
share the symmetrical pattern of incurrent pores.

## PELAGIC TUNICATE
*(Salpa sp.)*
2 in max. Transparent body with blue markings. Faint
muscles and neural ganglia (brain) can be seen.

 Pelagic tunicates are often mistaken for jellyfish, but they have a few distinguishing features, like wide incurrent and excurrent siphons that allow them to jet through the water. They also have a very simple nervous system, usually visible through their transparent bodies. A simple, round "brain" called the neural ganglia can often be seen. Even the tiny striations of the simple muscles are visible. Because they are pelagic, small larval animals and fishes can sometimes be found taking shelter in and around them.

Pelagic Tunicates take on many shapes and sizes. They all reproduce asexually by budding. Depending on the species, these buds will form long chains, discs or floral shapes, until individual tunicates break off and begin life on their own. They are most commonly seen in the summer months.

# TUNICATES : INVERTEBRATES

**MOTTLED ENCRUSTING TUNICATE**
*(Distaplia bermudensis)*
0.25 in max. Tiny individuals surrounding a shared excurrent siphon. Mottled in various colors.

**AZURE OVERGROWING TUNICATE**
*(Family: Didemnidae)*
6 in colony max. Thin, uniform blue mat of individuals encrusts over the substrate. Found on deeper reefs.

**ENCRUSTING SOCIAL TUNICATE**
*(Symplegma viride)*
0.25 in max. Tiny individuals growing from a common base that spreads across the substrate. Color varies.

**GLOBULAR ENCRUSTING TUNICATE**
*(Diplosoma glandulosum)*
4 in max. Tiny individuals empty into a common, deep excurrent siphon. Thin white markings.

**OVERGROWING MAT TUNICATE**
*(Trididemum solidum)*
12 in colony max. Hard, rough-textured mat that overgrows any substrate. Tiny excurrent siphons.

**OVERGROWING TUNICATE**
*(Family: Didemnidae)*
6 in colony max. Thin, colorful mat of individuals over the substrate, often upside-down under ledges.

## GIANT ANEMONE
*(Condylactis gigantea)*
12 in max. The largest of the anemone. Dozens of long tentacles with blue, red or green tips. Color is variable.

Anemones are very simple animals, similar to corals but more active. They are made up of a pedal disc, used for attaching to the reef, and an oral disc with a single opening in the middle, serving as both a mouth and an anus. Surrounding this opening are numerous tentacles, tipped with stinging cells called nematocysts. These can sting and immobilize prey, such as small fishes. Anemones can move slowly across the reef, at a few inches a day, or they can detach themselves from the reef and float away to a more productive spot.

👁 Look closer: some animals have evolved to make use of the stinging cells of the anemone as a shelter. The commonly found Pederson Cleaner Shrimp (p. 174) lives symbiotically with the Corkscrew Anemone and the Squat Anemone Shrimp (p. 179) is often found on the Giant Anemone. The eyes of the Banded Clinging Crab (pictured on the right) are perfectly camouflaged, poking out of the tentacles of the Knobby Anemone. These animals can resist the stings of the anemone, and in return they keep it clean of debris by foraging on the anemone's waste.

# ANEMONES : INVERTEBRATES

### GIANT ANEMONE (JUVENILE)
*(Condylactis gigantea)*
Younger anemones are often found attached to blades of Turtle Grass in lagoons or on shallow reef-tops.

### BERRIED ANEMONE
*(Alicia mirabilis)*
4 in max. Tightly packed knobs of stinging cells surround the mouth. Extends only at night to feed.

### HIDDEN ANEMONE
*(Lebrunia coralligens)*
2 in max. Tiny tentacles with rounded tips, poking from holes in the reef. Pale tips often have two lobes.

### BEADED ANEMONE
*(Epicystis crucifer)*
6 in max. Large, flattened oral disc with over 200 short tentacles, often with rings. Variable in color.

### SPONGE ANEMONE
*(undescribed, order Actinaria)*
2 in max. Brownish oral disc with a white mouth and long, white-banded tentacles. Found on sponges.

### PALE CLUMPING ANEMONE
*(Aiptasia sp.)*
1 in max. Numerous long, pointed tentacles around a darker oral disc. Often grows in dense groups.

## LAVENDER TUBE DWELLING ANEMONE
*(Unidentified, Order Ceriantharia)*
5 in max. Long, pointed tentacles with a central tuft
of pale lavender tentacles around a white oral disc.

Tube-Dwelling Anemones hide in the sand or in crevices on the reef until nightfall, when they extend their tentacles into the water to collect small animals as they swim by. They will often feed on the tiny worms attracted by a diver's light. If disturbed, they can retract in the blink of an eye.

## BANDED TUBE DWELLING ANEMONE
*(Arachnanthus nocturnus)*
3 in max. Whitish oral disc with brown and white
banded outer tentacles. Found in sand or on the reef.

## TRANSPARENT TUBE DWELLING ANEMONE
*(Unidentified, Order Ceriantharia)*
10 in max. Long, transparent body with long,
thin tentacles. Retreats quickly into the sand.

# ANEMONES : INVERTEBRATES

**WIDEBAND TUBE DWELLING ANEMONE**
*(Arachnanthus sp.)*
2 in max. Pale tentacles become maroon towards the mouth. The oral disc has large, pale blotches.

**TURTLE GRASS ANEMONE**
*(Viatrix globulifera)*
0.75 in max. Tiny body with long, speckled tentacles. Found in the shallows, attached to Turtle Grass.

**KNOBBY ANEMONE**
*(Lucida sp.)*
6 in max. Numerous long, transparent tentacles with densely-packed, small, pale knobs of stinging cells.

**RED WARTY ANEMONE**
*(Bunodsoma granulifera)*
5 in max. Reddish body covered with pale, warty knobs. Tentacles green, with red and yellow bands.

**CORKSCREW ANEMONE**
*(Bartholomea annulata)*
8 in max. Numerous transparent to greenish tentacles have pale, spiral patterns. Found in sandy areas.

**SUN ANEMONE**
*(Stichodactyla helianthus)*
6 in max. The oral disc is completely covered with short, rounded, green tentacles, like a carpet.

👁 Anemones are often be tough to identify on a dive because of the variety of colors and shapes that each species can display, depending on their location. Pictured above is a rare variation on the more common Club-Tipped Anemone. Some anemones seem to produce their own light, called fluorescing, as seen with the Beaded Anemone, pictured on the left. The fluorescence comes from a rare kind of algae that grows in the flesh of the tentacles. This symbiotic relationship with algae is another trait that many anemone species share with their close cousins, the hard corals.

Anemones have a multitude of ways to feed themselves. Some live in a symbiotic relationship with certain algae that live in their tissues, just like corals. The algae has a safe place to grow, while the anemone gets the oxygen and sugars that are produced by photosynthesis. Anemones also harbour smaller animals like the Sun Anemone Shrimp (p. 179) and can absorb and live on their wastes. They can also absorb vital nutrients directly from the seawater. Some species, like the Sun Anemone, can live to be over 100 years old.

# ANEMONES : INVERTEBRATES

### CLUB TIPPED ANEMONE
*(Telmatactis americana)*
4 in max. Flattened disc with large, rounded tips on the reddish tentacles. The disc is flecked with pale spots.

### BRANCHING ANEMONE
*(Lebrunia danae)*
12 in max. Small, brownish knobs on branching, finger-like tentacles, often with white to light brown highlights.

### HITCH-HIKING ANEMONE
*(Calliactis tricolor)*
3 in max. Found on Hermit Crabs. Variable in color. Smooth body with numerous dark spots near the base.

### LIGHTBULB ANEMONE
*(undescribed, order Actinaria)*
4 in max. As yet undescribed, this anemone has large, bulbous, white tentacles, often with pointed tips.

### UNKNOWN ANEMONE
*(undescribed, order Actinaria)*
There are still many species in the Caribbean that have yet to be described or possibly even discovered.

### SUNBURST ANEMONE
*(undescribed, order Actinaria)*
2 in max. Bright, radial pattern from a reddish central disc. Long tentacles. Color varies from yellow to red.

👓 Corallimorphs, once thought to be anemones, are also known as Mushroom Corals. Although they share features with both corals and anemones, they are now placed in a family by themselves. They can feed using symbiotic algae in their flesh, but unlike corals, they have no internal skeleton. They differ from anemones by remaining attached to the same place on the reef, using poisons in their tentacles to stop other animals from getting too close. They also feed by collecting plankton on a layer of mucus which is drawn into the mouth, and some are even able to capture and devour small prey.

**WARTY CORALLIMORPH**
*(Discosoma sanctithomae)*
4 in max. Flattened disc with a raised oral opening. Larger, bulbous tentacles, often with pointed ends.

**WARTY CORALLIMORPH (VARIETY)**
*(Discosoma sanctithomae)*
Varies greatly in color, but all have larger tentacles towards the mouth and a fringe of smaller tentacles.

# CORALLIMORPHS : INVERTEBRATES

### FLORIDA CORALLIMORPH
*(Ricordea florida)*
2 in max. Rounded tentacles around a pale mouth. Longer tentacles around body. Usually green to orange.

### FLORIDA CORALLIMORPH (VARIETY)
*(Ricordea florida)*
Grows singly or in large groupings, this corallimorph is also able to fluoresce, seeming to give off its own light.

### UMBRELLA CORALLIMORPH
*(Discosoma neglectum)*
3 in max. Flattened, pale oral disc with short, rectangular tentacles around the outer edges.

### FORKED TENTACLE CORALLIMORPH
*(Discosoma carlgreni)*
3 in max. Green to transparent body with small forked tentacles radiating outwards on the oral disc.

### PARACHUTE CORALLIMORPH
*(Order: Corallimorpharian)*
3 in max. Thin, flat oral disc with lines of small tentacles radiating out from the central mouth. Color varies.

### ORANGE BALL CORALLIMORPH
*(Pseudocorynactis caribbeorum)*
2 in max. Orange body and pale to transparent oral disc. All the tentacles end in bright orange balls.

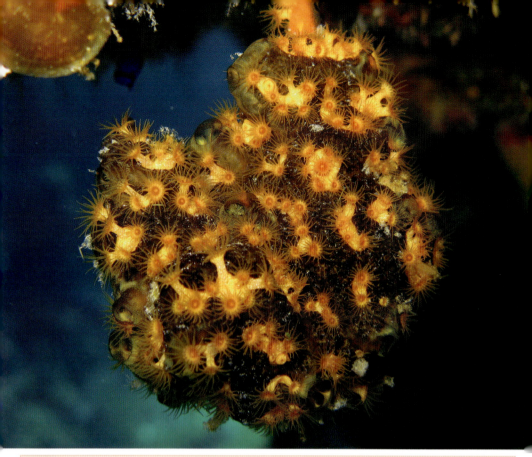

🥽 At first glance, zoanthids appear to be tiny coral polyps. On closer inspection you can see the tiny slit in the middle of the oral disc that acts a mouth for this tiny creature. They are also known as Button Polyps. The bright colors are not part of the animal itself, but come from different algae that live within the tissues, just as in the true, reef-building corals. They are most often found in clusters, growing on sponges or in dense mats on the top of the reef itself. They are very hardy animals; given enough sunlight they can spread across a reef quickly, adding two or three new polyps every week.

**MAT ZOANTHID**
*(Zoanthus pulchellus)*
0.5 in max. Grows in dense mats of individuals, gray to light brown. May fluoresce on deeper reefs.

**MAT ZOANTHID (VARIETY)**
*(Zoanthus pulchellus)*
Color and density is highly variable. Loose patches of individuals or dense clusters. Whitish to dark green.

# ZOANTHIDS : INVERTEBRATES

**GOLDEN ZOANTHID**
*(Parazoanthus swiftii)*
0.25 in max. Bright yellow body and tentacles. They are often found at depth on Thin Rope Sponges (p. 123).

**HYDROID ZOANTHID**
*(Parazoanthus tunicans)*
0.25 in max. Light brown to yellow tentacles and body. Only found encrusting the Feather Hydroid (p. 117).

**BROWN ZOANTHID**
*(Order: Zoanthidea)*
0.5 in max. Short, brown tentacles and green body with a single, white blotch inside. Grows in clusters.

**BROWN ZOANTHID (VARIETY)**
*(Order: Zoanthidea)*
Often found growing in tightly packed clusters with overlapping edges. All have white markings inside.

**SUN ZOANTHID**
*(Palythoa grandis)*
1.25 in max. The largest of all the Zoanthids. A flattened disc in dark and light brown. Short tentacles.

**SUN ZOANTHID (VARIETY)**
*(Palythoa grandis)*
Sun Zoanthids grow solitary or in small groups and have a range of colors from green to reddish.

🥽 The defining characteristics of zoanthids are the two rings of tentacles around the mouth, and their ability to capture and take in small particles of sand and debris to help them maintain their body shape. unlike the true corals that actually produce their own calcium carbonate skeletons to live in. Zoanthids are not reef-builders, they merely borrow tiny bits of it for their use.

A rare form of zoanthid is the Snake Polyp (pictured below). Once classified as sea cucumbers because of their tubular shape and long bodies, they are nocturnal animals, only opening their tentacles at night to feed. Like many members of the zoanthid family, they have yet to be fully described.

**SNAKE POLYPS**
*(Isaurus tuberculatus)*
2 in max. Stiff tubular body growing out of the reef.
Mouth usually bent inwards. Color highly variable.

**SNAKE POLYP (VARIETY)**
*(Isaurus tuberculatus)*
These nocturnal zoanthids are firmly rooted to
the reef and only open their tentacles at night to feed.

# ZOANTHIDS : INVERTEBRATES

### SPONGE ZOANTHID
*(Parazoanthus parasiticus)*
0.25 in max. Brown tentacles and a pale body with a brown circle inside. Often on vase and rope sponges.

### WHITE ENCRUSTING ZOANTHID
*(Palythoa caribaeorum)*
0.25 in max. Short tentacles around a circular disc. Grows in clusters within a common, fleshy base.

### SOLITARY ZOANTHID
*(Order: Zoanthidea)*
An undescribed species, found growing singly. Unusually long, tapering tentacles around the oral disc.

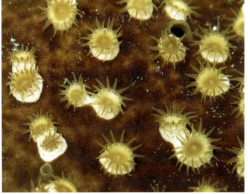

### BROWN SPONGE ZOANTHID
*(Parazoanthus catenularis)*
0.25 in max. Tentacles and body are pale brown. The base is white. Found on Encrusting Sponges (p. 32).

### MAROON SPONGE ZOANTHID
*(Parazoanthus puertoricense)*
0.25 in max. Tentacles and body are deep purple to maroon. Often found on Volcano Sponges (p. 37).

### YELLOW SPONGE ZOANTHID
*(Epizoanthus cutressi)*
0.25 in max. Twelve thin, yellow tentacles are arranged around a darker yellow oral disc and body.

### SOLITARY GORGONIAN HYDROID
*(Ralpharia gorgoniae)*
1 in max. Single, white polyp surrounded by thin, curling tentacles. Found on tips of Sea Plumes (p. 89).

Look closer: each individual polyp of a hydroid is like a tiny jellyfish, with a central mouth surrounded by stinging tentacles. Most have evolved to live together, each supporting and feeding the basic structure of the animal. They feed by stinging and capturing tiny plankton in the water.

### CHRISTMAS TREE HYDROID
*(Halocordyle disticha)*
3.5 in max. Branches alternate from a single stalk, with white polyps on the tips of each branch.

### SOLITARY SPONGE HYDROID
*(Zyzzyzus warreni)*
1 in max. Single polyps on long, thin stalks; each one surrounded by thin, straight, brown tentacles.

# HYDROIDS : INVERTEBRATES

### BRANCHING HYDROID
*(Sertularella speciosa)*
6 in max. Branches alternate at right angles from a single stalk. Polyps spread out on both sides of the branches.

### UNBRANCHED HYDROID
*(Cnidoscyphus marginatus)*
4 in max. An unbranched central stalk has yellowish, alternating polyps attached directly to it.

### FEATHER BUSH HYDROID
*(Dentitheca dendritica)*
14 in max. Thick, central stalks branch repeatedly to form a bush. Covered in Hydroid Zoanthids (p. 113).

### FEATHER HYDROID
*(Gymnangium longicauda)*
12 in max. Thin, whitish branches alternately spaced along a brownish central stalk, resembling a feather.

### THREAD HYDROID
*(Halopteris carinata)*
6 in max. Long, thin central stalks with tiny, alternating branchlets of polyps. Usually grows in clusters.

### WHITE STINGER
*(Macrorhynchia philippina)*
4 in max. Rigid stalk with few only a few branches. Distinctively bright white polyps run in pairs.

🤿 Bryozoans are often mistaken for marine plants, but they are actually small animal colonies. Millions of tiny animals called zooids, each specialized to perform a different function, are gathered together to make up one of the oldest and simplest life-forms on Earth. Some zooids are for defense, some for reproduction and others for producing food. Bryozoans are filter feeders and they have been found in fossils up to 450 million years old. Previously thought of as a nuisance for fouling the bottoms of ships, these tiny, disease-resistant animals are now essential to modern cancer research.

**BLEEDING TEETH BRYOZOAN**
*(Trematooecia aviculifera)*
8 in max. Encrusting layer of larger, pink to reddish zooids visible to the naked eye, with pale openings.

**TUBULAR HORN BRYOZOAN**
*(Schizoporella violacea)*
6 in max. Purple to brown, encrusting colonies with branching, tube-like projections. Often covered in algae.

# BRYOZOANS : INVERTEBRATES

### WHITE TANGLED BRYOZOAN
*(Bracebridgia subsulcata)*
6 in max. Tangled clumps of white, cylindrical tubes that branch often. Found under deeper ledges.

### BROWN FAN BRYOZOAN
*(Canda simplex)*
1.5 in max. Rounded, brown disc of interconnected branching stalks, each ending in a reddish tip.

### SEAWEED BRYOZOAN
*(Caulibugula dendrograpta)*
16 in max. Series of fine, white, fan-shaped colonies growing radially outwards from a common stalk.

### TAN FAN BRYOZOAN
*(Scrupocellaria sp.)*
1.25 in max. Light brown disc of tightly spaced, highly branched and interconnected stalks. No red tips.

### PURPLE REEF FAN
*(Bugula minima)*
2 in max. Rounded pink to purple disc of widely spaced stalks that rarely branch. Found on deeper reefs.

### WHITE FAN BRYOZOAN
*(Reteporellina evelinae)*
2 in max. White, branching, fan-shaped stalks that rarely connect. Branch outwards in a single plane.

## SPONGE BRITTLE STAR
*(Ophiothrix suensonii)*
8 in max. Five long, thin arms with long, thin spines.
Dark lines down each arm. Small central body.

Brittle stars are one of the most common creatures on a healthy reef; as many as twenty can be found on every square foot. Most active at night, they can also be seen in the daytime resting inside sponges or hiding under pieces of rubble in the shallows. They are surprisingly agile, walking on their five arms. They gather in late summer, in groups of many dozens, to spawn.

Although brittle stars are relatively small and can crawl quickly across the reef, they are often preyed upon by small carnivores, like the Yellowhead Wrasse (on the right). Just like lizards on land, they can shake off one of their limbs when attacked and it will continue to move about, distracting the hunter. After the brittle star crawls away it can easily regenerate this lost limb, and it can even regenerate lost internal organs after a serious attack. Brittle stars are some of the simplest and most successful creatures on Earth, with fossilized records going back over 500 million years.

# BRITTLE STARS : INVERTEBRATES

### RUBY BRITTLE STAR (VARIETY)
*(Ophioderma rubicundum)*
Smaller individuals often have a variety of colors on one animal, from green to red to orange to purple.

### RUBY BRITTLE STAR
*(Ophioderma rubicundum)*
9 in max. Long, thin arms have short spines and are banded with red. Color and patterns are highly variable.

### HARLEQUIN BRITTLE STAR
*(Ophioderma appressum)*
13 in max. Body is speckled with black or white. Arms are banded with gray, green, brown or white.

### RUBY BRITTLE STAR (VARIETY)
*(Ophioderma rubicundum)*
Larger individuals can often have a pattern of pale lines on the central disc, similar to the Slimy Brittlestar.

### BLUNT-SPINED BRITTLE STAR (VARIETY)
*(Ophiocoma echinata)*
Larger individuals can have contrasting colors on their central discs and arms.

### BLUNT-SPINED BRITTLE STAR
*(Ophiocoma echinata)*
12 in max. Smooth central disc in gray or black. The arms have thick, blunt spines, longer near the center.

**SPOTTED BRITTLE STAR**
*(Ophioderma guttatum)*
18 in max. Long arms have very short spines. The smooth central body and the arms have tiny spots.

> Brittle stars feed by secreting a mucous that is caught between the spines along their arms. This sticky substance can catch floating bits of debris and zooplankton from the water. The arms then transfer this substance, together with the food, to the small mouth underneath the central disc.

**CIRCLE-MARKED BRITTLE STAR**
*(Ophioderma cinereum)*
14 in max. The central body has ten spots, each outlined in black. The arms are often banded.

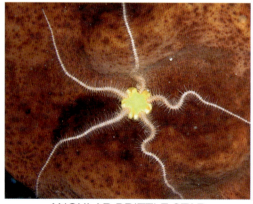

**ANGULAR BRITTLE STAR**
*(Ophiothrix angulata)*
8 in max. The central body has five distinct lobes between the arms. Color variable. Found on sponges.

# SEA STARS : INVERTEBRATES

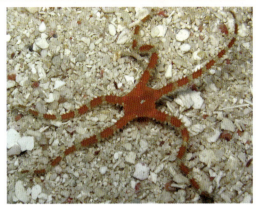

**SLIMY BRITTLE STAR**
*(Ophiomyxa flaccida)*
16 in max. The long arms have serrated edges.
They taper at the ends and are banded in red or tan.

**SLIMY BRITTLE STAR (VARIETY)**
*(Ophiomyxa flaccida)*
The central disc of some individuals has a mottled,
not striped, pattern of red and white to tan.

**CUSHION SEA STAR**
*(Oreaster reticulatus)*
14 in max. Five short, trinagular arms. Thick body
with a network of raised bumps in radiating lines.

**BLUNT-ARMED SEA STAR**
*(Asterina folium)*
1 in max. Five short, triangular arms with blunt
ends. Color varies from white to yellow, red or blue.

**COMMON COMET STAR**
*(Linckia guildingii)*
8 in max. Four to seven arms, all of different lengths,
with blunt tips. Color varies from orange to tan.

**COMET STAR**
*(Ophidiaster guildingii)*
4 in max. Five tubular arms, all of the same length,
with upturned tips. Color varies from tan to purple.

## GIANT BASKET STAR
*(Astrophyton muricatum)*
3 ft max. Long, repeatedly branching arms extend from a tangled mass of branchlets. Light brown to reddish.

👓 Basket stars only spread out their arms to feed at night. They remain in a tight protective ball in the daytime, digesting their evening meal. Sometimes they will wrap soft corals or sea fans around them like a cloak. They have no blood, but use filtered sea water inside their bodies to move nutrients around. Each can live for up to 35 years.

👓 Although crinoids are mostly found hiding deep inside cracks in the reef, they are able to move about on the reef floor to get to better feeding sites. Using the shorter "legs" under their bodies, they can move quite rapidly until they find a new hiding spot. At night they will venture high up onto the top of the reef, and feed by capturing plankton drifting by in the currents.

# CRINOIDS : INVERTEBRATES

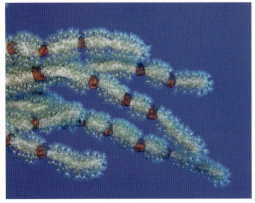

### SEA ROD BASKET STAR
*(Schizostella bifurcata)*
4 in max. Reddish-brown, banded arms that only branch once or twice. Found on sea rods (p. 84).

### LACE CORAL BRITTLE STAR
*(Sigsbeia conifera)*
0.5 in max. Cream to reddish-brown disc with five red-banded arms. Lives only on Rose Lace Coral (p. 59).

### BEADED CRINOID
*(Davidaster discoidea)*
8 in max. Twenty arms. Color is highly variable. Side branches are usually tinged with silver or gold.

### BLACK AND WHITE CRINOID
*(Nemaster grandis)*
12 in max. Forty arms. Branches are solid black and numerous side branches are tipped in white.

### GOLDEN CRINOID
*(Davidaster rubiginosa)*
12 in max. Twenty arms. Branches and side branches are usually golden; but also in green, yellow or black.

### SWIMMING CRINOID
*(Analcidometra armata)*
4 in max. Ten arms. Pale branches with red side branches. Can swim about by undulating the arms.

Sea urchins are some of the longest-living creatures on the planet: some species can live for over 200 years. They are protected by long, mobile spines. Even so, they rarely venture out in the day, hiding in crevices until nightfall, when they come out and clean the reef of decaying plant and animal matter. For this reason they are very important to reef ecosystems. In 1983 a mysterious disease killed off 97% of the Long-Spined Urchins. As a result, the Caribbean is still recovering from the vast algae bloom that took over the reef after this event. Sea urchins reproduce in the summer by releasing millions of jelly-covered eggs and then clouds of sperm into the water. The eggs can remain as plankton for up to 5 years until they develop enough to settle onto the reef.

Look closely between the spines of some sea urchins to see tiny tentacles, called podia, with miniature suction cups on their ends. They use these to move about the reef and even to climb sideways, up and over obstacles. Some will use these tentacles to grab onto loose bits of algae or empty shells to cover their body for extra protection.

# SEA URCHINS : INVERTEBRATES

### LONG-SPINED URCHIN (VARIETY)
*(Diadema antillarum)*
A less common, white-spined variety. Some individuals have black and white spines together.

### LONG-SPINED URCHIN
*(Diadema antillarum)*
10 in max. Numerous long, thin spines, longer towards the top of the animal. Nocturnal.

### MAGNIFICENT URCHIN
*(Astropyga magnifica)*
12 in max. Dark purple body with radiating red lines. Long spines run in radial bands down the body.

### LONG-SPINED URCHIN (JUVENILE)
*(Diadema antillarum)*
Juveniles are usually more colorful than the adults. The spines are often banded in contrasting colors.

### REEF URCHIN
*(Echinometra viridis)*
4 in max. Dark red body. The short, pointed spines all have darker tips and a pale ring around their base.

### SLATE PENCIL URCHIN
*(Eucidaris tribuloides)*
6 in max. Light red to brownish body with only a few, large, tapering spines; banded with brown rings.

### JEWEL URCHIN
*(Lytechinus williamsi)*
3.5 in max. Body and spines are white or light green.
Short podia end in small purple balls, others are clear.

> While some sea urchins use acids to slowly melt away holes into the reef, others will hide in the sand, waiting for nightfall. These are the sand dollars and sea biscuits. They have shorter, thicker spines that allow them to dig deep into the sand during the day.

### ROCK BORING URCHIN
*(Echinometra lucunter lucunter)*
4 in max. Short, brown spines from a rounded body that is either black to brown or reddish.

### SAND DOLLAR
*(Clypeaster subdepressus)*
6 in max. Flat, disc-shaped, brown body with a darker pentagonal design on the back. Very short spines.

# SEA URCHINS : INVERTEBRATES

**WEST INDIAN SEA EGG**
*(Tripneustes ventricosus)*
6 in max. Rounded, dark purple to black body.
The white spines are short and dense. Visible podia.

**VARIEGATED URCHIN**
*(Lytechinus variegatus)*
4 in max. Pale body with numerous white podia. Red or
white spines are short and dense, following plate lines.

**LONG SPINED SEA BISCUIT**
*(Plagiobrissus grandis)*
8 in max. Elongated oval-shaped body with short
brown spines. Long clear spines on the top and rear.

**INFLATED SEA BISCUIT**
*(Clypeaster rosaceus)*
8 in max. Flattened brown to red body with a
raised pentagonal design on the back. Short spines.

**SIX KEYHOLE SAND DOLLAR**
*(Leodia sexiesperforata)*
4 in max. Flat, disc-shaped body with six
elongated holes around the sides. Very short spines.

**RED HEART URCHIN**
*(Meoma ventricosa)*
8 in max. Dome-shaped body, flattened on
the bottom. Short, brown spines. Buried during the day.

　　　　　Most species of sea cucumbers will either be male or female, and they reproduce on certain nights of the year, usually in late summer. They make their way out onto the tops of the reef, stretching out into the current and releasing either sperm or eggs into the water. The eggs are fertilized and slowly develop near the surface, before settling onto a new patch of reef. The feeding tentacles develop first, followed by the tiny podia, or tube feet, used for locomotion.

Their role in the reef ecosystem is similar to that of earthworms on land. Sea cucumbers feed on algae, small animals and decaying organic matter, breaking these down into smaller particles. Bacteria can then re-introduce this waste into the food chain. Most sea cucumbers have tiny projections around the mouth for transferring the food into their stomachs. The Beaded Sea Cucumber (on the right) has a ring of even larger, moveable tentacles around its mouth, used for gathering food.

　　　　　Despite their unappetizing appearance and leathery skin, they can be eaten by larger, faster moving animals like the trunkfish on the left. Some species have developed an interesting defense strategy. If attacked, they can regurgitate a sticky mass from their stomachs onto the fish to entangle it. Others release a strong poison into the water, stunning attackers. There are some fish, crab and shrimp species that have evolved to live inside the stomachs of sea cucumbers for protection.

# SEA CUCUMBERS : INVERTEBRATES

### BEADED SEA CUCUMBER
*(Euapta lappa)*
3 ft max. Long, segmented body ends in thick tentacles around the mouth. Yellow stripes on the sides.

### CONICAL SEA CUCUMBER
*(Eostichopus arnesoni)*
16 in max. Dark brown with numerous, lighter, cone-shaped knobs along the back. The sole is reddish.

### FIVE-TOOTHED SEA CUCUMBER
*(Actinopyga agassizii)*
12 in max. The common name comes from the five, tooth-like appendages surrounding the mouth.

### FIVE-TOOTHED SEA CUCUMBER
*(Actinopyga agassizii)*
12 in max. Dark to light brown body, often with squared sides, covered with very small, pointed knobs.

### TIGER TAIL SEA CUCUMBER
*(Holothuria thomasi)*
7 ft max. The largest sea cucumber. A long, thin body extends from the reef. Short tentacles around mouth.

### DONKEY DUNG SEA CUCUMBER
*(Holothuria mexicana)*
14 in max. Dark brown to tan with numerous creases along the body. The sole is usually pink to white.

## THREE ROWED SEA CUCUMBER
*(Isostichopus badionotus)*
16 in max. Brown or tan body is covered in small,
sharp knobs, usually in sharply contrasting colors.

> Although there are relatively few different species of sea cucumbers in the Caribbean, they can often be difficult to identify because of the wide variety of colors and patterns they can display, depending on the size, depth and the food sources of each individual.

## THREE ROWED SEA CUCUMBER
*(Isostichopus badionotus)*
Sometimes each podia is a contrasting, darker
brown, like chocolate drops across the back.

## THREE ROWED SEA CUCUMBER
*(Isostichopus badionotus)*
Sometimes a solid brown body with bright yellow
spots surrounding each podia across the back.

# SEA CUCUMBERS : INVERTEBRATES

### FLORIDA SEA CUCUMBER
*(Holothuria floridana)*
10 in max. Tan body tapers towards the ends.
Often mottled. Numerous, sharp knobs along the back.

### GRUB SEA CUCUMBER
*(Holothuria cubana)*
6 in max. Pale body, often with patches of brown
along the sides. Numerous, sharp knobs along the back.

### SLENDER SEA CUCUMBER
*(Holothuria impatiens)*
10 in max. Thin, elongated body with long thin podia on
the back. Color varies from brown to yellow to reddish.

### FURRY SEA CUCUMBER
*(Astichopus multifidus)*
16 in max. Thick, fleshy body ranges from white to
brown. Surrounded by long, slender, pointed podia.

### FURRY SEA CUCUMBER
*(Astichopus multifidus)*
Can be mottled in light and dark brown with
light brown or white spots across the back.

### FURRY SEA CUCUMBER
*(Astichopus multifidus)*
The podia along the back are sometimes in
a contrasting, lighter color, each circled in white.

## BEARDED FIREWORM
*(Hermodice carunculata)*
12 in max. Long, segmented body lined with white tufts of bristles. Fleshy red appendage on the head.

Divers should be wary around fireworms. They get their name from the intense sting they can inflict on contact with the skin. If threatened, a series of white bristles that contain a powerful neurotoxin shoots out from along the sides of the body. This allows them to forage freely on the reef, even in the daytime. If a diver accidentally touches a fireworm, adhesive tape can be used to remove the bristles. Alcohol should neutralize some of the toxins.

The dark orange frills that line the body are actually gills, similar to those of the nudibranchs, that allow them to take up oxygen directly from the seawater.

Fireworms feed by extending their mouths over the corals and dissolving the fleshy parts. They get their sting by feeding on fire corals. The nematocysts (stinging cells) are not digested but transferred, still intact, to the rows of spines along their sides.

# WORMS : INVERTEBRATES

### BEARDED FIREWORM (JUVENILE)
*(Hermodice carunculata)*
Can be as small as 0.25 in. Often found on sponges, shallow rubble patches or on the floors of canyons.

### BEARDED FIREWORM (VARIETY)
*(Hermodice carunculata)*
Fireworms are most often reddish-orange but can also be found in a green and a whitish-gray variety.

### SCALE WORMS
*(Family: Polynoidae)*
A collective name for worms with overlapping, plate-like scales on the back. Often found under rubble.

### MEDUSA WORM
*(Loimia medusa)*
18 in max. Light pink body with numerous, thin, pale to transparent tentacles with faint white spots.

### THE THING
*(Eunice longisetis)*
18 in max. Long, segmented, red to brown body with five long tentacles at the head. Most active at night.

### POLYCHEATE WORMS
*(Family: Serpulidae)*
A collective name for segmented worms. Some have short legs on the sides. Often found under rubble.

## SEA FROST
*(Filograna huxleyi)*
6 in colony max. Encrusting tangles of thin, white tubes,
that the tiny worms build as shelter.

> Not all marine worms will look like their land-based cousins. They can range from the tiny, almost microscopic, individuals of the Sea Frost (pictured above), to the gigantic rounded worms of the Baseodiscus family (pictured below) that can reach lengths of over 6 ft!

## BASEODISCUS WORM
*(Baseodiscus sp.)*
6 ft max. A rounded body in pastel colors, with a
series of dark spots. Usually lives deep inside the reef.

## NEMERTINE WORM
*(Nemertea sp.)*
6 in max. Pale, soft-bodied worms usually hiding in
the daytime. Slightly flattened body with few markings.

# WORMS : INVERTEBRATES

### SOUTHERN LUGWORM
*(Arenicola cristata)*
6 in max. Only seen by the sand that it blows up to the sea-floor. Feeds by filtering nutrients from the sand.

### CAPITELLIDAE WORM
*(family: Capitellidae)*
12 in max. A nocturnal family of segmented, burrowing worms, hiding in the sand during the day.

### BLOOD WORMS
*(Glycera dibranchiata)*
Tiny, bright red worms, usually hiding in caves during the day. They can be attracted to a diver's light.

### SPAGHETTI WORM
*(Eupolymnia crassicornis)*
18 in max. Thin, white to transparent tentacles from a common hole in the reef. Feeds over sandy areas.

### SPONGE WORMS
*(Haplosyllis sp.)*
0.2 in max. A collective name for the tiny white worms usually found living inside sponge walls.

### SPINY CHRISTMAS TREE WORM
*(Spirobranchus sp.)*
1.5 in max. A rare species of reef-building worm, with twin crowns of thin, black spikes. Found in rubble.

## CHRISTMAS TREE WORM
*(Spirobranchus giganteus)*
1.5 in max. Two spiralling crowns of radioles. Usually in contrasting shades of purple, white and orange.

Christmas Tree Worms are abundant throughout the Caribbean and come in a wide variety of colors. They are most often found growing from the tops of stony corals. They have a whorl-like pattern of radioles that allows them to retract very quickly, in a spiral motion, when threatened. Under the crown is a sharp spike that will hurt any fish trying to take a bite, and discourage them from trying again. At the front of the animal, elongated sensory organs stick out into the water, protected by a tough plate. This plate will act as a lid to cover the hole when the animal is retracted.

Tube-dwelling worms usually grow inside coral heads, and they match the rate of growth in their host coral. As the coral grows outwards, the worm builds up more of its protective tube so that it can always have access to the seawater it needs to feed in. When found in caves, where no coral growth is taking place, the tube of the worm grows attached to the cave wall. This protective case is made up of calcium carbonate and small particles taken out from the filtered seawater.

# FANWORMS : INVERTEBRATES

**BROWN FANWORM**
*(Notaulax nudicollis)*
1.25 in max. Brown and white bands on a circular crown of radioles. The tube is usually hidden.

**YELLOW FANWORM**
*(Notaulax occidentalis)*
1.25 in max. Yellow crown of dense radioles, often with numerous, thin, dark purple bands.

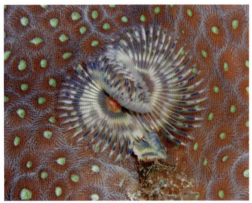

**STAR HORSESHOE WORM**
*(Pomatostegus stellatus)*
1.5 in max. Radioles form a U-shaped crown. Colors are highly variable, often in blue, red and yellow.

**STAR HORSESHOE WORM (VARIETY)**
*(Pomatostegus stellatus)*
Colors are highly variable, with blue, red and yellow the most common. All have a horseshoe shape.

**BLUSHING STAR CORAL FANWORM**
*(Vermiliopsis n. sp.)*
0.25 in max. Tiny, red crowns of radioles poking out from the surface of Blushing Star Corals (p. 69).

**RED SPOTTED HORSESHOE WORM**
*(Protula sp.)*
1.25 in max. Pale, white to yellow radioles folded into a U-shape. Distinctive red spots on the radioles.

Feather Dusters feed by keeping their fan-like arms, called radioles, waving in the currents to catch microscopic plankton drifting by. These crowns can sense when danger is near and quickly pull back into their protective tubes, which is then covered by the operculum. They even have light receptors down the length of the radioles, simple "eyes" on the lookout for danger. Divers can approach them slowly, but if there is any sudden movement they can detect the faintest of pressure waves, even from a diver's bubbles, and retract in less than 1/100th of a second. The patient diver can see the radioles slowly extending again after a minute or two.

**SOCIAL FEATHER DUSTER**
*(Bispira brunnea)*
1.25 in max. Radioles grow in circular patterns, often banded in white. Grow in clusters. Color variable.

**SOCIAL FEATHER DUSTER (VARIETY)**
*(Bispira brunnea)*
Like most feather dusters, these come in a variety of colors, usually white, tan or lavender.

# FEATHER DUSTERS : INVERTEBRATES

### GHOST FEATHER DUSTER
*(Anamobaea sp.)*
0.75 in max. Tiny, pale radioles with purple and brown bands towards the middle. Grow in groups on the sand.

### RUFFLED FEATHER DUSTER
*(Hypsicomus sp.)*
0.75 in max. An oblong crown of radioles is surrounded by a thin white line. Shy, retracts quickly.

### VARIEGATED FEATHER DUSTER
*(Bispira variegata)*
1.25 in max. Circular crown of radioles, sometimes banded or with tiny spots. Tubes are usually hidden.

### SPLIT CROWN FEATHER DUSTER
*(Anamobaea orstedii)*
2 in max. The oblong crown of radioles has a split down the middle, forming two sides. Colors are variable.

### MAGNIFICENT FEATHER DUSTER
*(Sabellastarte magnifica)*
6 in max. The largest of the Feather Dusters, with a double row of banded radioles. Tan, red and white.

### SHY FEATHER DUSTER
*(Megalomma sp.)*
1 in max. The crown of radioles is pinched in on one side, where they are longer. Shy, retracts quickly.

👓 One of the most common nudibranchs on a Caribbean reef is also one of the most fascinating. The Lettuce Sea Slug has two pronounced, curling rhinophores on its head, allowing it to sniff its way around the reef. There is an intricate mass of fleshy ruffles on its back, called parapodia. As a juvenile it is usually white and colorless, but it soon takes on the colors of the algae that it lives upon. It is a common find in the sunlit shallows, and this gives a hint as to its remarkable diet.

The Lettuce Sea Slug has developed a unique way of feeding itself. It will digest plant cells from the algae, but it actually keeps the chloroplasts alive and stored in the ruffles on its back. Chloroplasts are the part of the plant that use sunlight to produce sugars by photosynthesis. These chloroplasts will continue to work inside the nudibranch's flesh for up to a month, constantly producing food. Only now, the food is being used by an animal, rather than a plant. There is actually a higher concentration of this photosynthetic material in the Lettuce Sea Slug's body than there is in the plants that it feeds upon. By keeping its ruffled back always exposed to the sunlight, the Lettuce Sea Slug acts like a small, solar-powered battery moving about on the reef floor.

# NUDIBRANCHS : INVERTEBRATES

### LETTUCE SEA SLUG
*(Elysia crispata)*
4 in max. Fleshy ruffles on the back resemble a head of lettuce. It's color can be highly variable.

### ORNATE ELYSIA
*(Elysia ornata)*
2 in max. Body is light green with tiny black and white spots. Mantle lined with black and orange.

### STRIPED ELYSIA
*(Elysia sp.)*
0.75 in max. Light green body with white stripes. Thin brown lines on the edges of the mantle.

### SACOGLOSSAN SEA SLUG
*(Elysia tuca)*
1.5 in max. Pale green to gold body. White lines on head extend onto rhinophores. Mantle bulges on the back.

### PAINTED ELYSIA
*(Thuridilla picta)*
1.5 in max. Prominent, curling rhinophores tipped in red. Ruffled mantle with red, blue and green. Yellow on head.

### RETICULATED SEA SLUG
*(Oxynoe antillarum)*
0.75 in max. Light green body with a rough texture. Flaps of the mantle and rhinophores are paler green.

## TASSELED NUDIBRANCH
*(Bornella calcarata)*
4.5 in max. Dark orange to yellow body with white spots and netted pattern. Branching cerata.

Nudibranchs are often referred to as sea slugs, but this name does not do justice to these interesting and often flamboyant creatures. The word nudibranch comes from the Latin, meaning "naked lungs" and this is one of their characteristics. Their lungs are often literally outside their bodies, absorbing oxygen directly from the seawater. These lungs can be retracted quickly into the body if the animal senses danger. They have very poor eyesight. Instead, they use their long antennae, called rhinophores, to smell the water.

Some nudibranchs use camouflage to escape from predators, but many will rely on an ingenious system of poisons and chemical weaponry for protection. Their bodies absorb the unfired stinging cells of the hydroids (p. 116) that they feed upon. These weapons are stored in projections on the back called cerata, ready to be used against attackers.
Others will feed on poisonous sponges and store the poison in the skin. They have bold, contrasting colors to warn predators that they are poisonous, called aposematic coloration.

# NUDIBRANCHS : INVERTEBRATES

### LONG HORN NUDIBRANCH
*(Austraeolis catina)*
2 in max. Tapering body. Elongated rhinophores. Tufts of short cerata with tan to white markings.

### WHITE PATCH AEOLID
*(Flabellina engeli)*
1.5 in max. Rhinophores are tipped in white. Widely spaced cerata along the back, connected by white lines.

### CREUTZBERG'S SPURILLA
*(Spurilla creutzbergi)*
2.5 in max. Tan to transparent body with densely packed, curled cerata with white markings.

### PURPLE RING NUDIBRANCH
*(Flabellina sp.)*
1 in max. Body transparent to orange. Long, distinctly pointed cerata have white tips and purple rings.

### WHITE SPECKLED NUDIBRANCH
*(Pauleo jubatus)*
2.5 in max. Yellow to transparent body with tufts of thick, dense cerata with white speckles.

### LYNX NUDIBRANCH
*(Phidiana lynceus)*
1 in max. Distinctive blue line running down the middle from the head. Cerata have brown and white markings.

## ATLANTIC SIDEGILL SLUG
*(Pleurobranchus atlanticus)*
5 in max. Color variable, rusty red to purplish.
Numerous, same-sized papillae on the back and sides.

Sidegill Slugs only have one set of gills, on the right hand side, hidden between the mantle and the foot. They begin life with shells, which shrink or may even disappear completely as they grow. They are most active at night. If attacked, they can release a strong toxin, containing sulphuric acid.

## WARTY SIDEGILL SLUG
*(Pleurobranchus areolatus)*
5 in max. Rusty to bright golden body, covered in numerous short, warty projections. Hides in rubble.

## CROSS'S SIDEGILL SLUG
*(Pleurobranchus crossei)*
2 in max. Pale body with darker, irregular-sized papillae on back and sides. Often fringed with thin yellow lines.

# NUDIBRANCHS : INVERTEBRATES

### BROWN DORIS
*(Discodoris evelinae)*
5 in max. Uniform brown to red body with no markings. Large anal lungs and small, pointed rhinophores

### SLIMY DORIS
*(Dendrodoris krebsii)*
6 in max. Dome-shaped body with a ruffled mantle border. Color varies greatly. Large anal lungs.

### ANTILLEAN DORIS
*(Aphelodoris antillensis)*
1.5 in max. Translucent body with dark brown spots. The mantle is fringed with white and yellow.

### BLACK-LINED DORIS
*(Doriopsilla nigrolineata)*
2 in max. Light brown body with a warty texture, covered in irregular black lines. Pale rhinophores and lungs.

### ILO DORIS
*(Doris ilo)*
1.5 in max. Slightly mottled, cream to light brown body. Rhinophores and highly branched lungs are same color.

### LEATHER-BACKED DORIS
*(Platydoris angustipes)*
4 in max. Bright red, mottled body with thin, white mantle edges. Darker rhinophores and pale, branching lungs.

🤿 Nudibranchs can be hard to find on a reef, but they do leave clues that they are in the area. Nudibranchs often lay their eggs in a spiral pattern at the base of soft corals or on certain algae. By laying eggs on their favorite foods, the newly hatched animals can begin feeding immediately. Whenever a mass of eggs like this is found, have a closer look at the nearby reef for nudibranchs.

**BLACK SPOTTED NUDIBRANCH**
*(Phyllidiopsis papilligera)*
4 in max. White body with short, pointed, gray cerata, each one circled in black. Black-tipped rhinophores.

**TUFTED NUDIBRANCH**
*(Tritoniopsis frydis)*
1.75 in max. Cerata branch out repeatedly to form a tangled mass around the body. Color varies greatly.

# NUDIBRANCHS : INVERTEBRATES

### RED TIPPED SEA GODDESS
*(Glossodoris sedna)*
3 in max. White body lined in yellow. Red on the anal gills and rhinophores. A non-native, from the Pacific.

### GOLD CROWNED SEA GODDESS
*(Hypselodoris acriba)*
2.5 in max. Yellow body with purple spots and white ruffles around the edges. Yellow to golden anal gills.

### PURPLE CROWNED SEA GODDESS
*(Chromodoris kempfi)*
1 in max. Black and white pattern on back. Yellow mantle border. Purple anal gills and rhinophores.

### PURPLE SPOTTED SEA GODDESS
*(Hypselodoris marci)*
2 in max. Brownish body with small purple spots on the back and sides. White anal gills and rhinophores.

### CRISSCROSS TRITONIA
*(Tritonia bayeri)*
0.75 in max. Pink to transparent body with a fine network of white lines across the back. Short cerata.

### HAMNERS' TRITONIA
*(Tritonia hamnerorum)*
1 in max. Smooth, brown body with thin, white stripes. Short, widely-spaced, white cerata and rhinophores.

 With poor eyesight, relying on scent to move about the reef, one might think that these rare animals have a hard time reproducing. Nudibranchs are simultaneously hermaphroditic; they can act as both males and females at the same time. As they travel, they leave faint and unique scent trails that others of the same species can follow. When they mate, each nudibranch impregnates the other and each will be able to lay a fresh batch of eggs, doubling the chances that their genes will continue.

**CARIBBEAN SPANISH DANCER**
*(Hexabranchus morsomus)*
5 in max. Dark red body with small lumps and a thick mantle border. Can swim when disturbed.

**SARGASSUM NUDIBRANCH**
*(Scyllaea pelagica)*
2 in max. Light brown body with few large cerata on the back. Found in floating Sargassum Weed (p. 19).

# SEA HARES : INVERTEBRATES

### BLUE RING SEA HARE
*(Stylocheilus longicauda)*
3 in max. Long, tapering tail. Tan with white speckles. Thin, brown lines along the body and tiny blue spots.

### SMALL SEA HARE
*(Aplysia parvula)*
1.5 in max. Reddish-brown body with small white spots. Black markings on mantle lining and tips of rhinophores.

### WALKING SEA HARE
*(Aplysia juliana)*
3 in max. Color is highly variable. Thick, rounded tail with a large foot for holding on while feeding.

### RAMOSA SEA HARE
*(Petalifera ramosa)*
1.5 in max. Green to reddish-brown body with a pattern of paler, raised knobs outlined in white.

### RAGGED SEA HARE
*(Bursatella leachii)*
10 in max. Tan to dark brown body with numerous white spots and blotches. Covered in long filaments.

### SPOTTED SEA HARE
*(Aplysia dactylomela)*
12 in max. Tan to light green body with numerous dark circles and spots, each with a pale spot in the middle.

🤿 Flatworms are often confused with nudibranchs, but they form a separate group of animals. They are much more mobile, using an undulating motion to crawl across the sea floor, or even to swim to a new location. They have no respiratory system. Instead they absorb oxygen and expel carbon dioxide by simple diffusion through the skin. They are hermaphrodites, having both male and female sexual organs. Some can also reproduce by simply splitting in two, making a clone of themselves. Others can reproduce by budding. If a flatworm is cut into two pieces, a new head is formed on the tail section and each half can survive to become another adult.

### SPLENDID FLATWORM
*(Pseudoceros splendidus)*
2 in max. Dark purple to black body with a thin orange line around the edge. Short, orange-tipped antennae.

### STAINED FLATWORM
*(Acanthozoon maculosum)*
2 in max. Pale body, tapering towards the rear. Darker projections on the back, concentrated down the middle.

# FLATWORMS : INVERTEBRATES

### LEOPARD FLATWORM
*(Pseudoceros pardalis)*
5 in max. Dark purple body with orange spots outlined in black. The mantle border has small, white spots.

### RAWLINSON'S FLATWORM
*(Pseudoceros rawlinsonae)*
2 in max. The orange-rimmed mantle has widely-spaced white lines, pointing inwards over a black body.

### BLACK AGLAJA
*(Aglaja felis)*
0.2 in max. Jet black body with two lobes on the tail, one longer than the other. Found on sandy patches.

### BOLOOL FLATWORM
*(Pseudoceros bolool)*
3 in max. Uniformly black body and rhinophores. Tapers sharply towards the rear. Circumtropical.

### LEECH HEADSHIELD SLUG
*(Chelidonura hirundinina)*
1 in max. Flat head with two long, tapering tails. Orange and blue stripes with a white mid-body bar.

### BEROLINA HEADSHIELD SLUG
*(Chidonura berolina)*
0.5 in max. White body with black spots, denser towards the head. Orange stripes around the mantle.

## GOOSENECK BARNACLES
*(Lepas anatifera)*
1.5 in max. Pearly white shell attached by a long foot.
The fan is constantly moving in and out to catch food.

Barnacles are filter feeders. They remain attached to the reef and have fan-like arms that are constantly opening and closing, trapping microscopic food particles from the current. Each time they go back inside their shell, the food is cleaned off and sent out again to catch more.

## BLACK CORAL BARNACLES
*(Oxynaspis gracilis)*
0.5 in max. Distinctive hump on the back of the shell.
Attach to Black Corals (p. 78). Often encrusted.

## SESSILE BARNACLES
*(Order: Thoracica)*
1.5 in max. Thick walled, attaching directly to the reef.
Opening covered by two stony plates when not feeding.

# MOLLUSCS : INVERTEBRATES

### FUZZY CHITON
*(Acanthopleura granulata)*
3 in max. The mantle is gray to mottled pink.
Short tufts of hair-like spines surround the body.

### ORNATE CHITON
*(Tonicia schammi)*
1.5 in max. The mantle is reddish with white
bands or spots. Plates are green, brown or red.

### EASTERN ORANGE CHITON
*(Callistochiton shuttleworthianus)*
1 in max. Rounded, dome-shaped plates. Pale
orange to yellow with orange spots across the top.

### SLENDER CHITON
*(Stenoplax purpurascens)*
2 in max. Elongated body with narrower, rounded
plates. Plates are often gray when not encrusted.

### SQUAMOSE CHITON
*(Chiton squamosum)*
2 in max. Elongated oval body with light brown plates
speckled near the rim. The mantle is a pale brown.

### EASTERN BEADED CHITON
*(Chaetopleura apiculata)*
1 in max. Oval body with dark plates and mantle.
The rim of the mantle is speckled with white.

## ATLANTIC THORNY OYSTER
*(Spondylus americanus)*
6 in max. A deep red, rounded shell with numerous pointed spines on both sides. Spines longer at depth.

Oysters remain attached to the reef, while clams are able to swim about. This family of bivalves has been on Earth since the early Jurassic period. Oysters are either male or female, and being so widely spread about the reef, they reproduce in the late summer by "broadcast spawning". Each oyster throws out millions of eggs or sperm into the water, on a specific day for each species.

The Atlantic Thorny Oyster (above) has a total of 163 eyes lining its mantle. Oysters can close up their shells very quickly when they see something approaching.

As bivalves, oysters live by filtering seawater for food and minerals. They can live for decades and, as they grow, the sponges and algae of the reef grow around them, hiding them as they quietly filter the water. Often, only the outline of the shell opening is visible to divers.

# OYSTERS : INVERTEBRATES

### FROND OYSTER
*(Dendostrea frons)*
3 in max. The opening has a characteristic zig-zag pattern. Attach to soft coral, encrusted by sponges.

### ATLANTIC WING OYSTER
*(Pteria colymbus)*
3 in max. Dark brown shell, often encrusted by sponges, with a distinctive point near the hinges.

### AMBER PENSHELL
*(Pinna carnea)*
10 in max. Extremely thin shells with rounded tops. Often found on Giant Barrel Sponges (p. 53).

### LISTER PURSE OYSTER
*(Isognomon radiatus)*
2.5 in. Thin, yellowish shells with irregular, rounded openings. Often found in small clusters.

### MANGROVE OYSTER
*(Crassostrea gasar)*
3 in max. Flattened, rounded shell, often covered in algae. Found in mangroves and shallows.

### FLAT TREE OYSTER
*(Isognomon alatus)*
3 in max. Thin, flat shell with a rounded opening. Usually in shallow water, encrusted with sponges.

Unlike their oyster cousins, clams and scallops are able to detach themselves and swim about the reef by rapidly flapping their shells and mantle, either to escape predators or to find better feeding areas. They are filter feeders, taking nutrients directly from the seawater. Unmolested, some clams can live for decades (the oldest living clam was found in Japan: 405 years old). The age of a clam can be read using the rings on its shell, just like reading the age of a tree: one ring for each year of growth. Clams can attach onto the reef, secreting tiny threads of protein that harden on contact with seawater, while others have a muscular foot that allows them to bury deep into the sand.

### KNOBBY SCALLOP
*(Chlamys imbricata)*
1.5 in max. Thin shell with a rounded top. Numerous short, knobby projections extend from both sides.

### ORNATE SCALLOP
*(Caribachlamys ornata)*
2 in max. White shell with radial ribs. Broken pattern of reddish-brown bands. Found among shallow rubble.

# CLAMS : INVERTEBRATES

### ROUGH FILECLAM (VARIETY)
*(Lima scabra)*
The colors of the fileclam tentacles depend on the kind of proteins it filters from the water.

### ROUGH FILECLAM
*(Lima scabra)*
3.5 in max. Rounded shell with deep red mantle folds. Numerous long, white to red tentacles.

### SUNRISE TELLURIDE
*(Tellina radiata)*
3 in max. Lives beneath the sand in the shallows. The shell is cream to yellow with radiating pink lines.

### BUTTERCUP LUCINE
*(Anodontia alba)*
3 in max. Pale, rounded shell with faint growth lines. Brownish mantle with many short, white tentacles.

### ANTILLEAN FILECLAM
*(Lima pellucida)*
1 in max. Pale, oblong shell with tiny spines in ridges. Long, reddish tentacles with faint white banding.

### SPINY FILECLAM
*(Lima lima)*
3.5 in max. Tan to white shell with small radial ribs. Mantle and short tentacles are red to lavender.

## FLAMINGO TONGUE
*(Cyphoma gibbosum)*
1 in max. Pale, elongated shell is wider in the middle.
Creamy mantle has orange spots, circled in black.

Flamingo Tongues mating

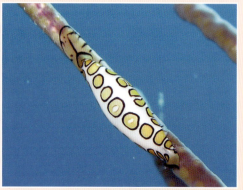

Juvenile Flamingo Tongue

With its bright orange spots, the Flamingo Tongue is often mistaken for a nudibranch (p. 142), but it actually has a hard shell that the mantle can retract into when threatened. The spots act as a warning to predators that the skin is toxic. Poisons from the soft corals that it feeds upon have been stored in the flesh. Look for them moving slowly along soft corals, especially where the outer layer of polyps has been stripped away.

# MOLLUSCS : INVERTEBRATES

### MARGIN SNAIL
*(Volvarina sp.)*
1 in max. Elongated, cream to brownish shell with a blunt spire. White to gray mantle and proboscis.

### SPOTTED CYPHOMA
*(Cyphoma mcgintyi)*
1 in max. Elongated shell is wider in the middle. The mantle has many dark brown spots, circled in black.

### BLACK SIMNIA
*(Simnia sp.)*
An undescribed species. Like all simnia they have elongated shells, pointed at both ends.

### COMMON WEST INDIAN SIMNIA
*(Cymbovula acicularis)*
0.75 in max. Pale mantle over an elongated shell. Thin orange line along its length. Found on soft corals.

### WORM SNAIL
*(Petaloconchus sp.)*
5 in max. Lives inside a long tube, in sponges or dead coral heads. Feeds by extending a long mucus thread.

### CHESTNUT LATIRUS
*(Leucozonia nassa)*
0.75 in max. Dark shell, pointed at both ends. Dark red body with tiny white spots. Often covered in algae.

### CHOCOLATE LINED TOPSNAIL
*(Calliostoma javanicum)*
1.5 in max. Pointed, conical shell with thin chocolate-brown
and gold lines that continue onto the body.

> Tiny molluscs, like snails, can move about the reef using a muscular foot. They have eye-stalks with simple vision and tentacles extend from their shell to sense the reef around them. They are most active at night. When threatened, they can pull their fleshy bodies into their shells for protection.

### WEST INDIAN STARSNAIL
*(Lithopoma tectum)*
2 in max. Robust, conical shell with spines around
the lower edge. Usually covered in red algae.

### LONGSPINE STARSNAIL
*(Astralium phoebium)*
3 in max. Round, flattened shell with curved spines
arranged spirally from the center. Faint brown bands.

# MOLLUSCS : INVERTEBRATES

### BARBADOS MITER
*(Mitra barbadensis)*
1 in max. Smooth, elongated shell with a long spire. Dark brown to reddish. Body and eyestalks are yellow.

### HARLEQUIN MITER
*(Vexillum histrio)*
0.5 in max. Dark red shell, highly ridged with yellow and black bands. Dark or black body with banded tentacles.

### BEAUTIFUL MITER
*(Vexillum pulchellum)*
0.5 in max. Bright orange shell with a pointed spire. Bands of black markings. Pale line near the opening.

### FILOSE TURBAN
*(Turbo cailletii)*
2 in max. Rounded, deep red, banded shell. Mantle is bright green with thin, darker lines. Eyestalks orange.

### IVORY CERITH
*(Cerithium eburneum)*
1 in max. Tiny, pointed shell with numerous small ridges. Usually pale, circled with dark brown spots.

### MUREX SNAIL
*(Muricopsis sp.)*
6 in max. Thick, pointed shell with many short, irregular, protruding spines. Often covered in red algae.

**KULKULCAN CONE**
*(Conus kulkulcan)*
1.5 in max. Cone-shaped body with short spire.
Deep red color with a lighter band towards the middle.

Cone shells should never be handled or removed from the reef, no matter how pretty the shell is. Some have a harpoon-like weapon that is used to immobilize prey like small fishes, but is also poisonous to humans. The venom of some cones has even been known to kill unwary collectors.

**CARDINAL CONE**
*(Conus cardinalis)*
1.5 in max. Cone-shaped body with short spire. Deep red with thin, red-speckled white band in the middle.

**MOUSE CONE**
*(Conus mus Hwass)*
2 in max. Very pointed spire. Thin brown rings around the shell. Upper rim has large white spots.

# MOLLUSCS : INVERTEBRATES

### STROMBOID SHELL (JUVENILE)
*(Strombus raninus)*
The juveniles of the Stromboid (conch) family look very much like cones, but with sharper spires.

### COLORFUL MOON SNAIL
*(Naticarius canrena)*
2 in max. Rounded shell with thin brown markings. White mantle with large brown and small orange spots.

### CARIBBEAN VASE
*(Vasum muricatum)*
8 in max. Short, pointed, conical spire. Often covered in alga and debris. The body is brown and speckled.

### ATLANTIC PARTRIDGE TUN
*(Tonna pennata)*
10 in max. Delicate, rounded shell with a short spire. The body is brown to black with white spots and lines.

### GRANULAR FROG SHELL
*(Bursa granularis)*
2 in max. Pointed shell with wide ridges and valleys. The pale body has brown spots. Antennae are banded.

### TRUE TULIP
*(Fasciolaria tulipa)*
10 in max. Elongated shell, pointed at both ends with thin, dark stripes. Body is pink with white speckles.

## SMOOTH SCOTCH BONNET
*(Semicassis cicatricosa)*
3 in max. Rounded shell with a sharp conical spire.
Reddish-brown, irregular bands. Body is light brown.

Larger molluscs, such as the Triton's Trumpet (on the left), are slow-motion hunters, smelling out and giving chase to even slower animals like starfish. Once captured, the hunter secretes a special saliva into the starfish, which paralyzes it. It can then feed at its leisure, often starting with the softer tissues around the mouth. The Triton's Trumpet has a serrated organ called the radula for sawing off pieces of its prey. It can also eat smaller molluscs whole, not bothering to cut them up first. After they have been digested, the spines or bits of shell are then spat out again.

Many larger molluscs carry a sharp blade near the mouth, called an operculum, that can perfectly cover the opening into their shells. When threatened, the animal can pull itself quickly inside its shell and the operculum closes like a door. It is attached to a strong muscular foot and can help the animal to move along the sea floor. This sharp appendage can also be used as a weapon, slashing sideways across a predator, such as an octopus, that might try to get into the shell.

# MOLLUSCS : INVERTEBRATES

### ATLANTIC DEER COWRIE
*(Cypraea cervus)*
5 in max. Rounded shell covered in white spots. Dark mantle with white spots and large, fleshy appendages.

### ATLANTIC GRAY COWRIE
*(Cypraea cinerea)*
1.5 in max. Smooth, dark brown shell with small black spots. The mantle is light brown. Tentacles are black.

### MEASLED COWRIE (JUVENILE)
*(Cypraea zebra)*
Juveniles have no spots, but a series of light and dark brown bands across the shell. Pale brown mantle.

### MEASLED COWRIE
*(Cypraea zebra)*
4 in max. Elongated brown shell with white spots that have brown centers. Pale mantle with many spikes.

### ATLANTIC TRITON'S TRUMPET
*(Charonia variegata)*
30 in max. Elongated shell, covered in rounded knobs. Body is cream to orange with dark brown whorls.

### RETICULATE COWRIE-HELMET
*(Cypraecassis testiculus)*
8 in max. Rounded shell with a short pointed tip. Broken lines of brown and white surround the shell.

## MILK CONCH
*(Strombus costatus)*
6 in max. Thick pale shell with cream inside. Pale green head and eye stalks, each with small tentacle.

A Chank Shell lays an egg case.   A Cameo Helmet lays its eggs onto the sand.

Conch have been a food source in the Caribbean for as long as there have been humans in the area. But with growing populations, this important link in the food chain is under threat in many areas. Conch are detritus eaters, meaning that they eat the debris that would otherwise choke off a healthy reef. Overharvesting quickly leads to a rapid growth in algae. This can smother and eventually destroy a reef ecosystem from the bottom up. Soon populations of fish and other food species dry up and humans must go farther afield to continue their harvest.

# CONCHS : INVERTEBRATES

### HAWKWING CONCH
*(Strombus raninus)*
5 in max. Orange to brown shell has two distinctively large spikes on the top. Inside of the shell is yellow.

### QUEEN CONCH
*(Strombus gigas)*
12 in max. Orange to brown shell with pink inside. The head and eye stalks are mottled, with a dark tentacle.

### CAMEO HELMET
*(Cassis madagascariensis)*
14 in max. Large, domed, cream to brown shell with a vertical opening in front. Lip is a solid cream color.

### KING HELMET
*(Cassis tuberosa)*
7 in max. Smooth shell has a wavy pattern of brown and cream whorls. Lip has distinct black bands.

### WEST INDIAN CHANK
*(Turbinella angulata)*
30 in max. Large shell with long, tapered opening. Body is mottled black and orange. Similar to Horse Conch.

### TRITON SNAIL
*(Cymatium sp.)*
5 in max. Most species of Triton snails have elongated spires and shell openings. Similar to Roostertail Conch.

Octopus are highly intelligent hunters. Research shows they have the same level of intelligence as the household cat. They are usually nocturnal hunters, feeding largely on crabs and shellfish. They have a sharp beak under their bodies that can slowly cut into even the hardest of shells, like the conch. They will also hunt fishes, creeping up on a small coral head and suddenly billowing out, not allowing any small fish under their bodies to escape. They use a tentacle to grab any prey trapped inside.

Experts at camouflage, an octopus can use tiny pigment cells on its skin to blend in with the reef, as seen on the post-larval octopus to the left, no larger than a fingernail. They can also mimic the color patterns of fish like parrotfish or flounder if they have to move about during the daytime.

# OCTOPUSES : INVERTEBRATES

### ATLANTIC PYGMY OCTOPUS
*(Octopus joubini)*
6 in max. Red to brown body with distinctively smooth skin. They are often found in empty shells.

### CARIBBEAN TWO-SPOT OCTOPUS
*(Octopus filosus)*
10 in max. Two dark blue, ocellated spots near the eyes (often hidden when camouflaged).

### LONG ARM OCTOPUS (JUVENILE)
*(Octopus defilippi)*
14 in max. Brownish body, often with widely-spaced white spots on long tentacles. Found in sandy areas.

### WHITE SPOTTED OCTOPUS
*(Octopus macropus)*
20 in max. Red to brown body with numerous white spots and bumps on the head and tentacles.

### COMMON OCTOPUS
*(Octopus vulgaris)*
3 ft max. The largest of the octopus. Dark edges around the suckers. No ring around the eyes.

### CARIBBEAN REEF OCTOPUS
*(Octopus briareus)*
20 in max. Green to blue body, mottled with brown. There is a distinctive dark ring around the eyes.

👓 Squid can be very social animals, often found in groups of up to a hundred individuals in shallow waters. They can swim either forwards or backwards and tend to align themselves with the rest of the group. They hunt singly or in pairs, often relying on camouflage in soft corals to surprise their prey; usually small fishes. Two of their ten tentacles are longer; arms with modified suckers for grabbing. The males have another modified arm that is used for putting packets of sperm into the females. A female can store up to seven or eight of these little packets, and then later decide which one she will use to fertilize herself.

👓 Just like the octopus, a squid can change its color rapidly, using thin cells on its skin called chromatophores. As each pigment-filled cell is activated, more pigment is squeezed towards the surface of the body and that color is seen. It is thought that squid use these changing patterns to communicate with one another in the group, especially while mating. They have even been seen communicating in small groups while they are hunting, sending special polarized messages to other squid in the group, while still projecting their normal camouflaged patterns towards their prey.

# SQUIDS : INVERTEBRATES

### CARIBBEAN REEF SQUID (JUVENILE)
*(Sepioteuthis sepioidea)*
Transparent body with large chromatophores (pigment cells). Hides in algae and soft corals.

### CARIBBEAN REEF SQUID
*(Sepioteuthis sepioidea)*
12 in max. Large eye. 10 tentacles. Thin, unbroken fin along the entire body length. Color highly variable.

### DIAMOND BACK SQUID EGG CASE
*(Thysanotheuthis rhombus)*
A long tubular mass of tiny, purple eggs encased in a transparent jelly. The squid is from very deep water.

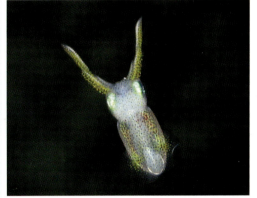

### GRASS SQUID
*(Pickfordiateunthis pulchella)*
1 in max. Smallest of the squid. Two sets of short tentacles on each side, not joining at the body.

Squid have excellent eyesight, with oversized pupils that allow them to hunt in low light conditions. They move about the reef by fluttering the fins on either side of the body, or by quickly pushing a jet of water from a siphon, at the bottom of their heads, for an extra burst of speed.

## PEDERSON CLEANER SHRIMP
*(Periclimenes pedersoni)*
1 in max. Transparent body with purple spots on the legs and tail. Lives in Corkscrew Anemones (p. 107).

🤿 Cleaner Shrimp such as these are given access to the most intimate parts of a fish in order to remove loose bits of food after a meal, or even bits of torn or decaying flesh. These shrimp advertise their cleaning services by frantically waving their antennae and dancing back and forth. The Pederson Cleaner Shrimp will be led towards the delicate parts like the gills, while the larger Banded Cleaner Shrimp will be used for tougher jobs, like clearing off parasites.

Patient divers can be rewarded with a "reef manicure" from these tiny creatures. Hold your hand steady in front of a cleaner shrimp and it may jump on to you and pick away under your nails. Breathe slowly and blow bubbles off to the side, away from the shrimp, so as not to scare it off.

# SHRIMPS : INVERTEBRATES

### BANDED CORAL SHRIMP (JUVENILE)
*(Stenopus hispidus)*
Transparent body with small red spots. The fan-like tail is tipped with white and red. Very long antennae.

### BANDED CORAL SHRIMP
*(Stenopus hispidus)*
2 in max. Body and claws are white with red bands. Long white antennae. Pale blue eggs are often visible.

### SPOTTED CLEANER SHRIMP
*(Periclimenes yucatanicus)*
1 in max. Transparent body with large white spots down the back. Often found in the Giant Anemone (p. 104).

### GOLDEN CORAL SHRIMP
*(Stenopus scutellatus)*
1.5 in max. Golden to yellow body. Claws are banded with red and yellow. Long white antennae.

### CROSSBANDED GRASS SHRIMP
*(Palaemon northropi)*
1 in max. Transparent body with faint brown bands. Often found in mangrove roots and under docks.

### SCARLET-STRIPED CLEANER SHRIMP
*(Lysmata grabhami)*
2 in max. Yellow body with two thick red stripes down the back. Long white antennae. Found on deeper reefs.

**SQUAT URCHIN SHRIMP**
*(Gnathophylloides mineri)*
0.75 in max. Darker sides with white stripes on the back
and claws. Lives only on West Indian Sea Eggs (p. 129).

🤿 Some shrimp have evolved to live on specific hosts, such as sea urchins, crinoids and corals. In this symbiotic relationship, the shrimp are able to live safely concealed from their predators, while they in turn keep the host animals clean of debris that could lead to infections.

**BLACK CORAL SHRIMP**
*(Periclimenes antipathophilus)*
0.5 in max. Transparent body with a thin red stripe.
Widely spaced eyes. Lives on Black Corals (p. 78)

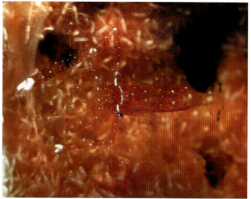

**WHITE-FOOTED SHRIMP**
*(Periclimenes harringtoni)*
1 in max. Reddish body with distinct white claws.
Found only in Touch-me-not Sponges (p. 55).

# SHRIMPS : INVERTEBRATES

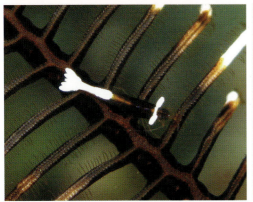

### BROWN FEATHERSTAR SHRIMP
*(Periclimenes meyeri)*
0.5 in max. Dark body with white eyes and tail. Found only on Black and White Crinoids (p. 125).

### ORANGE FEATHERSTAR SHRIMP
*(Periclimenes crinoidalis)*
0.5 in max. Pale body with golden eyes and body stripe. Found only on Golden Crinoids (p. 125).

### GORGONIAN SHRIMP
*(Periclimenes antillensis)*
0.5 in max. Generally takes on the color of it's host gorgonian. White eyes on distinctively short stalks.

### SWIMMING CRINOID SHRIMP
*(Periclimenes rincewindi)*
0.75 in max. White to tan body with serrated head and purple spots. Found only on Swimming Crinoids (p. 125).

### LONGTAIL GRASS SHRIMP
*(Periclimenes longicaudatus)*
0.75 in max. Transparent body with a hump towards the tail, which is long. Larger second set of claws.

### SARGASSUM SHRIMP
*(Latreutes parvulus)*
1 in max. Tan to light brown body with tiny darker spots. Found only in floats of Sargassum Seaweed (p. 19).

### WIRE CORAL SHRIMP
*(Pseudopontonides principis)*
0.5 in. Tapering body with lighter bands, mimicking
the white tentacles of the host Wire Coral (p. 79).

Soft corals, black corals and anemones are a good places to look for shrimps. Often a group of a dozen or more shrimps, sometimes from different species, can be seen to take up residence in the tentacles of the Giant Sea Anemone (p. 104) and other anemones.

### SEA PLUME SHRIMP
*(Neopontonides chacei)*
0.25 in max. Flattened head with hook-shaped claws
on the legs. No legs towards the tail. The eyes are large.

### SLIMY SEA PLUME SHRIMP
*(Periclimenes mclellandi)*
0.5 in max. Transparent purple body with white bands.
Color matches the Sea Plume. Eyes on short stalks.

# SHRIMPS : INVERTEBRATES

**WIRE CORAL SHRIMP (VARIETY)**
*(Pseudopontonides principis)*
Some Wire Coral Shrimp are banded in white, which exactly matches the spacing of the coral's white polyps.

**SQUAT ANEMONE SHRIMP**
*(Thor amboinensis)*
0.75 in max. Brownish body with yellow spots circled in white. Short antennae. Often found in anemones.

**SUN ANEMONE SHRIMP**
*(Periclimenes rathbunae)*
1 in max. Light brown body with small white and brown spots. Found on Sun Anemones (p. 107).

**SKELETON SHRIMP**
*(Pariambus typicus)*
0.5 in max. Tiny, thin-bodied shrimp living on Feather Hydroids (p. 117) and feeding on plankton.

**SLENDER CARIBBEAN SEA SPIDER**
*(Anoplodactylus spp.)*
0.5 in max. Very thin, barely visible bodies. Because of their size, their stomachs have to be in their legs.

**CARIBBEAN SEA SPIDER**
*(Anoplodactylus spp.)*
0.5 in max. Very thin, barely visible bodies. The female above is carrying an egg sac under its belly.

### RED NIGHT SHRIMP
*(Cinetorhynehus manningi)*
2 in max. Red to orange body with a single large, red spot in the middle. Large dark eyes. Moves very quickly.

> The wild shrimp industry is one of the most wasteful and damaging to marine environments in the Caribbean because the amount of other species that are brought up in the nets. As much as 10 pounds of this "by-catch" is killed for every pound of shrimp that makes it onto the market.

### RED NIGHT SHRIMP (JUVENILE)
*(Cinetorhynehus manningi)*
Transparent body with hints of red. Large bulbous eyes. A red spinal column is visible through the body.

### BUMBLE BEE SHRIMP
*(Gnathophyllum americanum)*
0.25 in max. Small, rounded body with brown and gold bands. Often found on or under sea cucumbers.

# SHRIMPS : INVERTEBRATES

### CIRCLED SQUAT SHRIMP
*(Gnathophyllum circellus)*
0.5 in max. Dark body with gold spots circled in black. Long, transparent legs and antennae. Extremely rare.

### PEPPERMINT SHRIMP
*(Lysmata wurdemanni)*
1.75 in max. Pink body with distinctive bright red and orange lines. Often found deep inside tube sponges.

### HIDDEN CLEANER SHRIMP
*(Lysmata rathbunae)*
1.75 in max. Pale, red to orange fine lines over a pale orange body. Often found in pairs, hiding in sponges.

### LONG-LEGGED SHRIMP
*(Janicea antiguensis)*
3 in max. Slender orange body banded in red. Long thin legs. Found on Giant Barrel Sponges (p. 53) at night.

### ARROW SHRIMP (VARIETY)
*(Tozeuma carolinense)*
1.5 in. Arrow Shrimp will take on the colors of their host, ranging from green to yellow to purple and more.

### ARROW SHRIMP
*(Tozeuma carolinense)*
1.5 in. Long slender body with a distinctive hump. The snout is tapered and curves upwards. Various colors.

## DARK MANTIS
*(Neogonodactylus curacaoensis)*
2 in max. Uniform, dark green color with a
fan-shaped tail. Colorful face and claws. Lobed eyes.

> 🤿 Snapping shrimps are often found hiding under the Corkscrew Anemone (p. 107), and get their name from the loud sound of their largest claw snapping shut. They use this to warn off intruders, and also to stun small fish that pass by, which they can then rush out to and eat.

## ORANGETAIL SNAPPING SHRIMP
*(Alpheus peasei)*
1 in max. Smooth, translucent body with red or orange
hints near head and tail. One claw is much larger.

## LARGE CLAW SNAPPING SHRIMP
*(Synalpheus sp.)*
0.75 in max. Colors are highly variable but uniform.
All have one smooth claw much larger than the other.

# SHRIMPS : INVERTEBRATES

### CILIATED FALSE SQUILLA (VARIETY)
*(Pseudosquilla ciliate)*
As this shrimp runs over sandy areas it takes on light and dark brown stripes as camouflage.

### CILIATED FALSE SQUILLA
*(Pseudosquilla ciliate)*
3.5 in max. Brown to light green body with spots or stripes. Can change colors quickly as it moves.

### SWOLLEN CLAW MANTIS
*(Neogonodactylus oerstedii)*
2 in max. Lobed eyes. The body ends in four pointed spikes. Final plate has a central ridge. Various colors.

### SCALY-TAILED MANTIS
*(Lysiosquilla scabricauda)*
1 ft max. Large eyes on movable stalks. Rounded golden plates over the shoulders. Light brown body.

### MANTIS SHRIMP (VARIETY)
*(Lysiosquilla sp.)*
An undescribed species of mantis shrimp that lives in a sandy burrow. Claws of equal size with red at the joints.

### RED SNAPPING SHRIMP
*(Alpheus sp.)*
2 in max. Bright red body with white markings. One claw is always larger. Long, red-banded antennae.

### TWO CLAW SHRIMP
*(Brachycarpus biunguiculatus)*
2.5 in max. Reddish brown body. The second pair of legs also has a long, slender set of claws.

> Most shrimps are nocturnal, and spend the daylight hours resting in caves and deep crevices within the reef. At night they will come out to forage, so they usually have very large eyes to make the most of limited light. They have long antennae and a highly developed sense of smell.

### DARK SNAPPING SHRIMP
*(Alpheus spp.)*
2 in max. Color variable from reddish brown to black. Banded tail. One large claw. Small eyes without stalks.

### FLORIDA PISTOL SHRIMP
*(Alpheus floridanus)*
2 in max. Grey body, small eyes. Lives in symbiotic relationship with the Orange Spotted Goby (p. 205).

# SHRIMPS : INVERTEBRATES

### VELVET SHRIMP
*(Metapenaeopsis goodie)*
2.5 in max. Transparent body with pale red markings. They bury themselves into the sand when disturbed.

### SOLDIERFISH ISOPOD
*(Renocila spp.)*
2.5 in max. Rounded, shrimp-like parasite found attached to the heads of Blackbar Soldierfish (p. 221).

### MYSID SHRIMP
*(Mysidium spp.)*
0.5 in max. Tiny, red-striped shrimp that gather under urchins and within the tentacles of sea anemones.

### POSSUM SHRIMP
*(Mysidium spp.)*
Almost microscopic, found in large groups swimming close together in front of recesses in the reef.

### BURROWING LOBSTER
*(Axius sp.)*
6 in max. Pale red to orange body with large, hairy claws. Usually found in burrows or buried under rubble.

### COMMON SQUAT LOBSTER
*(Munida pusilla)*
0.5 in max. The smallest of the lobster family. Red body and eyes, with long forearms and large claws.

## NECK CRAB
*(Podochela sp.)*
3 in max. Long legs and a long, tapered snout with small eyes on the sides. Covered in algae and hydroids.

Neck Crabs are often difficult to spot because they are well camouflaged in soft corals such as Sea Whips (p. 88). They are usually found in areas of moderate current, where they can grab plankton and small prey as it drifts by. They can cut off small branches from their hosts and attach them to their bodies by means of tiny hooked spines called setae. They will also attach stinging animals such as hydroids (p. 116) to keep them safe from predators. In shallow water they will often allow themselves to become encrusted with heavy coats of red algae, like the individual on the left.

Decorator Crabs must re-apply their camouflage each time they moult their shells. Different species prefer either algae, sponges or hydroids. During lean times on the reef, such as the long winter storms when they must take shelter, they can eat their own costumes if no other food source is available.

Newly moulted individual

Ready for a new moult!

# DECORATOR CRABS : INVERTEBRATES

**CURVED-NOSE NECK CRAB**
*(Podochela curvirostris)*
2 in max. Long legs and a long, upwardly-curving snout. Pale pink body with tiny purple spots.

**SPECK-CLAW DECORATOR CRAB**
*(Microphrys bicornuta)*
0.75 in max. Covered in sponges and other animals. The claws are speckled and often have lighter bands.

**SPONGY DECORATOR CRAB**
*(Marcocoeloma trispinosum)*
2 in max. Triangular body with a pointed snout and long spines to the rear. Yellow to brown legs.

**FURCATE SPIDER CRAB**
*(Stenocionops furcatus coelata)*
6 in max. Distinctively long, tapered snout. The body is reddish brown but usually completely covered.

**SOUTHERN TEARDROP CRAB**
*(Pelia rotunda)*
0.5 in max. Rounded body covered in sponges, often the legs as well. Claws are reddish brown.

**CRYPTIC TEARDROP CRAB**
*(Pelia mutica)*
0.75 in max. Covered in sponges, usually red and blue, and small zoanthids. Blue tips on the claws.

## GIANT HERMIT CRAB
*(Petrochirus diogenes)*
12 in max. The largest of the Hermit Crabs. The right claw is larger than the left. Red-banded antennae.

> 🤿 Hermit crabs have soft, vulnerable abdomens that they keep hidden inside a borrowed shell. As they grow, they can become too large to retract safely back into their shells, and they must find a larger one. Often two or more of these crabs can be found fighting over the rights to a prized shell.

## RED STRIPE HERMIT CRAB
*(Phimochirus holthuisi)*
1 in max. The right claw is much larger. Arms and claws are orange to cream, with wide, dark red bands.

## STAREYE HERMIT CRAB
*(Dardanus venosus)*
5 in max. Left claw is larger with hints of purple. Blue eyes with a distinctive star-shaped pattern.

# HERMIT CRABS : INVERTEBRATES

### RED BANDED HERMIT CRAB
*(Paguristes erythrops)*
4 in max. The claws are of equal size with red bands or spots. Golden antennae. The eyes are blue.

### RED REEF HERMIT CRAB
*(Paguristes cadenati)*
1 in max. The body, legs and claws are all a uniform dark red color. Green eyes on yellow eyestalks.

### BLUE EYE HERMIT CRAB
*(Paguristes sericeus)*
2.5 in max. Claws of equal size. Small, blue eyes on thin, white-speckled, red stalks.

### ORANGE CLAW HERMIT CRAB
*(Calcinus tibicen)*
1 in max. The left claw is larger, with pale yellow tips. Orange antennae and eyestalks. The eyes are black.

### WHITE SPECKLED HERMIT CRAB
*(Paguristes punticeps)*
5 in max. Claws of equal size. Body and legs covered in tiny white spots that form faint bands.

### BLUE LEGGED HERMIT CRAB
*(Clibanarius tricolor)*
1 in max. Pale blue legs are banded with red and yellow at the joints, tipped in yellow. Large dark claws.

## CHANNEL CLINGING CRAB (MALE)
*(Mithrax spinosissimus)*
12 in max. The male has very large claws, up to
the width of the body. Red upper body, white belly.

Channel Clinging Crabs are also known as King Crabs. The males have much larger claws and out-number the smaller females on the reef by 2:1. Triggered by a pheromone that the females release into the water, males begin to compete for the right to mate with a fertile female. They do this by approaching each other and stretching out their claws to see whose are the largest.

This ritualized competition ensures that neither crab is killed in the confrontation. The loser accepts his lot, and the winner is free to mate. He carries the female under his claws while she moults off her shell. Only then are her eggs ready to be fertilized. The female has a wide flap under her belly, where she keeps thousands of eggs, fanning them continuously to aerate them. As the eggs develop, she fans them more rapidly, until they are released as tiny larvae. They will float about for weeks in this stage until they settle onto a new patch of reef and begin to grow.

males fighting

mating couple

female with eggs

# CLINGING CRABS : INVERTEBRATES

**CHANNEL CLINGING CRAB (FEMALE)**
*(Mithrax spinosissimus)*
12 in max. The female has smaller, blunt claws and the abdominal plate is much wider than in males.

**RED RIDGED CLINGING CRAB**
*(Mithrax forceps)*
1 in max. The body has long indentations that form grooves. Sharp spines around body. Blunt claws.

**HAIRY CLINGING CRAB**
*(Mithrax pilosus)*
4 in max. Dark brown to red body. Short hairs cover the back and the arms. Slender, blunt claws.

**BANDED CLINGING CRAB**
*(Mithrax cinctimanus)*
0.75 in max. Body and legs are hairy. Smooth, red-banded claws. Found under anemones (p. 105).

**GREEN CLINGING CRAB**
*(Mithrax sculptus)*
0.75 in max. Smooth green body with green legs and claws with pale tips. Red spot inside joint of the claws.

**NODOSE CLINGING CRAB**
*(Mithrax coryphe)*
1 in max. Deep grooves and knobs cover the upper body. Four short spines on forearm of the claw.

## BATWING CORAL CRAB
*(Carpilius corallinus)*
6 in max. Smooth, bright red body with white spots.
Legs have hints of purple and yellow on the joints.

All crabs have a hard exoskeleton that they must continually shed in order to grow. First the crab absorbs sea water into its body, swelling up so that the outer shell cracks along the seams. The soft-bodied animal then slowly wriggles out of the shell, starting with the back legs, then the body and finally the front legs. Even the tiny mouth parts are pulled out of their protective casings. The outer layer of this swollen body slowly hardens into a new shell. The extra sea water is then expelled from the body and the crab has more room to grow inside its new, larger shell.

While the new shell is forming the crab is very vulnerable, so it will often hide down in the bottom of sponges for protection. The King Crab on the right will moult up to six times in its first year, four times in its second year and twice in its third year. By the time the crab is sexually mature, moulting will take place only once a year. If limbs are lost only three moults are needed in order to grow new ones. Moulting also gets rid of unwanted growths or harmful bacteria on the shell.

# CRABS : INVERTEBRATES

### MOTTLED SHORE CRAB
*(Pachygrapsus transversus)*
2 in max. Flattened green body with dark stripes. Yellow spots on leg joints. Found in the shallows.

### GAUDY CLOWN CRAB
*(Platypodiella spectabilis)*
1 in max. Smooth, bright orange to red body. Yellow markings lined in black on the face and the legs.

### NIMBLE SPRAY CRAB
*(Percnon gibbesi)*
1.5 in max. Very flattened body, circled by a thin green line. Yellow bands on the legs. Very shy.

### YELLOWLINE ARROW CRAB
*(Stenorhynchus seticornis)*
2.5 in max. Triangular body with a long, tapering snout. Long, thin legs with golden stripes. Tiny blue claws.

### SAND DOLLAR PEA CRAB
*(Dissodactylus mellitae)*
0.5 in max. Lives only under sand dollars (p. 128). Wide, flattened, pale pink to white body with tiny eyes.

### HEART URCHIN PEA CRAB
*(Dissodactylus primitivus)*
0.5 in max. Lives only under Red Heart Urchin (p. 129). Rounded, uniformly white body with hairy, white legs.

### GALL CRAB
*(Domecia acanthophora)*
0.5 in max. Smooth rectangular body with tiny
white spots. Found hiding in holes on Elkhorn Coral (p. 61).

> Tiny coral crabs, such as the Gall Crab, will move into natural hollows of the Elkhorn Coral. As the coral grows around it, the holes become deeper and safer for the Gall Crab. They will only venture out at night to forage for plankton and debris that has gathered on the surface of the coral.

### THORNY MUD CRAB
*(Micropanope urinator)*
0.75 in max. Rectangular body with short spines. Legs have small brown or white spots. On Fire Coral (p. 61).

### HAIRY CORAL CRAB
*(Domecia hispida)*
0.5 in max. Moult shown above: tan body with spots. The right claw is larger. All legs have fine hairs.

# SWIMMING CRABS : INVERTEBRATES

**SWIMMING CRAB (JUVENILE)**
*(Portunus sp.)*
Wide, flattened body. Usually camouflaged to blend in with the rubble of the lagoon or shallows.

**BLOTCHED SWIMMING CRAB**
*(Portunus spinimanus)*
3 in max. Wide, flattened body. Pale brown with dark lines and blotches. Sharp spines on the forearms.

**OCELLATE SWIMMING CRAB**
*(Portunus sebae)*
4 in max. Wide, flattened body with two dark reddish spots on the back, each circled in white.

**BLACK POINT SCULLING CRAB**
*(Cronius ruber)*
3 in max. Banded pincers of equal size. Red to tan blotches and stripes on all the legs and claws.

**BLUE CRABS**
*(Callinectes sp.)*
6 in max. The largest of the Swimming Crabs. Blue markings at the joints of all the legs and claws.

**SARGASSUM SWIMMING CRAB**
*(Portunus sayi)*
4 in max. Brown to gold with white blotches. Pelagic, usually hiding in floats of Sargassum Seaweed (p. 19).

### SPOTTED PORCELAIN CRAB
**(Porcellana sayana)**
1 in max. Pale red to orange body covered in
bright white and purple spots, each circled in red.

> Sponge crabs will carry around living sponges on top of their heads as camouflage. Their forelegs are modified to cut down fresh sponges as needed, and their back legs to hold the sponges firmly in place. Usually staying motionless on the reef, they can move very quickly if discovered.

### RED EYE SPONGE CRAB
**(Dromia erythropus)**
4 in max. Large spines next to the eyes and around
the body. The tips of the claws are sometimes reddish.

### LESSER SPONGE CRAB
**(Dromidia antillensis)**
3 in max. Small, dense spines cover the entire body.
The tips of the front claws are always bright crimson.

# CRABS : INVERTEBRATES

### PLUMED HAIRY CRAB
*(Pilumnus floridanus)*
1 in max. Flattened body is red with large brown blotches. Fine hairs on the back and the legs.

### NODOSE RUBBLE CRAB
*(Paractaea rufopunctata)*
1 in max. Wide, pale carapace covered in numerous red to orange bumps. Fine hairs on legs and claws.

### NODOSE BOX CRAB
*(Calappa angusta)*
1.5 in max. Pale, domed body is covered by numerous rounded projections, often in contrasting colors.

### FLAME BOX CRAB
*(Calappa flammea)*
5 in max. Dark red lines on the back form a pattern that dissolves towards the rear. Large claws cover the face.

### OCELLATED BOX CRAB
*(Calappa ocellata)*
5 in max. Dark red lines form circular patterns that will cover the entire shell. Large claws cover the face.

### ROUGH BOX CRAB
*(Calappa gallus)*
3 in max. Large claws cover the face, which is pinched inwards. Color varies, often heavily encrusted.

## RED BANDED LOBSTER
*(Justitia longimanus)*
8 in max. Red and orange patterns on the body.
The legs and antennae are banded with red and white.

Lobsters move about by walking or by using paddle-shaped swimmerets on their tails. They are essential parts of the Caribbean food chain, acting as reef cleaners. They feed on decaying matter, from algae to dead animals and even the feces of other reef inhabitants. Despite this, it has become an important, even iconic, food throughout the Caribbean. This was not always the case. In fact, lobsters were once widely used as fertilizer for farmers' fields. It was considered a very low-grade food. In the 18th century, in the southern American states, a law was passed forbidding farmers to feed their slaves lobster more than twice a week, because it was inhumane - a far cry from today's perception of a special seafood dinner.

Lobsters must moult continuously in order to grow. Juvenile lobsters are very vulnerable on the reef, especially to humans, as they hide in the more accessible shallows. By law, the minimum size a lobster tail can be served is 5.5 inches. This ensures that the lobster has been given a chance to reproduce at least once in its life. If left in peace these valuable reef cleaners can grow to reach a length of almost two feet and an age of up to 50 years!

# LOBSTERS : INVERTEBRATES

### CARIBBEAN SPINY LOBSTER
*(Panulirus argus)*
2 ft max. The body is reddish above and pale below. Two sharp horns above the eyes. Long antennae.

### SPOTTED SPINY LOBSTER
*(Panulirus guttatus)*
18 in max. A darker red to brown body covered with tiny white spots. Brown stripes on the lower legs.

### FLAMING REEF LOBSTER
*(Enoplometopus antillensis)*
5 in max. Red body with white stripes and a white circle on the sides. Rare: only the moult is shown above.

### COPPER LOBSTER
*(Palinurellus gundlachi)*
8 in max. Reddish body covered with fine hairs. Found deep in caves, crevices and on deeper reefs.

### SCULPTURED SLIPPER LOBSTER
*(Parribacus antarcticus)*
7 in max. Rough, tan to yellow body with numerous small spines. The round eyes are small and black.

### SPANISH LOBSTER
*(Scyllarides aequinoctialis)*
12 in max. Smooth brown to orange body. Yellow legs with brown spots. Distinctive, thin, purple antennae.

👓 In one of the best examples of symbiosis on a coral reef, tiny fishes, like the Neon Goby, will be allowed to jump onto larger fish and even to swim into their mouths safely, in order to feed on the dead skin and parasites there. They gather in areas called "cleaning stations" and the rules of predation are suspended here, to the benefit of all the fish involved. Instead of hiding on the reef, the obvious bright stripes on the gobies act as signals to larger fish to come in and enjoy their services. Neon Gobies often work in pairs or small groups to offer a more thorough cleaning.

👓 The main food source for gobies that live on a cleaning station are these tiny parasites that feed off of the mucus on a fish's skin. The gobies start at the tail and chase the parasites up and on to the chin, where they will be herded together and easier to catch.

While one fish is being cleaned a patient diver can often see other fishes circling nearby, waiting for their turn to come in. Some larger fish, like groupers, who can spend up to 8 hours a day getting cleaned, will sometimes jump the line and chase off smaller fish in order to get rid of some of their more pesky parasites.

# GOBIES : FISHES

### SPOTLIGHT GOBY
*(Elacatinus louisae)*
2 in max. Distinctive, bright yellow spot on the forehead. Two bright yellow lines run down the body.

### LINESNOUT GOBY
*(Elacatinus lori)*
1.75 in max. White bar between the eyes on the snout. Thin blue lines run through the eyes, down to the tail.

### COLIN'S CLEANING GOBY
*(Elacatinus colini)*
1.5 in max. Bright yellow stripe on the snout. Bright yellow lines run down body from behind yellow eyes.

### CARIBBEAN NEON GOBY
*(Elacatinus lobeli)*
2 in max. Two bright blue stripes run from the forehead, over the top of the eyes and towards the tail. Pale belly.

### PALLID GOBY
*(Coryphopterus eidolon)*
2 in max. Transparent body with bright orange line from the rear of the eye towards the tail.

### MASKED / GLASS GOBY
*(Coryphopterus personatus / hyalinus)*
1.5 in max. Both species are nearly identical, with white spots running down the lateral line. Black eyes

## RUSTY GOBY
*(Priolepis hipoliti)*
1.5 in max. Orange body with wide, darker bands. Orange spots on fins. Usually found upside down.

> Most gobies remain resting on the top of the reef, on the lookout for both food and predators. They are never far from a safe hole to dart into, but they can be approached by a slow and patient diver. Many are transparent enough to be able to see their internal organs.

## LEOPARD GOBY
*(Gobiosoma saucrum)*
1 in max. Transparent body with two darker squares near the belly, behind the pectoral fins. Red cheeks.

## WALL GOBY
*(Gobiosoma pallens)*
2 in max. Series of darker bands run down the body. Fins are clear. Found perched on dead coral heads.

GOBIES : FISHES

### SAND CANYON GOBY
*(Coryphopterus bol)*
3 in max. Transparent body. Lines run from the mouth. Spot at the base of the pectoral fin. Found on reeftops.

### COLON GOBY
*(Coryphopterus dicrus)*
2 in max. Transparent body with small brown spots. Two dark spots near the base of the pectoral fin.

### BRIDLED GOBY
*(Coryphopterus glaucofraenum)*
3 in max. Transparent body. Thin, white line runs from behind the mouth to the gill cover. Found in shallows.

### SPOTFIN GOBY
*(Oxyurichthys stigmalophius)*
6 in max. Large black spot at lower rear of foredorsal fin. Light brown blotches down the body. Usually at depth.

### PEPPERMINT GOBY
*(Coryphopterus lipernes)*
1.25 in max. Yellow to transparent body with bright blue markings on the face and around the eyes.

### GOLDSPOT GOBY
*(Gnatholepis thompsoni)*
3 in max. Thin dark bar runs from the top of the head across the eyes. Small, gold spot above pectoral fins.

## ORANGESIDED GOBY
*(Gobiosoma dilepis)*
1 in max. Transparent body. Two orange squares, outlined in black, behind the pectoral fins.

The dartfish, below, get their name from the fast escape they make into their burrows when threatened. They can usually be found in small colonies, each fish having its own hole. In this way they are similar to jawfish (p. 234), but dartfish will swim horizontally above the reef.

## HOVERING DARTFISH
*(Ptereleotris helenae)*
5 in max. Bluish body and fins. Blue line behind the eye. The tail is rounded. Hover over burrows in the sand.

## HOVERING DARTFISH (JUVENILE)
*(Ptereleotris helenae)*
The yellow on the fins and tail is more pronounced in juveniles. They hover closer to their burrows.

# GOBIES : FISHES

**TUSKED GOBY**
*(Risor ruber)*
1 in max. Long, tapering, transparent body with many tiny brown spots. The upper lip extends outwards.

**DWARF GOBY**
*(Lythrypnus elasson)*
1.5 in max. Orange body with bright orange spots below the eyes. Dark spot under the pectoral fin.

**FRILLFIN GOBY**
*(Bathygobius soporator)*
6 in max. Large, wide head. 5 or 6 wide, dark body bars. Can change color to match its surroundings.

**BARFIN GOBY**
*(Coryphopterus alloides)*
2 in max. Large eyes, reddish head and yellow body with small white spots. Dusky bar behind pectoral fin.

**ORANGESPOTTED GOBY**
*(Nes longus)*
4 in max. Pairs of dark patches with orange spots run down the body. Elongated foredorsal spine.

**DIPHASIC GOBY**
*(Lyhrypnus heterochroma)*
1 in max. Bright orange body with thin white bands. The eyes are green. Rare, it lives under ledges.

## QUILLFIN BLENNY
*(Labrisomus filamentosus)*
5 in max. Elongated foredorsal spines can be retracted.
Large ocellated spot on gill cover. Darker bars on body.

Blennies are smaller fishes that can most often be found resting on top of the reef, close to a safe hiding place. They usually have large pectoral fins that they use to hold themselves up with, and will dart away very quickly if disturbed. They are often the same size and found in the same habitats as gobies (p. 200). The most noticeable difference between a blenny and a goby is found on the dorsal fin. All gobies have two separate dorsal fins, while blennies have only one long, continuous dorsal fin. Triplefins (p. 211), pictured on the left, actually have three sets of dorsal fins.

Some blennies will live in holes in the reef, usually ones left over by burrowing worms (p. 138). These tube-dwelling blennies have small, pointed, transparent bodies that can swim backwards rapidly to get into their tiny holes. They are planktivores that will dart out only to grab a piece of food as it drifts by.

# BLENNIES : FISHES

### QUILLFIN BLENNY (JUVENILE)
*(Labrisomus filamentosus)*
Banded body with a rounded, bulbous head. Large foredorsal fin. Fan-shaped cirri above the eyes.

### PALEHEAD BLENNY
*(Labrisomus gobio)*
2.5 in max. Four or five body bars, wider in the middle. Spotted belly. Dark patch located behind the eyes.

### DOWNY BLENNY
*(Labrisomus kalisherae)*
3.5 in max. Red to dark brown body. Four or five faintly darker body bars. Large lips and eyes.

### OYSTER BLENNY
*(Hypleurochilus pseudoaequipinnis)*
3 in max. Large head covered in small orange spots. Branched cirri above the eyes. Found in shallows.

### HAIRY BLENNY (JUVENILE)
*(Labrisomus nuchipinnis)*
Juveniles have a dark spot on the front of the foredorsal fin that disappears over time. Shallow water only.

### HAIRY BLENNY
*(Labrisomus nuchipinnis)*
9 in max. Large ocellated spot on the gill covers. Body brownish with faint white spots. Found on shallow reefs.

### BLACKCHEEK BLENNY (FEMALE)
*(Starksia weigti)*
1.5 in max. Dark red body with irregular white patches and spots below the dorsal fins. The eyes are red.

The Arrow Blenny (facing page) is one of the few members of this family that hovers in mid-water close to the reef, although it will sometimes live in holes in deeper sponges. Most blennies remain perched on top of the reef, close to their shelters.

### REDLIP BLENNY
*(Ophioblennius macclurei)*
5 in max. Uniform dark red body and red lips. Remains perched on top of coral heads unless molested.

### REDLIP BLENNY (VARIETY)
*(Ophioblennius macclurei)*
The body behind the gill cover fades to white. Both varieties can exist side by side on a patch of reef.

# BLENNIES : FISHES

**BLACKCHEEK BLENNY (MALE)**
*(Starksia weigti)*
1.5 in max. Males will always have a series of white spots on the lips, sometimes absent in females.

**ARROW BLENNY**
*(Lucayablennius zingaro)*
2 in max. Tail is permanently cocked and ready to dart away. Long pointed face. Reddish body and yellow tail.

**RINGED BLENNY**
*(Starksia hassi)*
1.5 in max. Lighter bands down a long, tapering, red body. White spot on the cheek, down from the eye.

**RINGED BLENNY (VARIETY)**
*(Starksia hassi)*
The pale bands can be very faint, making identification difficult. There is always a white spot behind the eye.

**MARBLED BLENNY**
*(Paraclinus marmoratus)*
1.5 in max. The foredorsal spines join to form a short spike behind the head. Two green spots near the tail.

**DWARF BLENNY**
*(Starksia nanodes sp.)*
1.5 in max. White line on the forehead runs onto the snout. Dark bar under the eyes. White bands on back.

## BLACKEDGE TRIPLEFIN
*(Enneanectes atrorus)*
1.5 in max. Elongated foredorsal fins. First dorsal fins are the longest. Black edge on second dorsal fin.

Triplefins have a separate set of foredorsal spines that are connected by thin tissues. They often wave these about independently of the other dorsal fins, as a signal to other Triplefins in the area. They can stay perched on their large pectoral fins, motionless for hours.

## FLAGFIN BLENNY
*(Emblemariopsis carib sp.)*
1 in max. Distinctive short, mobile, foredorsal spine. Pale to transparent body with a faint red stripe.

## GOLDLINE BLENNY
*(Malacoctenus aurolineatus)*
2.5 in max. Three dark bars on yellow forebody. Pectoral fins are large and yellow, ventral fins are red.

BLENNIES : FISHES

**REDEYE TRIPLEFIN**
*(Enneanectes pectoralis)*
1.5 in max. The bar at the base of the tail is darker than the body bars, with a red bar behind it. The iris is red.

**LOFTY TRIPLEFIN**
*(Enneanectes altivelis)*
1.5 in max. The foredorsal fin is taller than the next dorsal fin. Perches on large, banded pectoral fins.

**ROUGHHEAD TRIPLEFIN**
*(Enneanectes boehlkei)*
1.5 in max. Foredorsal fin is shorter than the next dorsal fin. Usually reddish bars down the body.

**DIAMOND BLENNY**
*(Malacoctenus boehlkei)*
2.5 in max. Ocellated blue spot on foredorsal spine. Pointed snout. Often found near sea anemones.

**BLUETHROAT PIKEBLENNY**
*(Chaenopsis ocellata)*
5 in max. Rarely found in more than 10 ft of water. Long, thin body with orange iris. Blue ring under the chin.

**YELLOWFACE PIKEBLENNY**
*(Chaenopsis limbaughi)*
3.5 in max. Elongated body with single yellow to brown mid-body stripe. Long flattened snout.

Sailfin blennies use their massive foredorsal arrays to warn other fish away from their territories and to signal to females in elaborate courtship displays. The males are darker and more noticeable against the sandy backgrounds they prefer to hide in. Usually only their heads are seen poking out of holes in the sand or rubble. A diver must be very still and patient to see this behavior; the rapid flashing of their sails is over in the blink of an eye. They can be distinguished from other blennies by the characteristic teardrop shape of their pupils, and the long cirri above their heads.

**SAILFIN BLENNY (MALE)**
*(Emblemaria pandionis)*
2.5 in max. Very tall foredorsal spines that can be extended. "Sail" has darker concentric lines.

**SAILFIN BLENNY (FEMALE)**
*(Emblemaria pandionis)*
Lighter brown. Foredorsal spines form a "sail", with broken lines running parallel to the body.

## BLENNIES : FISHES

### RIBBON BLENNY (VARIETY)
*(Emblemaria vitta sp.)*
This blenny can rapidly change color as it flicks it's sail up and down when approached or threatened.

### RIBBON BLENNY
*(Emblemaria vitta sp.)*
2 in max. Pointed snout. Elongated foredorsal array is rounded, with a bright, pointed yellow spot at the base.

### SADDLED BLENNY
*(Malacoctenus triangulatus)*
2.5 in max. Four dark, triangular bars usually run from the dorsal fin to the belly. Red spots along the body.

### SADDLED BLENNY (VARIETY)
*(Malacoctenus triangulatus)*
Highly variable in color, all Saddled Blennies are found in shallower water and have bright yellow ventral fins.

### ROSY BLENNY
*(Malacoctenus macropus)*
2.5 in max. Distinctive red markings beneath the eye and gills. Sharply pointed snout. Found in shallows.

### GOATEE BLENNY
*(Paraclinus barbatus)*
2.5 in max. Red body and eyes. Fleshy appendage on the chin. Three blue, ocellated spots towards the tail.

🤿 Tube-dwelling blennies often live in the holes left behind by burrowing worms (p. 138). Often many of these holes are found on the same coral head, and the holes nearest the top get more bits of plankton floating by, and so are prized by the largest and strongest blenny in the group.
It is usually the male blenny that lives inside the hole, leaving the female outside on the surface of the coral head. She will deposit her eggs into the bottom of the hole. The male will then fertilize these eggs and remain there with only his head poking out, guarding them until they are ready to hatch.

FILAMENT BLENNY
(Emblemaria hyltoni)
1 in max. Distinctive long, mobile foredorsal spine. Found only in the Bay Islands, Honduras.

SECRETARY BLENNY
(Acanthemblemaria maria)
2 in max. White markings below the eyes. Two large cirri above the eyes. Orange eyes, never green or yellow.

# TUBE-DWELLING BLENNIES : FISHES

### SEA FAN BLENNY (FEMALE)
*(Emblemariopsis pricei)*
1 in max. Transparent body with a thick line down the center, alternating in red and white bands.

### SEA FAN BLENNY (MALE)
*(Emblemariopsis pricei)*
1 in max. Remains inside its hole. Black head with occasional white spots. Bulbous eyes and large lips.

### ROUGHHEAD BLENNY
*(Acanthemblemaria aspera)*
1.5 in max. Numerous branching cirri above the eyes. Darker body with numerous white spots.

### ROUGHHEAD BLENNY (VARIETY)
*(Acanthemblemaria aspera)*
Golden yellow body with numerous white spots. The distinctive irises of the eyes are always orange.

### SPINYHEAD BLENNY
*(Acanthemblemaria spinosa)*
1.5 in max. Numerous short spines on the forehead, which is white. Large greenish eyes. Serrated lips.

### SPINYHEAD BLENNY (VARIETY)
*(Acanthemblemaria spinosa)*
Shorter cirri are less branched; previously classified as the Secretary Blenny. Both have white eye markings.

## GREEN RAZORFISH (MALE)
*(Xyrichtys splendens)*
5.5 in max. Rounded tail. One or two dark mid-body spots.
Variable colors, mainly with greenish tints.

Razorfishes get their name from their sharp foreheads. They all belong to the wrasse family but their bodies and behavior have become adapted to live in a specific habitat: sand patches. There is usually no place for a fish to hide in open sandy areas. So, when startled, they will use their sharp foreheads to dart directly into the sand for shelter. They live in large family groups with one dominant male on each sand patch, protecting a harem of smaller females. Generally unafraid of divers, they will even try to feed off the debris that can be kicked up by a diver's fins.

Post-larval (newly hatched) razorfish will settle onto the reef from their pelagic, larval stage and will remain hidden close to the bottom, usually among tufts of brown algae (p. 18), in which they try to camouflage themselves. They will even swim differently, tumbling back and forth like a piece of algae or debris, even in calm water.

## RAZORFISHES : FISHES

**GREEN RAZORFISH (JUVENILE)**
*(Xyrichtys splendens)*
Mottled or barred in brown, with longer dorsal and ventral fins. Hovers close to algae on the bottom.

**GREEN RAZORFISH (FEMALE)**
*(Xyrichtys splendens)*
Reddish brown to pink, females have no distinctive markings, but can be identified by their reddish iris.

**ROSY RAZORFISH (FEMALE)**
*(Xyrichtys martinicensis)*
Pearly white head. Gray to pink body with no markings. White patch with small red lines just above the belly.

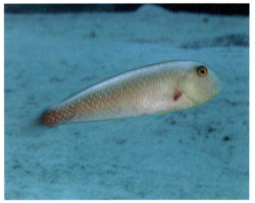

**ROSY RAZORFISH (MALE)**
*(Xyrichtys martinicensis)*
6 in max. Straight edge on the tail. Rounded head. Distinct darker spot at the base of the pectoral fin.

**PEARLY RAZORFISH (FEMALE)**
*(Xyrichtys novacula)*
Pale green to pink. Smaller dark eye with no red iris. Flattened head. Whitish area on the upper belly.

**PEARLY RAZORFISH (MALE)**
*(Xyrichtys novacula)*
15 in max. The largest of the razorfish. Small eye and a blunt head. Single small, dark body bar.

## WHITESTAR CARDINALFISH
*(Apogon lachneri)*
3 in max. Elongated dorsal and anal fins. Two small spots at the base of the dorsal fin, first black then white.

Cardinalfish are nocturnal animals and spend the daylight hours hidden in caves and crevices on the reef. Large eyes help them to pluck food out of the water at night and their red color makes them harder to see in the dark. Male cardinalfish will incubate their eggs in their mouths.

## BELTED CARDINALFISH
*(Apogon townsendi)*
2.5 in max. Dark bar from last dorsal fin to ventral fin. Two more dark bars towards the tail.

## BRIDLE CARDINALFISH
*(Apogon aurolineatus)*
2.5 in max. Solid orange to light brown color with no distinctive markings. Lives near anemones.

# CARDINALFISHES : FISHES

### BROADSADDLE CARDINALFISH
*(Apogon pillionatus)*
4 in max. Dark bar behind the last dorsal fin is followed by one or two white bars towards the tail.

### DUSKY CARDINALFISH
*(Phaeoptyx pigmentaria)*
3.5 in max. Pale body with darker speckles behind each scale. Single wide bar at the base of the tail.

### BARRED CARDINALFISH
*(Apogon binotatus)*
2.5 in max. Dark band from the last dorsal fin, down to the ventral fin. Single wide dark bar towards the tail.

### FLAMEFISH
*(Apogon maculatus)*
4.5 in max. Two distinctive white lines across the eyes. Dark spots just behind the eyes and under the dorsal fin.

### MIMIC CARDINALFISH
*(Apogon phenax)*
3 in max. Dark bar under rear dorsal fin narrows to a point near the belly. Often a dark bar near the tail.

### ROUGHLIP CARDINALFISH
*(Apogon robinsi)*
4 in max. Dark body bar below last dorsal fin. Often a wide bar near the tail. Upper body has yellowish hue.

## LONGSPINE SQUIRRELFISH
*(Holocentrus rufus)*
1 ft max. Reddish body with faint white stripes. The tips of the dorsal spines have white, triangular spots.

> 🤿 Soldierfish are nocturnal and can be found during the day hiding in caves and under ledges. They are planktivores and will also eat shrimp and larvae. Their red coloration makes them less visible to predators at night, when they will leave the safety of their caves in search of food.

## SQUIRRELFISH
*(Holocentrus adscensionis)*
16 in max. Red body with paler yellow or white stripes. Front dorsal spines are tipped with yellow.

## DUSKY SQUIRRELFISH
*(Sargocentron vexillarium)*
7 in max. Bronze to reddish and silver stripes. Red borders on anal fins and tail. Found in shallows.

# SQUIRRELFISHES : FISHES

### DEEPWATER SQUIRRELFISH
*(Sargocentron bullisi)*
5 in max. Red and white stripes with thin brown stripes in between. Always found on deeper reefs.

### BLACKBAR SOLDIERFISH
*(Myripristis jacobus)*
9 in max. Distinctive black bar and white bar behind the gill covers. White margins on the ventral fins.

### BIGEYE
*(Priacanthus arenatus)*
16 in max. Uniform red to reddish-brown. May have slightly darker margins on the fins and the tail.

### LONGJAW SQUIRRELFISH
*(Neoniphon marianus)*
7 in max. Golden stripes on a red body. Dorsal fins have white spots and white spine tips. Long anal fin.

### CARDINAL SOLDIERFISH
*(Plectrypops retrospinis)*
9 in max. Pale body with larger scales with red margins. The tail is rounded. The belly may be a paler pink color.

### REEF SQUIRRELFISH
*(Sargocentron coruscum)*
6 in max. White stripes run down the length of the body. Distinctive black spot on the first foredorsal spines.

# SILVERSIDES
*(Atherinidae, Clupeidae, Engraulididae)*
6 in max. Small, silvery collections of fish with forked tails, often mixed together in shallows and caves.

Every year in the late summer, lucky divers can be treated to an explosion of these tiny fishes.
Silverside schools consist of tiny herrings, anchovies and others, all hatching onto the reef at the same time in a process called "broadcast spawning". They can be found in their millions, inside caves and canyons in shallow water. By hatching onto the reef at the same time, their natural predators are overwhelmed, becoming literally sated on fish, and so some will survive to carry on the process the following year. In a few short weeks almost all of these tiny fishes will be eaten.

Silversides try to stay as close to each other and to the walls of the reef as possible, moving in unison to confuse predators, such as groupers, jacks and barracudas. It is a time of plenty for these carnivores, with a seemingly endless supply of prey available. Even humans will cash in on this annual event; the commercial name for this catch is "whitebait".

# LIONFISH : FISHES

**LIONFISH**
*(Volitans Pterois)*
1 ft max. Large ventral arrays. Long dorsal and
anal spines. Striped body with fleshy appendages.

It has been called one of the most devastating marine invasions in history. Although they can now be seen throughout the Caribbean, the Lionfish is not native to the area. Originally from the Indo-Pacific region, they have no natural predators in the Caribbean. They are highly poisonous, with venom in their dorsal, ventral and anal fins. The wide, fan-shaped pectoral fins are not poisonous, and only used for cornering their prey. They are voracious hunters, able to swallow prey at least half their own body size. They often hunt the juveniles of other species, making their impact on the reef even worse. They have even been known to feed on the local cleaner species.

It is believed they were introduced from aquariums in Florida, and in a few short years they have spread to cover the whole Caribbean, playing havoc with local ecosystems as they spread. Every month an adult lionfish can release 300,000 larvae into the water, which can be carried for miles. The juveniles (below left) are nearly transparent, but still have the same venomous spines.

## SPOTTED DRUM (JUVENILE)
*(Equetus punctatus)*
White body with black bars and stripes on all fins.
Small black spot on the snout. Long foredorsal fin.

In the water, it is often difficult to tell the juveniles of these drum species apart without seeing their faces. The Spotted Drum has a single black spot on its forehead, the Jackknife Fish has a thin black line down its snout, and the Highhat has a black bar between its eyes.

## SPOTTED DRUM
*(Equetus punctatus)*
11 in max. The foredorsal fin becomes a spike and the spots reach up the body and onto the dorsal fins.

## REEF CROAKER
*(Odontoscion dentex)*
1 ft max. Large, reddish eyes. Dark spot at the base of the pectoral fin. Often hides in deeper crevices.

# DRUMS : FISHES

### HIGHHAT (JUVENILE)
*(Pareques acuminatus)*
Long dorsal fin, similar in length to the tapering tail. There is a black band running between the eyes.

### HIGHHAT (INTERMEDIATE)
*(Pareques acuminatus)*
Body develops black stripes along the body, black band remains between the eyes. Dark spot on foredorsal fin.

### HIGHHAT
*(Pareques acuminatus)*
9 in max. Body has numerous black and white stripes. The dorsal fin is shorter and is black, edged in white.

### JACKKNIFE FISH (JUVENILE)
*(Equetus lanceolatus)*
Elongated foredorsal spine is black and white. Small line down the snout (the Spotted Drum has a spot).

### JACKKNIFE FISH (INTERMEDIATE)
*(Equetus lanceolatus)*
Foredorsal spine remains erect but shortens. Tail remains pointed with no spots. Long ventral fins.

### JACKKNIFE FISH
*(Equetus lanceolatus)*
9 in max. Foredorsal fin is black in front and white behind. Fills out to form a wide blade-shaped fan.

## LONGLURE FROGFISH
*(Antennarius multiocellatus)*
9 in max. Highly variable in color. Three dark
spots near the tail. Skin has a sponge-like texture.

One of the most difficult fish to spot on a reef, the Frogfish, camouflages itself as a sponge. They can take on almost any color and even have fake sponge pores on their skin. They rarely move and when they do it is by hopping on fins that look more like legs, and by jetting water out of their gills behind them. The Longlure Frogfish entices prey in by "fishing" for them with an attractive lure, bobbing it up and down in front of their concealed mouths.

Frogfish can open their jaws wider than their heads, increasing the volume of their mouths twelvefold. It is one of the fastest strikes in the ocean, measured at 1/30th of a second. This sucks prey, sometimes half their own size, into their mouths. The prey is swallowed whole, without chewing. If their lure gets damaged it can be regrown.

## BOTTOM DWELLERS : FISHES

### SARGASSUMFISH
*(Histrio histrio)*
8 in max. Fleshy tabs around its body. Resembles the Sargassum Seaweed (p. 19) on which it lives.

### FLYING GUNARD
*(Dactylopterus volitans)*
18 in max. Blunt snout and tapering body. Oversized pectoral fins. Two thin fans in front of foredorsal fin.

### FLYING GUNARD (JUVENILE)
*(Dactylopterus volitans)*
Darker body with shortened pectoral rays. Found in shallow lagoons and reef tops.

### FLYING GUNARD (DISPLAY)
*(Dactylopterus volitans)*
When threatened, they spread their pectoral fins into wings. The bright blue spots startle predators.

### COMMON SNOOK
*(Centropomus undecimalis)*
4.5 ft max. Sloping forehead and distinctive, dark lateral line. Found in shallow lagoons and mangroves.

### BONEFISH
*(Albula vulpes)*
3.5 ft max. Long, silvery body with forked tail. Short mouth. Prefers to feed in lagoons or sandy inshores.

🤿 Scorpionfish are masters of camouflage. Their fleshy skin can take on both the color and even the texture of their surroundings, while they lie in wait for a meal to swim by. They are a close relative of the Lionfish, with their main defense being a row of sharp dorsal spines that can be quickly raised when threatened. These contain a powerful neurotoxin, causing intense pain, swelling, nausea and fainting. Divers should be careful of getting too close to the bottom while moving over shallow, rubble-covered bottoms, as this is where the common Spotted Scorpionfish prefers to lay in wait.

🤿 The wide mouth of the scorpionfish can gulp in prey almost as large as itself. Relying on stealth to hunt from the reef floor, these ambush predators move only rarely and for short distances, bouncing along on their fan-shaped pectoral fins. When a scorpionfish is disturbed, these fins can flash a vivid warning sign.

# BOTTOM DWELLERS : FISHES

### MUSHROOM SCORPIONFISH
*(Scorpaena inermis)*
3 in max. Smallest of the scorpionfishes. Fleshy growths above the eyes. Dark bars on the fins.

### REEF SCORPIONFISH
*(Scorpaenodes caribbaeus)*
5 in max. Dark brown to red body. Yellow spots on large pectoral fins. Black spot on rear of dorsal fin.

### SPOTTED SCORPIONFISH
*(Scorpaena plumieri)*
1.5 ft max. Largest and most common of the scorpionfishes. It has three darker bands on its tail. Color varies.

### PLUMED SCORPIONFISH
*(Scorpaena grandicornis)*
7 in max. Long fleshy growths above each eye and many fleshy tabs down the length of the body.

### SHORTNOSE BATFISH
*(Ogcocephalus nasutus)*
15 in max. Long spine on snout. Darker body with a reddish underbelly. Two dark bands on the tail.

### SHORTNOSE BATFISH (VARIETY)
*(Ogcocephalus nasutus)*
The colors of the Batfish are highly variable, sometimes with yellow or white. The long snout shortens with age.

## BEARDED TOADFISH
*(Sanopus barbatus)*
1 ft max. Flattened head with distinctive, fleshy barbels around the chin. Large blue eyes.

Toadfish live in well-tended burrows on the reef, usually under ledges with sandy bottoms, with only their heads sticking out to catch fish as they swim by. The fleshy barbels around the head help them to blend in. They communicate with each other using deep, croaking sounds.

## ATLANTIC FLASHLIGHT FISH
*(Kryptophanaron alfredi)*
10 in max. Dark body with white spots along lateral line. Glowing white light under the eye. Seen on new moons.

## REEF-CAVE BROTULA
*(Grammonus claudei)*
3 in max. Brown to black body. Dorsal and anal fins join onto the tail. Found deep inside caves.

# BOTTOM DWELLERS : FISHES

### CUSK EEL
*(Ophidion sp.)*
6 in max. Long, tapering body. Rounded head with large eyes and barbels under the chin. Buries in sand.

### LANCER DRAGONET
*(Paradiplogrammus bairdi)*
4.5 in max. Foredorsal fin is longer and can move up and down. Large bulbous eyes and a tapering body.

### SPOTTED DRAGONET
*(Diplogrammus pauciradiatus)*
2 in max. Large eyes and pointed snout. Long foredorsal fin. White spots down the belly to the tail.

### LANCER DRAGONET (VARIETY)
*(Paradiplogrammus bairdi)*
Mostly white and found on sand, the Dragonet can also change its color to blend in with algae or corals.

### TONGUEFISH
*(Symphurus sp.)*
3 in max. Flattened, elongated body with eyes close together on the top. Extremely rare. Shallow waters.

### RED CLINGFISH
*(Arcos rubiginosus)*
1.5 in max. Large, flattened head with bulbous red eyes. Lighter bands down the cheeks from the eyes.

 Sand Divers and Lizardfish are quite common, but often hard to spot on the reef, as they rarely move. They are ambush predators, relying on patience and camouflage to feed. They can sit motionless on the reef floor for hours until their prey comes to them. They can open their mouths very wide to suck in their prey, and rows of sharp teeth keep the prey from escaping. They feed mostly on smaller fishes and shrimps.

**SAND DIVER**
*(Synodus intermedius)*
18 in max. Large, wide mouth with prominent teeth. Dark spot on the gill cover. Diamond pattern on back.

**SAND DIVER (JUVENILE)**
*(Synodus intermedius)*
Juveniles tend to live partly buried in the sand or hiding in algae. Their color matches their background.

# BOTTOM DWELLERS : FISHES

### BLUESTRIPED LIZARDFISH
*(Synodus saurus)*
12 in max. Thin, pale blue stripes run down the length of the body. No yellow stripes, as on the Sand Diver.

### RED LIZARDFISH
*(Synodus synodus)*
13 in max. Series of reddish bars down the body. Small dark spot just behind the snout.

### DWARF SAND PERCH
*(Diplectrum bivittatum)*
12 in max. Pale blue markings on face. Dark body stripe continues to the tail. Builds burrows in sand.

### RED SPOTTED HAWKFISH
*(Amblycirrhitus pinos)*
4 in max. Tall, barred body. Red spots on face and dorsal fin. Red tassels on the dorsal spines.

### YELLOW GOATFISH
*(Mulloidichthys martinicus)*
16 in max. Distinctive yellow stripe down the body. The tail is bright yellow. Two barbels under the chin.

### SPOTTED GOATFISH
*(Pseudupeneus maculatus)*
11 in max. Three dark, rectangular patches down the length of the body. Two barbels under the chin.

## YELLOWHEAD JAWFISH
*(Opistognathus aurifrons)*
4 in max. Yellowish head and pale blue to white body.
Dark lines under the jaw. Fins and tail are rounded.

Yellowhead Jawfish are found in small colonies of around a dozen fish, each with their own burrow. Their heads have no scales and are hardened for digging. They make elaborate dens, lining them with larger pieces of rubble to avoid cave-ins, and can sometimes be seen raiding another's hole for choice pieces of building material. They feed on plankton that drifts over their burrows. Never straying far from the entrance, they swim slowly backwards into them, or may dart in, head first, when alarmed.

Jawfish are mouth-brooders: once eggs are fertilized, the male Jawfish will incubate them in its mouth for about two weeks, sometimes churning them about to keep the eggs supplied with fresh oxygen. They are typically shy when they are brooding, and have to forego feeding while their mouths are full. After all the eggs are hatched, the tiny fish are released all at once. This usually happens just as night begins to fall, giving the post-larval jawfish more protection as they find a place to hide. Each Jawfish can live for up to five years.

# BOTTOM DWELLERS : FISHES

### YELLOWHEAD JAWFISH (JUVENILE)
*(Opistognathus aurifrons)*
The yellow head is darker with a dark band through the eye. Found among the adults in smaller burrows.

### YELLOW JAWFISH
*(Opistognathus gilberti)*
3 in max. Black spot on dorsal fin. Black tail with transparent edges. Found burrowing on deeper reefs.

### DUSKY JAWFISH
*(Opistognathus whitehursti)*
4 in max. Dark brown with a black mottled pattern. The dorsal fin has a black edge. Large eyes and mouth.

### BANDED JAWFISH
*(Opistognathus macrognathus)*
8 in max. Light brown body with faint markings. Black spot far down on dorsal fin. Large eyes and mouth.

### SAND TILEFISH (JUVENILE)
*(Malacanthus plumieri)*
Elongated body, yellow towards the tail. Black spot near base of the tail. Buries itself into the sand for shelter.

### SAND TILEFISH
*(Malacanthus plumieri)*
2 ft max. Pale blue to white, elongated body. Darker spot on upper tail. Hovers over a sandy burrow.

## PEACOCK FLOUNDER
*(Bothus lunatus)*
18 in max. Pattern of blue circles on the back.
Small blue spots on head and fins. Notched forehead.

Looking closely over sandy areas, a diver may see flounders, usually only when they move. Often all that can be seen is an eye poking out of the sand. They are flattened ventrally, with both eyes on the tops of their heads. Their mouths open to the side to gulp in their prey. All flounders start life like normal fishes, with an eye on either side of their heads and a tall body. But as they develop, one eye slowly grows around to the side of the head, and they start to hunt by camouflage.

Flounders use special pigment cells on their skin to change color very rapidly, even while swimming over different types of reef floor. They may start out green or yellow as they swim over patches of algae, then turn almost white as they move over the sand, and then just as quickly, they turn brown or blue as they settle themselves onto a coral head.

# FLOUNDERS : FISHES

### CHANNEL FLOUNDER
*(Syacium micrurum)*
1 ft max. Elongated body, with brown spots covering the back. Eyes are distinctively very close together.

### EYED FLOUNDER
*(Bothus ocellatus)*
7 in max. Covered in brown circular markings with no blue. Widely spaced eyes. Dark spots near the tail.

### MACULATED FLOUNDER
*(Bothus maculiferus)*
10 in max. Blue rings and spots all across the back as well as the fins. Blunt, rounded forehead.

### SPOTFIN FLOUNDER
*(Cyclopsetta fimbriata)*
12 in max. Two large spots on both dorsal and anal fins. Single spots on both the tail and the pectoral fin.

### SPINY FLOUNDER
*(Engyophrys senta)*
4 in max. Large pale blotch on the back, mid-body. Often two more dark spots near tail and head.

### LINED SOLE
*(Achirus lineatus)*
4 in max. Dark, rounded body with thin, faint black bars across the back. Eyes are fringed and small.

## LONGSNOUT SEAHORSE
*(Hippocampus reidi)*
6 in max. Highly variable in their color, usually
with tiny black spots on the head and body.

Seahorses are able to camouflage themselves in many different colors. Their latin name means "the bent horse". They swim very slowly between their hiding places, with a prehensile tail, which is not used for swimming but only for grabbing onto the reef. They swim by fluttering their delicate, transparent dorsal fins very rapidly, up to 35 times a second.

It is the male seahorse that becomes pregnant. The female places her eggs in a brood pouch on the male's belly. After fertilizing the eggs, the males will carry them for up to 6 weeks until they are released, already fully formed. Seahorses can live for up to 5 years and can meet up with the same female in the same shallow area for mating every year. Seahorses have to eat constantly to stay alive because they have no stomachs to hold their food. A single seahorse can eat up to 3000 brine shrimp a day. They are endangered because they are often caught and dried to sell as ornaments. In some areas they are sold to Asian markets, because of a belief in their medicinal properties.

## SEAHORSES : FISHES

**LONGSNOUT SEAHORSE (JUVENILE)**
*(Hippocampus reidi)*
Seahorses are born fully formed and they cling to anything they can on the reef while they grow.

**LINED SEAHORSE**
*(Hippocampus erectus)*
6 in max. Reddish brown to black in color. Highly variable markings. Radiating lines from the eyes.

**SHORTFIN PIPEFISH**
*(Cosmocampus elucens)*
6 in max. Pale bands down length of the body. Two short, dark lines behind each eye. Long snout.

**SHORTFIN PIPEFISH (VARIETY)**
*(Cosmocampus elucens)*
A rare lavender variety of Shortfin Pipefish is found in shallower water. Darker varieties exist up to 1000 ft.

**BANDED PIPEFISH (VARIETY)**
*(Halicampus crinitus)*
In shallower water, closer to the sunlight, a light yellow or golden color can offer better camouflage.

**BANDED PIPEFISH**
*(Halicampus crinitus)*
9 in max. Short snout. Pale, irregular body bars and a thin brown central line runs the length of the body.

## PIPEHORSE
*(Acentronura dendritica)*
3 in max. Distinctive, fleshy appendages resemble tufts of algae, in which it hides. Small fins on a curved tail.

🤿 Pipefishes have a long and slender snout that is used to suck up prey like tiny shrimp. Pipefishes are difficult to spot on a dive and it can be even more difficult to tell the species apart. They are similar to seahorses, but do not have the prehensile tail for holding onto the reef, so they remain lying on the bottom. Like seahorses, the male of the pipefish will carry fertilized eggs in a special brood pouch on its belly, keeping them safe from scavengers until they can hatch.

Pipefish rely on camouflage to keep them safe from predators. They are often overlooked by divers, as they can look just like twigs or small blades of Manatee Grass (p. 7) lying motionless on the reef floor. They move very slowly, using tiny fin rays along the length of their bodies.

## PIPEFISHES : FISHES

**PIPEHORSE (VARIETY)**
*(Acentronura dendritica)*
Pipehorses are most often dark brown to black.
The fleshy appendages on the head are the longest.

**SARGASSUM PIPEFISH**
*(Syngnathus pelagicus)*
8 in max. Brownish body with pale bars. Hides in floats
of Sargassum Seaweed (p. 19). Rare on coral reefs.

**CARIBBEAN PIPEFISH**
*(Syngnathus caribbaeus)*
10 in max. Thicker body with squared sides.
Lightly banded. Color varies from brown to reddish.

**DIAMOND PIPEFISH**
*(Syngnathus sp.)*
8 in max. Pale, diamond-shaped markings down
the length of the body. Pale bands on the nose.

**WHITENOSE PIPEFISH**
*(Cosmocampus albirostris)*
8 in max. Distinctive white snout. Pale bands down
the length of the body. Found on sandy bottoms.

**HARLEQUIN PIPEFISH**
*(H. crinitus forma ensenadae)*
9 in max. Contrasting dark and light brown bars run
from the snout to the tail. Found in branching corals.

## SERGEANT MAJOR
*(Abudefduf saxatilis)*
7 in max. Five wide, black body bars tapering towards the belly. Yellowish towards the upper sides.

Damselfish are highly territorial, maintaining small patches of algae that they defend fearlessly, pecking away at much larger fishes that get too close to their food supply, often going for the eyes. The Sergeant Major gets his name from the five black body bars on its sides. Like all members of the damselfish family, they care for their eggs after they have been laid, usually in shallower water, under ledges and overhangs. Males will sometimes take on a darker blue coloration while they tend these nests. A female can lay thousands of tiny eggs in a dense patch on the reef, and the male will swim constantly back and forth, chasing off other fish looking for an easy meal. They will swim close to the incubating eggs and wave their fins across them to aerate the eggs, as well as picking away the slow-growing or unhealthy eggs in the batch. This ensures that the rest have the best chance for survival. The newly hatched, post-larval Sergeant Majors already have the distinctive body bars.

# DAMSELFISHES : FISHES

### SERGEANT MAJOR (VARIETY)
*(Abudefduf saxatilis)*
Males protecting a patch of eggs will take on a darker, bluish color and stay close to the reef and the eggs.

### NIGHT SERGEANT
*(Abudefduf taurus)*
10 in max. Brownish body with five dark body bars. Long upper lip. Prefers shallow, rocky inshores.

### BEAUGREGORY (JUVENILE)
*(Stegastes leucostictus)*
Blunt snout. Blue spots often centered in the scales. Often a faint black spot on the rear of the dorsal fin.

### BEAUGREGORY
*(Stegastes leucostictus)*
4 in max. Blunt snout. Often a small black spot on rear of dorsal fin. Yellowish highlights on the scales.

### THREESPOT DAMSELFISH (JUVENILE)
*(Stegastes planifrons)*
Yellow to golden body with black spots on upper body and dorsal fin. Smaller black spot at the base of the tail.

### THREESPOT DAMSELFISH
*(Stegastes planifrons)*
5 in max. Large dark spot at the base of the tail. Dark spot at the base of the pectoral fin. Yellow above eyes.

## YELLOWTAIL DAMSELFISH (JUVENILE)
*(Microspathodon chrysurus)*
Dark blue with bright blue spots over the entire body and head. Blue border on fins. The tail is transparent.

The juvenile Yellowtail Damselfish (below left) is found only up in the shallows, where it hides in the blades of both Lettuce Coral (p. 63) and fire corals (p. 61). It is sometimes colloquially known as "the disco fish" for its bright, flashing colors and its fast, continuous movements.

## YELLOWTAIL DAMSELFISH
*(Microspathodon chrysurus)*
7.5 in max. Dark body with scattered, bright blue spots on the forehead and back. Bright yellow tail.

## YELLOWTAIL DAMSELFISH (VARIETY)
*(Microspathodon chrysurus)*
Shallow water variety. Yellow to brown body, no yellow tail and only occasional small blue spots on the body.

# DAMSELFISHES : FISHES

**LONGFIN DAMSELFISH (JUVENILE)**
*(Stegastes diencaeus)*
6 in max. Black spot on the dorsal fin, ringed in blue. Blue lines run backwards from a darker head.

**LONGFIN DAMSELFISH**
*(Stegastes diencaeus)*
6 in max. Both dorsal and anal fins extend beyond the base of the tail. Bright blue edge on the anal fin.

**DUSKY DAMSELFISH (JUVENILE)**
*(Stegastes adustus)*
Orange area from snout to the end of the dorsal fins. Dark spots on dorsal fin and tail, edged in blue.

**DUSKY DAMSELFISH**
*(Stegastes adustus)*
5 in max. Dorsal and anal fins extend only to the end of the base of the tail. Thin dark border on anal fin.

**BROWN CHROMIS**
*(Chromis multilineata)*
6.5 in max. Uniform brown body. Yellow on dorsal fin and tail tips. White spot near upper base of the tail.

**BLUE CHROMIS**
*(Chromis cyanea)*
5 in max. Bright blue or purple body. Darker area from the snout across the top. Forked tail has dark borders.

### COCOA DAMSELFISH
*(Stegastes variabilis)*
5 in max. Belly, lower fins and tail are yellow. Dark borders on the scales. Often a dark spot just before tail.

> When damselfish protect their territory they are actually guarding their small supply of algae, like a little farm. Schools of Blue Tang (p. 248), avid herbivores, will sometimes descend on the small "farm" in a pack, overwhelming the damselfish and eating everything in sight.

### COCOA DAMSELFISH (JUVENILE)
*(Stegastes variabilis)*
Large black spot at the rear of the dorsal fin extends onto the body. Blue lines and spots run from snout.

### COCOA DAMSELFISH (VARIETY)
*(Stegastes variabilis)*
A darker variety, sometimes with a small dark spot near the base of the tail. Scales form diagonal lines on sides.

## DAMSELFISHES : FISHES

**BICOLOR DAMSELFISH (JUVENILE)**
*(Stegastes partitus)*
Distinct contrast between front and rear parts of the body. Fins edged in bright blue. Blue under eyes.

**BICOLOR DAMSELFISH**
*(Stegastes partitus)*
4 in max. Dark head and foredorsal fins. Pale to white body towards the tail. The belly is yellow.

**BICOLOR DAMSELFISH (VARIETY)**
*(Stegastes partitus)*
Males guarding eggs have a territorial display of black fins and tail and a white body. Moves rapidly.

**PURPLE REEF FISH**
*(Chromis scotti)*
4 in max. Gray with bright blue spots on the head. Blue crescent above the eye. Found on deeper walls.

**SUNSHINE FISH (JUVENILE)**
*(Chromis insolata)*
Yellow upper body and a bright blue or purple belly. Often has a bright blue line above the eyes.

**SUNSHINE FISH**
*(Chromis insolata)*
4 in max. Green to brown upper body. Belly is usually white. Pale or yellow edge on rear dorsal fin and tail.

🤿 Tang are sociable animals, almost always travelling in large groups across the reef, feeding on algae. Their role in a reef ecosystem should not be underestimated. They keep the algae levels down by their constant grazing, and without them the coral reef would soon be smothered. A group of Blue Tang can clear as much as 6 acres of reef algae in a day. They are as voracious as the algae is determined to grow, so the two are kept in a constant balance on a healthy coral reef. Blue Tang can live for a long time for such a small fish, between 12 and 15 years. They get their name from the small, razor-sharp protrusions at the bases of their tails, which they can use to defend themselves.

**BLUE TANG**
*(Acanthurus coeruleus)*
15 in max. Uniform blue body with a small yellow spine on the base of the tail. May lighten in shallow waters.

**BLUE TANG (JUVENILE)**
*(Acanthurus coeruleus)*
Bright yellow body with blue around the eyes and thin, bright blue margins on the fins.

# TANGS : FISHES

### DOCTORFISH
*(Acanthurus chirurgus)*
14 in max. A series of darker bars (may be faint) start behind the pectoral fin, which is edged in a darker color.

### DOCTORFISH (VARIETY)
*(Acanthurus chirurgus)*
Sometimes lighter with a white band at the base of the tail. (Note: Surgeonfish may also have white bands.)

### OCEAN SURGEONFISH (POST-LARVAL)
*(Acanthurus tractus)*
Transparent body with a silvery head. The larvae will usually begin to settle onto the reef in summer.

### DOCTORFISH (VARIETY)
*(Acanthurus chirurgus)*
The body bars may be very faint, looking similar to the surgeonfish. Pectoral fins are always darker.

### OCEAN SURGEONFISH (JUVENILE)
*(Acanthurus tractus)*
Uniform blue to greenish body with no dark bars. They may also have a white bar at the base of the tail.

### OCEAN SURGEONFISH
*(Acanthurus tractus)*
15 in max. Uniform dark to light blue body with no bars. The tail and fins edged in blue. Yellow on pectoral fins.

## BANDED BUTTERFLYFISH
*(Chaetodon striatus)*
6 in max. Wide, black bars on the body, across
the eyes and across the dorsal and ventral fins and tail.

  Butterflyfish have developed a tall, thin body plan that allows them to get deep into crevices to hide from their predators, and also to get at their food: tiny crustaceans and shrimps. The long snout and jaws have also been adapted to pinch off individual coral polyps, making them one of the few animals that will feed directly on living corals. Butterflyfish will often stay with the same mate for life, and they can live for up to 10 years.

Butterflyfish offer a perfect example of how patterns on a fish can confuse predators. Most will have a bold vertical bar passing through the eye, so it becomes harder to tell which end of the fish is which, or in which direction it will try to escape. Some even have a false eye-spot near the tail. The Spotfin Butterflyfish will go even further and display an extra eye-spot at night, when it becomes more vulnerable. If under attack, it's better to get a bite on the tail than on the head. This simple defense increases the chance that this fish will make it safely through the night.

# BUTTERFLYFISHES : FISHES

**SPOTFIN BUTTERFLYFISH (JUVENILE)**
*(Chaetodon ocellatus)*
Similar to the adult, but with a more rounded body and a longer yellow ventral fin. Black spot is more diffuse.

**SPOTFIN BUTTERFLYFISH**
*(Chaetodon ocellatus)*
8 in max. Black bar across eyes. Body white, fins yellow. Small black spot on the rear of the dorsal fin.

**FOUREYE BUTTERFLYFISH (JUVENILE)**
*(Chaetodon capistratus)*
Two black spots, circled in white, near the tail.
Two darker body bars. Black bar across the eyes.

**FOUREYE BUTTERFLYFISH**
*(Chaetodon capistratus)*
6 in max. Single, large black spot, circled in white, near the tail. Black bar across eyes. Thin diagonal stripes.

**LONGSNOUT BUTTERFLYFISH**
*(Chaetodon aculeatus)*
4 in max. Elongated snout. Yellow bar above the eye.
Dorsal fins are darker, ventral fins are yellow.

**REEF BUTTERFLYFISH**
*(Chaetodon sedentarius)*
6 in max. Wide, dark bar near the tail runs onto dorsal and ventral fins. Body yellow above and white below.

🤿 Rather than hiding from larger fish, juvenile angelfish will make themselves more visible, fluttering back and forth just off the bottom of the sea floor. They are trying to attract larger fish that will come in to get cleaned. The juvenile will eat the tiny parasites and dead skin that collects on their hosts. Above, a Gray Angelfish cleans a butterflyfish. Pictured on the left: a Queen Angelfish cleans a Reef Squirrelfish, and in a rare display of cleaning behavior, a juvenile Rock Beauty is cleaning a Green Moray.

🤿 Angelfish are often found in monogamous pairs, and they show a great degree of loyalty to their partners. They will spend their lives, swimming and feeding, never further than a few feet from their partner. They feed during the day and at night the couple will always return to the same den to sleep. They become highly territorial during mating season, keeping all other fishes away. During the breeding cycle a female can release as many as 10 million eggs into the water. Angelfish can live for up to 10 years in the wild.

ANGELFISHES : FISHES

### QUEEN ANGELFISH (JUVENILE)
*(Holacanthus ciliaris)*
Orange face and tail and ventral fin. Dark band across eye lined in blue. Three bright blue or white body bars.

### QUEEN ANGELFISH (INTERMEDIATE)
*(Holacanthus ciliaris)*
Yellow body with bright blue edges on dorsal and anal fins. Faint blue body bars fade over time.

### QUEEN ANGELFISH (ADULT)
*(Holacanthus ciliaris)*
18 in max. Dark blue "crown" on the forehead, circled in light blue. Blue lips and gill covers. Yellow tail.

### GRAY ANGELFISH (JUVENILE)
*(Pomacanthus arcuatus)*
Three bold yellow body bars. Bright blue spots on fin tips. Squared tail with a pale or transparent margin.

### GRAY ANGELFISH (INTERMEDIATE)
*(Pomacanthus arcuatus)*
Three wide, light yellow body bars and one on the tail. Uniform rounded scales with pale edges. White lips.

### GRAY ANGELFISH (ADULT)
*(Pomacanthus arcuatus)*
2 ft max. The largest of the angelfish family, gray body with a square-cut tail with a pale margin. White lips.

The flattened body plan of the angelfish allows it to hide in narrow spaces on the reef during the night, where it will keep a regular den, usually in the company of its partner. The flattened shape also makes it more difficult for larger predators to get a hold of.

The bright colors of the angelfishes are actually an advertisement that its flesh is poisonous to most carnivores. An angelfish will eat poisonous sponges and algae, and instead of making the angelfish sick, the poisons are transferred, undigested, to the rest of the body. It is these poisons that give them their characteristic bright colors.

Up to 70% of an angelfish's diet is sponges. Angelfish especially love the fleshy insides of the Leathery Barrel Sponge (p. 53) but their jaws can't break open the tough skin. Hawksbill Turtles (p. 325) also eat this sponge, and with their specially adapted beak, opening the sponges is no problem. Divers will often find angelfish of different species following turtles to their meals and picking up the scraps that fall from the turtle's beak. If a large group of angelfish is found hovering over the reef, it could mean there is a Hawksbill Turtle feeding somewhere in the area.

ANGELFISHES : FISHES

**FRENCH ANGELFISH (JUVENILE)**
*(Pomacanthus paru)*
Three bold yellow body bars. Blue spots on fin tips.
Rounded tail with yellow margin forming an oval.

**FRENCH ANGELFISH (INTERMEDIATE)**
*(Pomacanthus paru)*
Three wide body bars fade over time as scales develop
yellow edges. Long yellow dorsal fin. Tail rounded.

**FRENCH ANGELFISH (ADULT)**
*(Pomacanthus paru)*
18 in max. Rounded body with large scales edged in
yellow. Yellow around eyes and base of pectoral fin.

**CHERUBFISH**
*(Centropyge argi)*
3 in max. Smallest of the angelfishes. Yellow face and
chest. Dark blue body with pale blue margins on fins.

**ROCK BEAUTY (JUVENILE)**
*(Holacanthus tricolor)*
Yellow body with dark mid-body spot. Inside this is
a blue-ringed black spot. Blue ring around the eyes.

**ROCK BEAUTY**
*(Holacanthus tricolor)*
12 in max. Yellow head and belly with a dark body.
Fins may be edged with red. Yellow tail. Black lips.

## QUEEN TRIGGERFISH
*(Balistes vetula)*
2 ft max. Two blue stripes across the face. Black lines radiate outwards from the eyes. Elongated dorsal fin.

🤿 Triggerfish and filefish get their name from a long foredorsal spine that can be raised up and locked into position to deter larger fish from attacking. The spines can also help lodge them into the reef while they are sleeping or hiding from predators. They are not fast swimmers and eat less mobile prey, such as crustaceans and brittle stars. Larger triggerfish can be very territorial, especially during mating season. Males will clear away small patches of the reef to make a nest for the female, who will then lay eggs. Both will guard the nest until the eggs hatch.

🤿 Like many fishes, the post-larval filefish may float in the ocean for weeks before they mature, hiding near pieces of flotsam (far left). When they are finally blown over a reef, they will settle to the bottom and use their highly adaptive skin as camouflage (left) until they are big enough to forage openly.

## TRIGGERFISHES : FISHES

### QUEEN TRIGGERFISH (JUVENILE)
*(Balistes vetula)*
Usually found on deeper reefs. Gray to blue body with thin, dark, diagonal stripes. Stays close to the reef.

### OCEAN TRIGGERFISH
*(Canthidermis sufflamen)*
2 ft max. Uniform gray in color. Black spot at the base of the pectoral fin. Small ventral spike.

### BLACK DURGON
*(Melichthys niger)*
16 in max. Dark body with two pale blue or white lines at the base of the dorsal and anal fins.

### BLACK DURGON (VARIETY)
*(Melichthys niger)*
Nesting males will become paler and display bright green, orange or blue markings, especially on the face.

### SLENDER FILEFISH
*(Monacanthus tuckeri)*
4 in max. Elongated snout. Large dewlap on the belly. White, reticulated body pattern. Found in soft corals.

### ROUGH TRIGGERFISH
*(Canthidermis maculata)*
13 in max. Dark body covered in bright blue spots and broken lines. Pelagic, rarely seen on reef-tops.

## SARGASSUM TRIGGERFISH
*(Xanthichthys ringens)*
10 in max. Purple body with rows of small black spots.
Three black lines on the face. White above the eyes.

Triggerfish have small mouths with only a few short teeth in front, but they do have very strong jaws. Their back teeth have become fused together into bony plates, which helps them to crack open the shells of molluscs and other invertebrates that make up the bulk of their diet.

### WHITE SPOTTED FILEFISH
*(Cantherhines macrocerus)*
18 in max. Orange body, sometimes with white spots.
Two hooked, bright orange spines near the tail base.

### WHITE SPOTTED FILEFISH (VARIETY)
*(Cantherhines macrocerus)*
White spots are not always seen, usually when the fish is startled or threatened. Often swim in mated pairs.

# FILEFISHES : FISHES

### SCRAWLED FILEFISH
*(Aluterus scriptus)*
3 ft max. Yellowish to gray body covered with bright blue lines and black spots. Elongated tail.

### SCRAWLED FILEFISH (VARIETY)
*(Aluterus scriptus)*
Sometimes darker bands randomly across the body to help blend in with the reef, especially at night.

### PYGMY FILEFISH
*(Stephanolepis setifer)*
7 in max. Its color matches its surroundings, with darker, broken lines running down the sides.

### ORANGE SPOTTED FILEFISH
*(Cantherhines pullus)*
8 in max. Orange spots on the body. Small white patch at the upper base of the tail. Found close to the reef.

### FRINGED FILEFISH
*(Monocanthus ciliatus)*
8 in max. Large dewlap on the belly and large hump under the dorsal fin. Fleshy tabs cover the body.

### UNICORN FILEFISH
*(Aluterus monoceros)*
2 ft max. Elongated snout, distinctly concave below the mouth. Scattered with small, brown spots along the body.

## WEB BURRFISH
*(Chilomycterus antillarum)*
1 ft max. Honeycomb pattern over the back and sides.
Four large, black spots on the rear of the body.

🤿 Balloonfish have a unique defense mechanism to deter predators, one that divers should be aware of. When threatened, they will gulp in large amounts of seawater and inflate their bodies. Modified scales form sharp spines that will stick out. This will usually put off an attack, but if not, the spines also contain a deadly poison called tetrodotoxin. This poison is collected from various types of algae, and they keep the toxin levels in their bodies up, in case of attack. The poison is more deadly than cyanide and, in some species, there is enough to kill 30 humans in a single fish.

Balloonfish and their cousins have a varied diet. They only have four teeth, which are fused to form hard plates that can be used to crush molluscs. They also supplement their diets by nibbling on corals and sponges. They are usually most active at night and so they have developed very large, light-sensitive eyes.

# PUFFERFISHES : FISHES

### PORCUPINEFISH
*(Diodon hystrix)*
3 ft max. Wide head with a tapering body. Small black dots over all fins as well as the body. Fins are darker.

### BRIDLED BURRFISH
*(Chilomycterus antennatus)*
1 ft max. Elongated darker patches above pectoral fins, outlined in white. Spots on body and tail.

### BALLOONFISH
*(Diodon holocanthus)*
20 in max. Rounded head with pointed snout. Spines on head and body. Fins are pale to transparent.

### SHARPNOSE PUFFER
*(Canthigaster rostrata)*
4.5 in max. Darker upper body and pale belly. Lighter tail has black borders. Blue lines behind the mouth.

### CHECKERED PUFFER
*(Sphoeroides testudineus)*
1 ft max. White underbelly. Back has numerous darker patches. Prefers sandy, shallow areas. Orange eyes.

### BANDTAIL PUFFER
*(Sphoeroides spengleri)*
1 ft max. Distinctive row of black spots runs from the mouth down to the tail. Tail has two black bars.

## SMOOTH TRUNKFISH
*(Lactophrys triqueter)*
1 ft max. Dark body with white spots. Pectoral fins
are yellowish. Elongated snout and obvious lips.

Trunkfish have a hard outer skeleton of bony plates. They have a varied diet and have adapted to make the most of food available on a reef. Their hard jaws can break open the raw limestone of the reef to get at invertebrates, or they can blow away layers of sand if something is hiding there.

The post-larval or juvenile trunkfish is colloquially known as simply "the pea" because of its small size. They are very difficult to spot, not only because they are so tiny, but also because of the habitats in which they choose to hide. In mid to late summer, look closely into the Fire Corals (p. 61) and within the folds of Lettuce Corals (p. 63) and you may find these elusive fish. They do have tails, but they are curled flat around the back of the body. Tiny, fan-shaped pectoral fins move them about.

# TRUNKFISHES : FISHES

### SMOOTH TRUNKFISH (POST-LARVAL)
*(Lactophrys triqueter)*
About the size of a pea. Dark body with pale yellow or white spots. The tail is tucked in against the body.

### SMOOTH TRUNKFISH (VARIETY)
*(Lactophrys triqueter)*
A rare color variation. Spots may become elongated and connect to form a reticulated pattern on the sides.

### SPOTTED TRUNKFISH (POST-LARVAL)
*(Lactophrys bicaudalis)*
About the size of a pea. Yellow body with black or brown spots. The tail is tucked in against the body.

### SPOTTED TRUNKFISH (INTERMEDIATE)
*(Lactophrys bicaudalis)*
Yellow or white body with black spots. Often a darker band runs between the eyes or on the upper back.

### SPOTTED TRUNKFISH
*(Lactophrys bicaudalis)*
16 in max. White to yellowish body covered in dense black spots. White area around the pointed mouth.

### SPOTTED TRUNKFISH (VARIETY)
*(Lactophrys bicaudalis)*
At night or when resting they can darken their skin color to blend in with their backgrounds.

## HONEYCOMB COWFISH
*(Acanthostracion polygonia)*
18 in max. Bright blue or brown honeycomb pattern over the body. Can pale or darken dramatically.

Cowfish are generally slow-moving fish, foraging close to the sea floor. Their mouths have been adapted to pluck out little invertebrates and algae from crevices in the reef, with the teeth fused together to form a long, tubular beak. They will sometimes feed on actual coral polyps. Inside the mouth there are two bony plates, top and bottom, that are used to crush their food before swallowing.

Their bodies are made up of fused plates that protect everything but the stomach, which is why they will always remain close to the reef while swimming. The only flexible part of the body is the tail, which is only rarely used to swim quickly away from danger. They swim using fan-like movements of their large pectoral fins, and the two fins near the tail.

Cowfishes get their name from the two pointed "horns" sticking out from the tops of their heads, just above the eyes. They have no scales, just a covering of skin that is poisonous to other fish. There are pigment cells in the skin that allow them to darken or lighten, or change colors to blend in with the reef.

# TRUNKFISHES : FISHES

### HONEYCOMB COWFISH (VARIETY)
*(Acanthostracion polygonia)*
Bright blue or brown honeycomb pattern over the body. Can pale or darken dramatically.

### SCRAWLED COWFISH
*(Acanthostracion quadricornis)*
18 in max. Blue lines and spots over a yellowish body. Continuous blue line runs from the snout to the tail.

### SCRAWLED COWFISH (VARIETY)
*(Acanthostracion quadricornis)*
At night or while resting, the skin can darken to blend in with the reef. The blue spots becomes brighter.

### BUFFALO TRUNKFISH
*(Lactophrys trigonus)*
19 in max. Gray body, sometimes with light blue spots. Rounded hump on the back. Elongated tail base.

### BUFFALO TRUNKFISH (VARIETY)
*(Lactophrys trigonus)*
Closer to the reef or at night the skin will darken to help the Trunkfish camouflage itself against the reef.

### BUFFALO TRUNKFISH (VARIETY)
*(Lactophrys trigonus)*
In the shallow water of the lagoons they will take on a golden or green color to hide in the seagrass.

Hogfish have large jaws that are adapted to feed on a wide variety of foods. There are sharp teeth near the front that are used to hold prey, like small fishes and crabs. They also have two large bony plates at the back of the jaws that are used for crushing shells. They can sift through the sand, digging to find clams and scallops, which are crushed and swallowed. Sand and pieces of shell are pumped out through the gills. Juveniles live as cleaners and will often take up residence with other cleaning species like the Neon Goby (p. 201) and the juvenile Bluehead Wrasse (p. 280). Juvenile Hogfishes tend to concentrate on removing the larger and more stubborn parasites from their hosts.

**HOGFISH**
*(Lachnolaimus maximus)*
3 ft max. Dark forehead and upper body stripe. Three distinctive, long foredorsal spines. Black bar on the tail.

**HOGFISH (INTERMEDIATE)**
*(Lachnolaimus maximus)*
Three long foredorsal spines. Mottled in brown or red. Sloping forehead. Can darken or lighten dramatically.

# HOGFISHES : FISHES

### SPOTFIN HOGFISH (JUVENILE)
*(Bodianus pulchellus)*
Uniform yellow body with two darker lines running through the eye. Black spot on the foredorsal fin.

### SPOTFIN HOGFISH (INTERMEDIATE)
*(Bodianus pulchellus)*
Reddish to purple head and front body, yellow towards the tail. Reddish eyes with two dark stripes

### SPOTFIN HOGFISH
*(Bodianus pulchellus)*
9 in max. Red body with white areas below the eyes and onto sides. Yellow patch on rear dorsal fin and tail.

### SPANISH HOGFISH (JUVENILE)
*(Bodianus rufus)*
Blue or purple upper body. Yellow sides, belly and tail. They act as cleaner fish, removing larger parasites.

### SPANISH HOGFISH (INTERMEDIATE)
*(Bodianus rufus)*
Purple to red upper body from the eyes to the back of the dorsal fin. Yellow underbelly, sides and tail.

### SPANISH HOGFISH
*(Bodianus rufus)*
2 ft max. Yellow body fading to purple around the dorsal and ventral fins. Reddish tints on the tail.

Grunts are one of the most common fish on a Caribbean reef and tend to stick together in large schools in the shallows. Their strong, low-slung jaws give a hint as to their diet: they are bottom feeders. They feed mostly on crustaceans hiding in the sand and smaller, bottom-dwelling fish.

Grunt are territorial animals. Male grunts will compete with one another for the right to mate, by swimming rapidly together and seeing who has the largest set of jaws. This ritualized fighting decides who is the dominant fish without actually fighting and wounding another member of the school, who can then try again later, or join another school.

Grunts of all ages will school together for protection. Some have long stripes across their bodies that help to distract predators. The shifting lines of a school of grunt makes it difficult for the eyes of a reef predator, like a Barracuda, to lock on to one specific individual in the school.

# GRUNTS : FISHES

### BLUESTRIPED GRUNT (JUVENILE)
*(Haemulon sciurus)*
Two brown stripes run down the body, one through the eye and another above it. Small spot near the tail.

### BLUESTRIPED GRUNT
*(Haemulon sciurus)*
18 in max. Blue stripes on a yellow body. Black tail and rear dorsal fin. The ventral and anal fins are yellow.

### FRENCH GRUNT (JUVENILE)
*(Haemulon flavolineatum)*
Brown stripe along the body passes through the eyes. Small brown spot at the base of the tail.

### FRENCH GRUNT
*(Haemulon flavolineatum)*
1 ft max. Wide yellow stripes are straight above and diagonal below the lateral line. All fins are yellow.

### TOMTATE (JUVENILE)
*(Haemulon aurolineatum)*
Brown stripe runs along the body and a shorter one just above the eye. Faint horizontal lines on the belly.

### TOMTATE
*(Haemulon aurolineatum)*
10 in max. Yellow stripe runs through the eyes to the base of the tail. Large black spot continues onto the tail.

🤿 A healthy coral reef is actually a very noisy place, and a big part of the sounds of the reef comes from the grunt. They make a grunting sound by rubbing together two bony plates in the back of their throats to warn away predators. Not all grunts live in schools. As they enter adulthood some will break away from the group and live solitary lives on the reef, each with its own territory. The White Margate will live over sandy areas, where it feeds on molluscs hiding in the sand. The Black Margate can be found at the entrance to caves and canyons. Spanish Grunts are usually found under ledges and overhangs in areas of stronger current.

### SPANISH GRUNT
*(Haemulon macrostomum)*
15 in max. Black stripes are only on the upper body. Yellow patch under dorsal fin. White spot at base of tail.

### CAESAR GRUNT
*(Haemulon carbonarium)*
15 in max. Copper stripes run down a pale body. Rear dorsal fin, anal fin and tail are all dark. Eyes are blue.

## GRUNTS : FISHES

### SMALL MOUTH GRUNT
*(Haemulon chrysargyreum)*
10 in max. Silvery with wide yellow stripes running down the length of the body. All fins are yellow.

### WHITE GRUNT
*(Haemulon plumierii)*
18 in max. There are a series of blue stripes only on the head, breaking up into small blue spots on the body.

### WHITE MARGATE
*(Haemulon album)*
2 ft max. Uniform silvery body with large scales. The eye is small with a white ring. Long sloping forehead.

### BLACK MARGATE
*(Anisotremus surinamensis)*
2 ft max. Large black patch on the side. All the fins are black. Found in or near the entrance to caves.

### PORKFISH
*(Anisotremus virginicus)*
14 in max. Two wide black bars on face, one across the eyes and the other behind the gills. All fins are yellow.

### COTTONWICK
*(Haemulon melanarum)*
13 in max. Wide black stripe from foredorsal fin runs onto the tail and forms a "V". Faint yellow body stripes.

Parrotfish are some of the most colorful and iconic reef fishes in the Caribbean. They get their name from their fused front teeth, which resemble a parrot's beak. Parrotfish are all born as females and live in harems of up to dozens of fish, all controlled by a single dominant male. They go through dramatic color changes as they grow from juveniles, on to larger females and then to the final stage, which is called the "supermale" that is in charge of the school. It is in this final stage that the colors of a parrotfish become the most vibrant. The males will fight each other, sometimes to the death, for control of the harems. If the male dies, then the strongest and most advanced of the females turns into a male and takes over. This transformation can take place in as little as two weeks. Parrotfish are sexually mature after about three years and can live for up to ten years.

Parrotfish are the largest and some of the most important herbivores in a reef ecosystem, keeping levels of algae in check. As they feed on the marine plants covering the reef, some coral gets scraped off and eaten too. In fact up to 75% of the parrotfish's gut contents is inorganic material. After the nutrients are digested out of this mixture, the rest is expelled as a fine sand. A single adult parrotfish can pass a ton of sand every year. So the next time you lay your towel down on a white sand beach in the Caribbean, remember that what you are lying on is mostly fish poop!

# PARROTFISHES : FISHES

**BLUE PARROTFISH (JUVENILE)**
*(Scarus coeruleus)*
Large yellow patch from the snout to the forehead and upper body. Yellow eyes and a pale underside.

**BLUE PARROTFISH (FEMALE)**
*(Scarus coeruleus)*
Pale blue body with a faint area of yellow above the eyes. The dorsal fin is edged in a brighter blue.

**BLUE PARROTFISH (MALE)**
*(Scarus coeruleus)*
4 ft max. Uniform light blue body. Distinctive blunt head with prominent white teeth. All the fins are blue.

**REDBAND PARROTFISH (JUVENILE)**
*(Sparisoma aurofrenatum)*
Striped body with a pale belly. Large red eyes. Distinctive black spot located behind the gill cover.

**REDBAND PARROTFISH (FEMALE)**
*(Sparisoma aurofrenatum)*
Solid greenish-blue body with large scales, edged in black. All of the fins and the tail are red.

**REDBAND PARROTFISH (MALE)**
*(Sparisoma aurofrenatum)*
11 in max. A red band runs under the eye from the mouth. Small black and yellow spots behind the gills.

🥽 Parrotfish are only active in the daytime. Some species, such as the Queen Parrotfish, will not only find a safe crevice in the reef to sleep, but they will also secrete a thin membrane of mucus around their bodies, like a sleeping bag. It is thought that this membrane will mask their scent from predators that are more active at night, such as Moray Eels and Nurse Sharks, which rely on smell to find fishes hiding in the darkness. In the morning the parrotfishes will wriggle out of these sleeping bags and continue with their daily feeding.

🥽 Rather than spending the night in a sleeping bag, most parrotfish will simply change their color at night to blend in with the reef, and rely solely on this camouflage to get safely through the night. Specialized skin cells have pigments that can be pressed up against their scales to change their color, sometimes dramatically. They can blend in with corals, algae, sponges or even the white of the sand.

## PARROTFISHES : FISHES

### PRINCESS PARROTFISH (JUVENILE)
*(Scarus taeniopterus)*
Three black stripes down the body with a pale belly. Dark borders on the tail, unlike the Striped Parrotfish.

### PRINCESS PARROTFISH (FEMALE)
*(Scarus taeniopterus)*
Indistinct, pale stripes run from behind the eyes towards the tail. The fins are yellow. The tail has dark borders.

### PRINCESS PARROTFISH (MALE)
*(Scarus taeniopterus)*
14 in max. Distinctive yellow body stripe fades towards the tail. The tail is bordered by two pink stripes.

### STRIPED PARROTFISH (JUVENILE)
*(Scarus iseri)*
Black and white stripes run the length of the body. The eyes are red. The tail is transparent with no borders.

### STRIPED PARROTFISH (FEMALE)
*(Scarus iseri)*
Dark upper body with two white stripes. White belly. Distinctive yellow patch in front of the eyes.

### STRIPED PARROTFISH (MALE)
*(Scarus iseri)*
10 in max. Distinctive orange to yellow stripe runs from above the pectoral fin. Yellow patch under the chin.

### STOPLIGHT PARROTFISH (MALE)
*(Sparisoma viride)*
2 ft max. Green body with pink markings on the face.
Yellow dot on the gill cover. Yellow markings on the tail.

> The Stoplight Parrotfish is the perfect example to show how dramatically these fish can change their appearance as they grow older. All three stages in this fish's life look like they are from completely different species. It only takes a few weeks for each color change to take place.

### STOPLIGHT PARROTFISH (FEMALE)
*(Sparisoma viride)*
Large brown to grey scales are edged in black. The belly is a pale red. All fins and the tail are a dark red.

### STOPLIGHT PARROTFISH (JUVENILE)
*(Sparisoma viride)*
Three rows of small white spots run down the length of the body. Black spot on gill cover. White bar on the tail.

# PARROTFISHES : FISHES

### QUEEN PARROTFISH (FEMALE)
*(Scarus vetula)*
No markings on a gray face. A wide, white stripe runs from the pectoral fin, down the body towards the tail.

### QUEEN PARROTFISH (MALE)
*(Scarus vetula)*
2 ft max. Distinctive blue to green makings around the mouth. Single pale bar on the pectoral fins.

### GREENBLOTCH PARROTFISH (FEMALE)
*(Sparisoma atomarium)*
Uniform dark red body and dorsal fin. Ventral and anal fins are yellow. The eyes are green and red.

### GREENBLOTCH PARROTFISH (MALE)
*(Sparisoma atomarium)*
4.5 in max. Distinctive, large, green spot above the pectoral fin. Red body with green highlights. Red eyes.

### REDTAIL PARROTFISH (FEMALE)
*(Sparisoma chrysopterum)*
Distinctive red and gray patterns to the scales. Dark patch under the pectoral fin. The tail has hints of yellow.

### REDTAIL PARROTFISH (MALE)
*(Sparisoma chrysopterum)*
18 in max. Light blue patch behind the pectoral fin. Black spot on pectoral fin base. Red crescent on tail.

### MIDNIGHT PARROTFISH
*(Scarus coelestinus)*
3 ft max. Dark blue body and fins with pale blue facial markings. The large beak is often covered in algae.

> Midnight and Rainbow Parrotfishes are the largest members of this family. They can actually be heard by divers as they feed, when their massive jaws make contact with the reef. The Rainbow Parrotfish can live for up to 10 years and, unmolested, can grow to be the same size as a diver.

### RAINBOW PARROTFISH (MALE)
*(Scarus guacamaia)*
5.5 ft max. The largest of the parrotfish. Lobed red forehead and face, bright green towards tail. Large scales.

### RAINBOW PARROTFISH (FEMALE)
*(Scarus guacamaia)*
Sloping forehead. Large scales are edged in red. The tail is usually more squared in shape.

# PARROTFISHES : FISHES

**YELLOWTAIL PARROTFISH (FEMALE)**
*(Sparisoma rubripinne)*
Large gray scales have dark edges. Yellow tail. Ventral and anal fins are red. Pinkish underbelly.

**YELLOWTAIL PARROTFISH (MALE)**
*(Sparisoma rubripinne)*
1.5 ft max. Uniform greenish color. Dorsal, anal and ventral fins are red. Black spot behind the gill cover.

**BLUELIP PARROTFISH (FEMALE)**
*(Cryptotomus roseus)*
Slender, tapering body with a pointed snout. Two white stripes down the body. Found in shallow lagoons.

**BLUELIP PARROTFISH (MALE)**
*(Cryptotomus roseus)*
5 in max. Slender, tapering body. Bright pink stripe runs from behind the pectoral fin towards the tail.

**PARROTFISH (POSTLARVAL)**
*(Sparisoma sp.)*
Just after hatching, parrotfish are highly variable in color, blending into algae and shallow reeftops for protection.

**BUCKTOOTH PARROTFISH (MALE)**
*(Sparisoma radians)*
8 in max. Green upper body and tail, white underbelly. Distinctive black spot on the base of the pectoral fin.

## BLUEHEAD WRASSE
*(Thalassoma bifasciatum)*
6 in max. Dark blue head and a bright green
body, separated by thick bars of black and white.

Bluehead Wrasse are one of the most common fish seen in the Caribbean. Yet the terminal phase (shown above) is hardly ever seen on the reef. This is because, unlike most fish, they become sexually active long before they reach their oldest and most colorful stage of life. They live in schools of up to thousands of individuals, usually in the shallow, sunlit areas of the reef. The tiny yellow fish live as cleaners, eating parasites off other fish, as well as taking plankton out of the water. They are often seen mating for hours, in what is known as a "spawning rise". One female will be surrounded and followed by dozens of males, and a complicated dance begins. When the female is ready, she puts on a burst of speed and races towards the surface, releasing her eggs. The strongest and fastest males keep up with her, releasing sperm to fertilize the eggs. Sergeant majors often hover above this mating dance to feed on the eggs.

# WRASSES : FISHES

**BLUEHEAD WRASSE (JUVENILE)**
*(Thalassoma bifasciatum)*
Striped upper body and a white underbelly. Large black spot at the front of the foredorsal fin. Fins are clear.

**BLUEHEAD WRASSE (FEMALE)**
*(Thalassoma bifasciatum)*
The yellow phase with a darker mid-body stripe. Acts as a cleaner species, in schools on shallow reef tops.

**CLOWN WRASSE (JUVENILE)**
*(Halichoeres maculipinna)*
Striped upper body and white underbelly. Two yellow body stripes meet to form a "V" on the forehead.

**CLOWN WRASSE**
*(Halichoeres maculipinna)*
7 in max. Large, dark mid-body spot. Darker head and back. Yellow near the tail. Red or pink lines on the face.

**RAINBOW WRASSE (JUVENILE)**
*(Halichoeres pictus)*
Yellow upper body and a white underbelly. Brown line runs through the eye to the tail, darker near the snout.

**RAINBOW WRASSE**
*(Halichoeres pictus)*
7 in max. Black spot near base of tail. Fins transparent except for an orange center. Blue lines on face.

### YELLOWHEAD WRASSE
*(Halichoeres garnoti)*
8 in max. Bright yellow head and back. Dark bar mid-way down the body. Two small lines radiate from eyes.

Wrasse can live in schools of up to a thousand fish. These are planktivores, preferring areas of stronger current that bring in more food. They can be seen swimming in long lines across the reef to get to better feeding areas. Other wrasse can be solitary foragers, though they sometimes join other fishes and eat their scraps.

Wrasse are in the same family as the parrotfish, but they are carnivorous and this affects their behavior, making them much more active and aggressive. All wrasse are born female, and they live in harems, usually of around twenty females controlled by a single dominant male. These males patrol their territory, rounding up all the females and defending them from the advances of other males. A challenger will approach the dominant male and a ritualized fight begins. They will open their mouths wide to see who has the bigger jaws and teeth. If the dominant male dies, one of the more mature females will then change into a male and take control of the harem.

# WRASSES : FISHES

### YELLOWHEAD WRASSE (JUVENILE)
*(Halichoeres garnoti)*
Yellow body. Brilliant blue stripe, outlined in black, runs from behind the eye to the tail. Fins are transparent.

### YELLOWHEAD WRASSE (FEMALE)
*(Halichoeres garnoti)*
Bright blue stripe from the eye to the tail. Another runs above the dorsal fin. Small, dark lines from the eyes.

### YELLOWCHEEK WRASSE (JUVENILE)
*(Halichoeres cyanocephalus)*
Two occelated blue spots, one below the dorsal fin and one at the base of the tail. Yellow face and dorsal fin.

### YELLOWCHEEK WRASSE
*(Halichoeres cyanocephalus)*
10 in max. Blue body with a bright yellow forehead and upper body stripe. Pale belly and a yellow tail.

### BLACKEAR WRASSE (JUVENILE)
*(Halichoeres poeyi)*
Uniform bright green to yellow body with no distinctive markings. Bright yellow eyes. Found on shallow reefs.

### BLACKEAR WRASSE
*(Halichoeres poeyi)*
8 in max. Distinctive orange spot behind the eye. There is a tiny black spot near the base of the tail.

## PUDDINGWIFE
*(Halichoeres radiatus)*
18 in max. The largest of the wrasse. Wide, pale mid-body bar. Yellow margin on tail. Blue margins on fins.

> Despite its strange name, the Puddingwife is one of the more aggressive wrasse on a Caribbean reef. The males will actively round up their females for protection when divers come too near to the harem, and he will watch over them until the divers move away.

## PUDDINGWIFE (JUVENILE)
*(Halichoeres radiatus)*
Large occelated blue spot on the dorsal fin. Orange and white body bars. White line from the eye to the tail.

## PUDDINGWIFE (FEMALE)
*(Halichoeres radiatus)*
Yellow to green. Body and fins are covered in brilliant green to blue lines and dots. Tail is bordered in blue.

# WRASSES : FISHES

### CREOLE WRASSE (JUVENILE)
*(Clepticus parrae)*
Bright purple body with a line of darker spots along the back. Single dark spot on the foredorsal fin.

### CREOLE WRASSE (FEMALE)
*(Clepticus parrae)*
Uniform purple body with hints of red towards the back. Large black spot on the forehead and snout.

### CREOLE WRASSE (MALE)
*(Clepticus parrae)*
1 ft max. Pointed snout. Purple fore-body and dorsal fin. Large yellow patch from mid-body to the tail.

### SLIPPERY DICK (JUVENILE)
*(Halichoeres bivittatus)*
Upper body is light brown, lower body is white with a dark stripe. Occelated blue spot on dorsal fin.

### SLIPPERY DICK (FEMALE)
*(Halichoeres bivittatus)*
Pale body with a wide, reddish-brown stripe from the eye to the tail. The fins and tail are transparent.

### SLIPPERY DICK (MALE)
*(Halichoeres bivittatus)*
9 in max. Body striped in shades of green and pink. Pink markings on the face. Black spot above gill cover.

## FAIRY BASSLET
*(Gramma loreto)*
3 in max. Front of the body is purple, yellow toward tail.
Dark spot on the dorsal fin. Often found upside-down.

Fairy Basslets are planktivores, picking their food out of the water column. They are usually found in areas of moderate current, such as along walls. They always orientate themselves to the reef and so they are often seen hanging upside-down under ledges, waiting for food to drift by.

## BLACKCAP BASSLET
*(Gramma melacara)*
4 in max. Purple body with a dark stripe from the face to the dorsal fin. Often found on deeper walls.

## YELLOWCHEEK BASSLET
*(Gramma linki)*
4 in max. Yellow lines across the cheeks. Yellow spots on a light gray body. Yellow ring around the eyes.

# BASSLETS : FISHES

### BANTAM BASS
*(Parasphyraenops incisus)*
1.5 in max. Black spot on the foredorsal fin. White line down the length of the body. White "V" on the tail.

### CAVE BASSLET
*(Liopropoma mowbrayi)*
3.5 in max. Uniform red color. Black band at the tip of the tail. Small black spot on the tip of the dorsal fin.

### CANDY BASSLET
*(Liopropoma carmabi)*
2 in max. Striped body. Darker spot only on rear dorsal fin. Spots on tail do not join. Found on deeper reefs.

### PEPPERMINT BASSLET
*(Liopropoma rubre)*
3.5 in max. Striped body. Darker spots on both rear dorsal and ventral fins. Spots on tail are joined.

### TOOTHLESS BASSLET
*(Schultzea beta)*
2 in max. Pale body with darker stripes. Yellow tail. Often in small groups; also known as School Bass.

### THREELINE BASSLET
*(Lipogramma trilineatum)*
1.5 in max. Yellow body with three blue lines from the front of the face. Found on deeper reefs, under ledges.

### GREATER SOAPFISH
*(Rypticus saponaceus)*
1 ft max. Grayish-brown body with white blotches and a pointed snout. Rounded fins. Often lies on its side.

Soapfish get their name from a unique defense mechanism. They release a frothy poison from their skin when they are threatened, that puts off any attacker. They can usually be found lazing on their sides under ledges and overhangs.

### ORANGEBACK BASS
*(Serranus annularis)*
2.5 in max. Two orange squares behind the eyes, circled in black. White line down length of the body.

### SNOW BASS
*(Serranus chionaraia)*
2 in max. Large white marking on belly up to sides. Dark spots along back and onto the transparent tail.

# SMALL BASSES : FISHES

### GRAYSBY (JUVENILE)
*(Cephalopholis cruentatus)*
A thin white line runs from under the lower lip, over the back of the head. Forehead and back is yellowish.

### GRAYSBY
*(Cephalopholis cruentatus)*
1 ft max. Rusty brown color with spots that continue onto fins. Several spots line the base of the dorsal fin.

### LANTERN BASS
*(Serranus baldwini)*
3 in max. Series of dark orange bars on belly. Dark spots at the base of the tail. Inhabits rubble beds.

### HARLEQUIN BASS
*(Serranus tigrinus)*
4 in max. Pointed head. Upper body white, lower body yellow. Dark body bars and dark spots on the tail.

### TOBACCOFISH
*(Serranus tabacarius)*
7 in max. Orange-brown body with lighter belly and dark markings above. Tail bordered in black lines.

### CHALK BASS
*(Serranus tortugarum)*
3.5 in max. Bluish body with alternating dark bars across the top of the back. Found on deep rubble.

## CONEY (BICOLOR VARIETY)
*(Cephalopholis fulva)*
An uncommon color variety. Brown-speckled body with reddish-brown above and white below.

All members of the bass family are carnivores, and competition is intense. All are born female, but as they mature, one bass will slowly change into a male and begin to dominate the others in the area, defending his group from younger males trying to approach. Divers can often see them chasing away rivals. They are even known to be cannibals if their territory is threatened. Before mating season the males will try to dominate a group of females and engage in ritualized battles to decide who gets to mate. Weaker males will be driven off or eaten.

Bass are successful ambush predators, lying motionless on the reef, waiting for their prey to come to them. Spots or stripes make their outline hard to see against the backdrop. They have oversized mouths that can open very quickly, creating a powerful suction, pulling in their prey. Short, backward-facing teeth help keep the prey locked in place.

# LARGE BASSES : FISHES

### CONEY (JUVENILE)
*(Cephalopholis fulva)*
Light brown body, darkening towards the top. White spots on base of tail and back. Spots on bottom lip.

### CONEY (RED VARIETY)
*(Cephalopholis fulva)*
16 in max. The most common color variety. Brown to reddish body, speckled with dark and light blue spots.

### CONEY (YELLOW VARIETY)
*(Cephalopholis fulva)*
A rare color variety usually found on shallower reefs. Solid, bright yellow body with tiny, bright blue spots.

### CREOLEFISH
*(Paranthias furcifer)*
1 ft max. Color varies from red to purple. Red spot at base of pectoral fins. Usually found in deeper water.

### ROCK HIND
*(Epinephelus adscensionis)*
2 ft max. Brown to red spots on body and fins. Darker blotches under the dorsal fin and at the base of the tail.

### RED HIND
*(Epinephelus guttatus)*
2 ft max. Large, red spots cover the body. Reddish underbelly. The dorsal fin starts far down the back.

👓 Hamlets are also members of the bass family, which includes groupers and hinds. Like all bass, they are carnivores and have wide, large-lipped mouths they use to suck in their prey whole. They have short, backward-facing teeth that keep their prey firmly in their mouths until they can be swallowed. Unlike most other bass, they have developed a tall, thin body plan that also gives them access to other food sources hiding in the reef, like shrimps and small crustaceans. They are common in the Caribbean, with one species tending to dominate a given area. They tend to live and hunt alone or in pairs.

👓 Hamlets are a diurnal species, meaning that they are active only in the daytime. At night they will find a place to hide in the coral and will darken their bodies to blend in with the colors of the reef, extending their sharp dorsal spines for protection.

# HAMLETS : FISHES

### BUTTER HAMLET
*(Hypoplectrus unicolor)*
5 in max. Uniform, pale yellow body. Large black spot on base of the tail. Often two black spots on the snout.

### INDIGO HAMLET
*(Hypoplectrus indigo)*
5.5 in max. Dark blue body with numerous paler blue to white body bars. Blue ventral fins, all others are pale.

### BLACK HAMLET
*(Hypoplectrus nigricans)*
6 in max. Uniform black color, sometimes with brown or blue shading around the head. Long ventral fins.

### BARRED HAMLET
*(Hypoplectrus puella)*
6 in max. Wide black or blue body bar, narrower near the belly. Thin blue lines and spots on the face.

### YELLOWTAIL HAMLET
*(Hypoplectrus chlorurus)*
5 in max. Body is highly variable between brown, blue and black. The tail is always a bright yellow color.

### GOLDEN HAMLET
*(Hypoplectrus gummigutta)*
5 in max. Deep golden color with bright blue lines and marks across the snout. Found on deeper reefs.

Hamlets have a bizarre love life. There are no males or females in this species. They are simultaneous hermaphrodites, meaning that they have both male and female sexual organs. Once they find a mate they will take turns at both the male and the female role, in multiple mating sessions over the course of many nights. One night any given hamlet could play the role of the male, and then the next night it could be the female. They also have the ability to breed with all the other hamlet species on a reef, giving rise to confusing hybrids (see below). This makes identification on a dive very difficult. Because of this ability to mate with all other hamlets, there is some debate about whether there are actually different species of hamlet, or just one species with color variations. Many scientists are now looking to hamlets as an example of evolution in action, witnessing the births of new species.

# HAMLETS : FISHES

### MASKED HAMLET
*(Hypoplectrus providencianus)*
5 in max. Dark triangular shape below the eyes. Dark spot near base of tail. Ventral fins blue, pectorals dark.

### SHY HAMLET
*(Hypoplectrus guttavarius)*
5 in max. Dark body from dorsal fins to tail. Yellow head, belly and fins. Dark spots lined in blue on snout.

### TAN HAMLET
*(Hypoplectrus randallorum)*
5 in max. Uniform grey to light brown color. Front of ventral fin is always blue. Other fins are pale in color.

### YELLOWBELLY HAMLET
*(Hypoplectrus aberrans)*
5 in max. Bright yellow belly extends toward and onto the tail. Sometimes blue markings on the head.

### HAMLET (JUVENILE)
All juvenile hamlets appear similar until they reach a certain size and begin to differentiate. They all have two white spots on the base of the tail.

### HAMLET (INTERMEDIATE)
As the two white spots near the base of the tail begin to fade, the coloration of each individual becomes apparent and the hamlet is ready to mate.

Groupers are the largest members of the bass family. Some can grow to over 1000 lbs and live up to 30 years. They all have wide, oversized mouths that create lots of suction as they open. Prey is literally sucked into the mouth whole, rather than being bitten or chewed.

All groupers start out life as females, and only much later in life will they turn into males. Because of the high mortality rate in a reef ecosystem, this means there will always be more fertile females available for spawning and only the strongest will be able to reproduce.

🤿 Groupers are not always easy to spot on the reef. They are ambush predators, relying not on speed but on concealment to catch their prey. They will lie in wait for hours, either hidden in soft corals or sponges or under ledges. Juveniles will scavenge for slower prey like crustaceans, but as they get older and develop their hunting techniques, their diet consists mostly of smaller fish and squid.

# GROUPERS : FISHES

**BLACK GROUPER (JUVENILE)**
*(Mycteroperca bonaci)*
Light brown body with darker, rectangular patches on the sides. Tips of the dorsal spines are pale yellow.

**BLACK GROUPER**
*(Mycteroperca bonaci)*
4.5 ft max. Brown to black body with dark rectangular patches. Tail has a black margin with a thin white edge.

**YELLOWMOUTH GROUPER (JUVENILE)**
*(Mycteroperca interstitialis)*
The top half of the body is black, the bottom half is white. White line runs from the lower lip to the dorsal fin.

**YELLOWMOUTH GROUPER**
*(Mycteroperca interstitialis)*
2.5 ft max. Yellow patches at the corners of the mouth. Pale edges on the pectoral fins. Sloping forehead.

**YELLOWMOUTH GROUPER (VARIETY)**
*(Mycteroperca interstitialis)*
During mating season they take on a dramatic, two-tone pattern. Compare: Nassau Grouper (p. 298).

**YELLOWMOUTH GROUPER (VARIETY)**
*(Mycteroperca interstitialis)*
A rare, reddish color with no other markings. This can be seen when they are resting or in deep water.

## GOLIATH GROUPER
*(Epinephelus itajara)*
8 ft max. Easily the largest fish on Caribbean reefs.
Small dark spots cover the body. Rounded tail.

Groupers have been over-fished for decades, and as top predators they are crucial to a healthy reef system. The Nassau Grouper, below, has now made it on to the CITES Endangered Species List, and the Goliath Grouper, above, is considered Critically Endangered.

## NASSAU GROUPER
*(Epinephelus striatus)*
4 ft max. Dark brown to red body bars. Distinct black spot at the upper base of the tail. Gold-tipped dorsal fin.

## NASSAU GROUPER (VARIETY)
*(Epinephelus striatus)*
During mating season they take on a dramatic two-tone pattern. Compare: Yellowmouth Grouper (p. 297).

# GROUPERS : FISHES

### TIGER GROUPER (JUVENILE)
*(Mycteroperca tigris)*
Bright yellow body with darker stripes running from the lower lip, through the eyes and towards the tail.

### TIGER GROUPER
*(Mycteroperca tigris)*
3.5 ft max. Distinct white bars across the top of the back, becoming irregular spots towards the belly.

### TIGER GROUPER (VARIETY)
*(Mycteroperca tigris)*
During mating season, or when distressed, the head pales and the bars darken, in a show of aggression.

### YELLOWFIN GROUPER
*(Mycteroperca venenosa)*
3 ft max. Distinct yellow band on the tips of the pectoral fins. Thin dark margins on the edges of all other fins.

### YELLOWFIN GROUPER (VARIETY)
*(Mycteroperca venenosa)*
Rounded, dark, rectangular patches over a lighter background. Dorsal fin has patches of red and gold.

### YELLOWFIN GROUPER (VARIETY)
*(Mycteroperca venenosa)*
A rare red phase of the Yellowfin Grouper, usually found in deeper waters or when threatened.

## MUTTON SNAPPER
*(Lutjanus analis)*
2.5 ft max. Faint blue lines under the eye. Small black spot on upper mid-body. Tail and pectoral fins are red.

The Mutton Snapper, above, is a favorite of fishermen and is considered a threatened species in many areas of the Caribbean. It is a top predator that can live for up to 40 years. A very slow reproduction rate means that their numbers are falling dramatically.

## MUTTON SNAPPER (VARIETY)
*(Lutjanus analis)*
Often during mating season, or when its territory is threatened, the Mutton will show darker body bars.

## DOG SNAPPER
*(Lutjanus jocu)*
3 ft max. Heavy body. Distinctive, long, white triangle below the eye. Two long upper "canine" teeth.

# SNAPPERS : FISHES

### CUBERA SNAPPER
*(Lutjanus cyanopterus)*
5 ft max. The largest of the snapper. Heavy body with a large head and wide lips. May show dark bars.

### GLASSEYE SNAPPER
*(Heteropriacanthus cruentatus)*
1 ft max. Deep red to pale pink with silver body bars. Large red eyes. Compare to Bigeye (p. 221).

### GRAY SNAPPER
*(Lutjanus griseus)*
2 ft max. Uniform grey to brown body with a sloping head. May darken dramatically. Anal fin is rounded.

### MAHOGANY SNAPPER
*(Lutjanus mahogani)*
15 in max. Silvery color with a sloping forehead. Dark or red margin on the tail and the dorsal fins.

### MAHOGANY SNAPPER (JUVENILE)
*(Lutjanus mahogani)*
Pale body with a single, dark, mid-body spot. The tail is edged in red. The ventral and anal fins are clear.

### MAHOGANY SNAPPER (VARIETY)
*(Lutjanus mahogani)*
In deeper water or at rest the body is more reddish, with bright red edges on the tail and dorsal fins.

## BLACK SNAPPER
*(Apsilus dentatus)*
2 ft max. Solid dark blue body and tail. High, curving
lateral line. Found on deeper reefs and headlands.

> The Black Snapper (pictured above) is rarely seen at diving depths, preferring deeper walls. They will sometimes come up to shallower water when currents move around headlands, and upwelling brings their food source closer to the surface, where they may be spotted by divers.

## SCHOOLMASTER
*(Lutjanus apodus)*
2 ft max. Body gray to red or yellow. All fins are yellow.
Found under ledges or schooling in the shallows.

## SCHOOLMASTER (JUVENILE)
*(Lutjanus apodus)*
Distinctive lines down the snout, brown through the eye
and blue below it. Younger juveniles have body bars.

# SNAPPERS : FISHES

### YELLOWTAIL SNAPPER (JUVENILE)
*(Ocyurus chrysurus)*
Found in shallow waters and lagoons, the juvenile looks similar to the adult, but with wider yellow stripes.

### YELLOWTAIL SNAPPER
*(Ocyurus chrysurus)*
2.5 ft max. A bright yellow line runs from the eye to the tail, which is also yellow. Yellow spots across the back.

### BLACKFIN SNAPPER (JUVENILE)
*(Lutjanus buccanella)*
Pale gray body. Yellow patch on the upper base of the tail. A small black spot at the base of the pectoral fin.

### BLACKFIN SNAPPER
*(Lutjanus buccanella)*
2.5 ft max. Red body. Yellow patch on the upper base of the tail. Generally found below safe diving limits.

### LANE SNAPPER (JUVENILE)
*(Lutjanus synagris)*
Reddish tints on the dorsal fin and the edge of the tail. Ventral and anal fins are always yellow. Mid-body spot.

### LANE SNAPPER
*(Lutjanus synagris)*
15 in max. Several yellow body stripes. Sometimes with a large, dark, mid-body spot. The fins are transparent.

## JOLTHEAD PORGY
*(Calamus bajonado)*
2 ft max. Silvery body. Large eyes and large lips with
a distinctive orange blotch at the corner of the mouth.

> The Porgy has developed large lips and strong jaws for feeding on molluscs, such as clams and other hard-shelled invertebrates. They are often found hovering over the sandy areas where this kind of prey tries to take shelter, often in pairs or in small family groups.

### SAUCER EYE PORGY
*(Calamus calamus)*
16 in max. Blue spot at the base of pectoral fin. Blue line under the eye. Yellow in the corner of the mouth.

### BERMUDA CHUB
*(Kyphosus sectatrix)*
2.5 ft max. Pointed snout on oval-shaped body. Silver with faint orange stripes down the sides. Fins darker.

# SILVERY : FISHES

### SLENDER MOJARRA
*(Eucinostomus jonesii)*
8 in max. Long, slender body, sometimes with darker, mottled, body bars. Found in lagoons and shallows.

### FLAGFIN MOJARRA
*(Eucinostomus melanopterus)*
7 in max. Slightly brownish tint on a silvery body. Distinctive black tips on the foredorsal spines.

### MOTTLED MOJARRA
*(Eucinostomus lefroyi)*
9 in max. The foredorsal fin and tail have slightly darker edges. Darker spot above the iris of the eyes.

### YELLOWFIN MOJARRA
*(Gerres cinereus)*
16 in max. The largest of the mojarra. Yellow ventral fins. The sides have broken, vertical, body bars.

### SHORTFIN SWEEPER
*(Pempheris poeyi)*
4 in max. Hatchet-shaped. Found schooling in caves and caverns. No distinctive markings.

### GLASSY SWEEPER
*(Pempheris schomburgkii)*
6 in max. Hatchet-shaped. Found schooling in caves and caverns. Dark stripe at the base of anal fin.

## TRUMPETFISH
*(Aulostomus maculatus)*
3 ft max. Long rounded body with eyes set far back from an extended snout. Color is highly variable.

Trumpetfish are highly adaptable hunters found in all tropical seas around the world. They can change their colors to blend in with their surroundings, or even to swim unseen with other fishes. In the bright shallows they can be a vibrant yellow or they can become a deep red to hunt among the soft corals of the deeper reef. They can even turn blue, allowing them to swim among a school of harmless Blue Tang (p. 248) and sneak up on unsuspecting prey. Their long body will curve into an S-shape before they strike, with lightning speed.

With their long, thin bodies the Trumpetfish have a very small profile as they approach their prey. They will often swim alongside other fish, such as the Hogfish on the left, in a tactic known as shadow hunting. This gives them an extra element of surprise while their prey is distracted.

# SILVERY : FISHES

### HOUNDFISH
*(Tylosurus crocodilus)*
5 ft max. Dark bar on the gill cover. Snout can be red. The lower lobe of the tail is longer than the upper.

### KEELTAIL NEEDLEFISH
*(Platybelone argalus)*
20 in max. Lateral keel on either side of the tail. Long and slender snout. Found just under the surface.

### BALAO
*(Hemiramphus balao)*
15 in max. Long, thin body with purple tints on the tail. The lower jaw is elongated with an orange or red tip.

### BLUESPOTTED CORNETFISH
*(Fistularia tabacaria)*
6 ft max. Long, thin body with faint blue spots. A long filament trails behind the tail. Often found in lagoons.

### ATLANTIC THREAD HERRING
*(Opisthonema oglinum)*
14 in max. Silvery body with pale belly and a small head. Black tips on the tail. Thin filament behind the dorsal fin.

### BOGA
*(Inermia vittata)*
9 in max. Silvery blue with darker stripes. The snout is often pale yellow. School in hundreds along walls.

## GREAT BARRACUDA
*(Sphyraena barracuda)*
6 ft max. Long silvery body with darker blotches.
Longer lower jaw. Can pale and darken quickly.

Post-larval Barracuda in the seagrass.

One of the most voracious and successful piscivores on the reef, the Barracuda, has been around for 50 million years. It can grow up to 100 lbs and live for up to 15 years. Although they often hunt alone they will sometimes school, called a battery of Barracuda. They are often caught, but because they are at the top of their food chain there is a danger of poisons accumulating in their flesh, called ciguatera. Local fishermen look out for this by leaving some of the meat near ants. If the ants begin to feed on the meat, it will also be safe for humans.

Barracudas rely on short bursts of speed to catch their prey and have been recorded striking at over 30 mph. They prefer to hunt in stronger currents, where their streamlined shape gives them an advantage. Their large eyes are best suited for hunting in the low-light conditions around dusk and dawn. Some teeth face inwards to keep hold of their prey.

# SILVERY : FISHES

### SOUTHERN SENNET
*(Sphyraena picudilla)*
18 in max. Silvery, with faint yellow body stripes. Two dorsal fins are widely separated. Often schooling.

### CERO
*(Scomberomorus regalis)*
4 ft max. Long, silvery body with a dark yellow stripe and spots. Dorsal fin is towards rear and usually darker.

### KING MACKEREL
*(Scomberomorus cavalla)*
5 ft max. Uniform silvery body with no markings. Distinctive lateral line drops down after the dorsal fins.

### WAHOO
*(Acanthocybium solandri)*
7 ft max. Long, silvery, cigar-shaped body often with darker bands on the sides. Sharply pointed snout.

### DOLPHINFISH (MAHI-MAHI)
*(Coryphaena hippurus)*
5.5 ft max. Large head and thick, tapering body. Males have especially pronounced foreheads. Mostly pelagic.

### TARPON
*(Megalops atlanticus)*
8 ft max. Large, shiny scales and a large, upturned mouth. Most often found in channels and canyons.

## PERMIT
*(Trachinotus falcatus)*
3.5 ft max. Tall, silvery body with darker, pointed fins.
Orange patch above the anal fin. Large, rubbery lips.

👓 Jacks are fast, silvery fishes; carnivores that can grow up to 70 lbs (in the case of the Crevalle Jack), and are sought after by fishermen. The most common is the Bar Jack, which can be found in all areas of the Caribbean. It often forms hunting partnerships with other species of fish in a tactic called nuclear hunting. At other times a Bar Jack will darken its color dramatically and swim under other, slower fish like the Hogfish on the left. This technique, called shadow hunting, involves hiding behind a less threatening fish, one that slowly forages on the seabed, and then darting out to catch a meal.

👓 As juveniles, Bar Jacks are one of the most sociable fishes in the Caribbean, sometimes in schools of a hundred or more. They will often surround a larger fish such as a grouper. Rather than putting themselves in harm's way, it is a form of protection. Few predators on the reef will come close to a fully grown Black Grouper like the one on the right. The grouper itself feeds only on larger fishes. To chase after the small, agile Bar Jack would be a waste of energy for very little food. This strategy gives the juveniles a bump up the food chain.

# JACKS : FISHES

**BAR JACK**
*(Caranx ruber)*
2 ft max. Blue and black stripes run from the head, on the top of the body and onto the lower lobe of the tail.

**YELLOW JACK**
*(Caranx bartholomaei)*
3 ft max. Silvery with a yellowish tint. Fins and tail are pale yellow. Yellow around the mouth and eyes.

**LEATHERJACK**
*(Oligoplites saurus)*
1.5 ft max. Long, silvery body with a sloping forehead. Distinctive yellow tail and a straight lateral line.

**COTTONMOUTH JACK**
*(Uraspis secunda)*
1.5 ft max. Rounded, silvery body with no markings. The dorsal fin and the tail are often darker.

**BLUE RUNNER**
*(Caranx crysos)*
2.5 ft max. Faint, darker bars across the body. The tips of the tail have distinctively black tips.

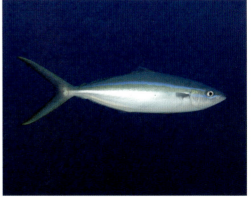

**RAINBOW RUNNER**
*(Elagatis bipinnulata)*
4 ft max. Elongated body with a large tail. Two blue stripes, with yellow in between, from eye to tail.

### ATLANTIC SPADEFISH
*(Chaetodipterus faber)*
3 ft max. Rounded silvery body with dark bars. Dark margins on the anal fins and tail. Often schooling.

> 🥽 Some species of Jack continue schooling even after they have grown to maturity, such as the Atlantic Spadefish, above, and the Horse-Eye Jack, which can be found in their hundreds. Horse-Eye Jacks are true piscivores, usually hunting in co-ordinated teams along areas with stronger current.

### ATLANTIC SPADEFISH (JUVENILE)
*(Chaetodipterus faber)*
Tall, oval body with a pronounced foredorsal spine. Dark bands over a gray to orange body.

### AFRICAN POMPANO
*(Alectis ciliaris)*
3.5 ft max. Distinctive, long filaments run from behind the dorsal and anal fins. Widely forked tail.

## JACKS : FISHES

**HORSE-EYE JACK**
*(Caranx latus)*
2.5 ft max. Distinctively large eye. Yellow tail with black edges. Dark scutes (ridges) run towards the tail.

**CREVALLE JACK**
*(Caranx hippos)*
3.5 ft max. Large blunt head. Silvery body with yellowish fins and tail. High lateral line. Black spot on gill cover.

**GREATER AMBERJACK**
*(Seriola dumerili)*
5.5 ft max. Largest of the jack. Dark band on forehead running through the eye. Short, pale dorsal and anal fins.

**ALMACO JACK**
*(Seriola rivoliana)*
3 ft max. Silvery body with dark, prominent fins. Dark band across the eye to the dorsal fin. Mostly pelagic.

**BIGEYE SCAD**
*(Selar crumenophthalmus)*
2 ft max. Oval, silvery body. Large eyes. Forked tail. Scutes (ridges) on the rear of the lateral line.

**MACKEREL SCAD**
*(Decapterus macarellus)*
1 ft max. Elongated, silvery body. Black spot on upper gill cover. Often greenish with a yellow mid-body stripe.

🦈 Sharksuckers are often mistakenly called remoras by divers, whereas the two are really a distinctly different species. True remoras have no stripes anywhere on their bodies and are usually found on pelagic animals such as whales, sharks and larger oceanic rays. As such they are rarely seen on a Caribbean reef. More commonly seen are the two Sharksucker species, that will attach themselves to any flat surface, including turtles, groupers and even boats or divers. The Sharksucker gets a free lift around the reef and the protection of a larger animal. They slow their hosts down and offer little benefit in return. Larger Sharksuckers can be seen free-swimming, without a host.

These fish attach by means of a modified set of scales located on the tops of their heads. As such they are often forced to swim upside down, depending on where they are attached to the host. Fish will often try to pass their Sharksuckers off onto other fish. They can also do themselves a great deal of harm trying to scrape them off onto the reef, opening their skin up to infections.

# SHARKSUCKERS : FISHES

### SHARKSUCKER (INTERMEDIATE)
*(Echeneis naucrates)*
Black, mid-body stripe bordered in white. Thin white borders on a dark tail. White border on dorsal fins.

### SHARKSUCKER (ADULT)
*(Echeneis naucrates)*
3.5 ft max. Often found free-swimming. The stripe is only on the face. Thin white border on dorsal fins.

### SHARKSUCKER (JUVENILE)
*(Echeneis naucrates)*
Pale blue body with a large head. Lighter blue stripes run down to the tail. Attaches to smaller fishes.

### WHITEFIN SHARKSUCKER
*(Echeneis neucratoides)*
30 in max. Often yellowish. Black mid-body stripe with pale borders. Wide white borders on a dark tail.

Sharksuckers can be an annoyance to turtles and reef fish when they attach, but they are fast and nimble swimmers and may stay on a given host for years. If a Sharksucker attaches itself to a diver, it can easily be removed by pushing it forwards to release the suction.

315

## GREEN MORAY
*(Gymnothorax funebris)*
8 ft max. The largest of the eels. Uniform green.
Constantly opens and closes its mouth to breathe.

Green Morays have a series of backward facing teeth on the roofs of their mouths to help keep prey from escaping. They are actually brown in color but are covered with a yellow slime that protects their skin. They can live for up to 30 years. Eels are constantly opening and closing their jaws to breathe, forcing the water back onto their gills. Eels are carnivores, and mostly hunt at night. They have large, extended nostrils and a very keen sense of smell to help them find their food in the darkness. During the day, eels will usually find a safe place to rest, with only their heads sticking out to breathe.

Eels have evolved a very flexible and elongated body shape that allows them access to more food sources than other fishes: animals that are hiding deep within crevices of the reef. Some can even swim under the sand. To help with this, they have no pectoral fins or lobed tails. Instead, they have a single, long, dorsal fin running the length of their bodies. As they swim, they will twist their bodies 90 degrees and undulate to move them forward. They are fast enough to catch fish free-swimming in the water, but they usually hunt by trapping their prey in small crevices of the reef, into which they can easily fit.

# EELS : FISHES

### CHAIN MORAY
*(Echidna catenata)*
2.5 ft max. Dark body with bright yellow markings and bars down the sides, in a chain-like pattern.

### SPOTTED MORAY
*(Gymnothorax moringa)*
4 ft max. Body is covered with dark brown to black spots. Often hide at the base of larger sponges.

### BLACKSPOTTED EEL
*(Quassiremus ascensionis)*
2.5 ft max. Thin body with reddish spots with black centers. Black spots on the face and the head.

### GOLDENTAIL MORAY
*(Gymnothorax miliaris)*
2 ft max. The body is covered in bright yellow spots, denser towards the tail. Yellow ring around the eye.

### SHARPTAIL EEL
*(Myrichthys breviceps)*
3.5 ft max. Thin body with short dorsal fin. Large white spots on the body, small yellow spots on the head.

### GOLDSPOTTED EEL
*(Myrichthys ocellatus)*
3.5 ft max. Thin body with short dorsal fin. Bright yellow spots with black borders run along the body.

## VIPER MORAY
*(Enchelycore nigricans)*
2.5 ft max. Olive-green body. Jaws only close at the tip of the snout, with numerous, long teeth always visible.

Hunting on the reef is not always about competition over the same food source. Sometimes different species that would normally be in competition will work together to have a better chance of getting a meal. Divers are sometimes surprised to see eels and other carnivores swimming together, side by side across the top of the reef. This tactic is known as team hunting.

A common pairing is a large Green Moray and a large grouper. As they hunt, one fish will distract the prey while the other fish goes in for a strike. When prey is cornered the two will spread out and cover all the possible escape routes. The eel can even use its thinner body to go in and chase the prey out for the grouper to snatch up. In the end, both species stand a better chance of getting a meal.

# EELS : FISHES

### CONGER EEL (JUVENILE)
*(Ariosoma sp.)*
After hatching, eels are pelagic, until they reach about 1 in. Then they settle onto the reef and begin to forage.

### BANDTOOTH CONGER
*(Ariosoma balearicum)*
15 in max. Brownish body, paler on the bottom. Dark mark under the eye. Red around a small pectoral fin.

### CHESTNUT MORAY
*(Enchelycore carychroa)*
13 in max. Golden to reddish-brown color. Series of tiny white spots on the upper and lower jaws and snout.

### MANYTOOTH CONGER
*(Conger triporiceps)*
3.5 ft max. Light blue or purple in color. Dark borders on both the dorsal and anal fins. Small, dark pectoral fins.

### PURPLEMOUTH MORAY
*(Gymnothorax vicinus)*
4 ft max. Yellowish brown body. Dark stripe down the length of the dorsal fin. The eyes are bright yellow.

### BROWN GARDEN EELS
*(Heteroconger longissimus)*
1.5 ft max. Only the head and forebody extend from the sand. Found in colonies on deeper sand patches.

👓 Eagle Rays and Southern Stingrays have their mouths under their bodies for digging into the sand, where they find their food, such as molluscs and other invertebrates. They sense prey by using electroreceptors similar to those of sharks. Some will bury themselves into the sand with only eyes and gill openings showing, as they wait to ambush prey. Their skeletons are made of cartilage, except for two bony plates in their mouths for crushing their food. Stingrays have one or more sharp barbs on their tails. Each barb contains a powerful neurotoxin and has backwards facing spines. These are the ray's only defense from predators.

👓 Eagle Rays look very different from below and above. This helps them to move about without being noticed by their main predators, the sharks. The white belly makes them hard to spot from below, looking up toward the light. The pattern of spots on their backs breaks up their outline when seen from above.

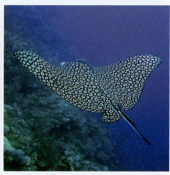

# RAYS : FISHES

### SOUTHERN STINGRAY
*(Dasyatis americana)*
5.5 ft max. Gray body with protruding eyes. The snout and tips of the fins are pointed. Found in sand.

### SPOTTED EAGLE RAY
*(Aetobatus narinari)*
8 ft max. The top of the body is dark with white spots and circles. The belly is white. Flattened snout.

### ROUGHTAIL STINGRAY
*(Dasyatis centroura)*
7 ft max. Rows of darker spines run up from the tail and across the lower back. Pointed nose and wings.

### YELLOW STINGRAY
*(Urolophus jamaicensis)*
15 in max. Small eyes. The body is covered in dark spots and yellow blotches. Often hides under ledges.

### MANTA RAY
*(Manta birostris)*
22 ft max. Black body above, white below. Large mouth with two cephalic lobes. Pelagic, rarely on coral reefs.

### CARIBBEAN WHIPTAIL STINGRAY
*(Himantura schmardae)*
4 ft max. Gray, circular body with large openings behind the eyes. Snout and tips of fins are rounded.

321

## NURSE SHARK
*(Ginglymostoma cirratum)*
14 ft max. Grey body with small black and white dots.
Small white eyes. Dorsal fins closer towards the tail.

Nurse Sharks feed mainly on smaller fishes, lobsters and conch. These are also, unfortunately, the food species that humans are most likely to take off a reef, and their numbers are dwindling in many areas. Nurse sharks can live up to 25 years. The fleshy barbels on the shark's snout help it to sniff out molluscs hiding in the sand. The mouth of a nurse shark is adapted to fit over the opening of conch shells; they literally suck the animal out of its shell, with a force of over 1000 lbs per square inch, the power of twelve vacuum cleaners.

Shark populations are in decline all around the world. An estimated 38 million sharks are killed each year, mostly as bycatch, or for the Chinese delicacy of shark-fin soup. It is estimated that in the last few decades as much as 70% of all the ocean's sharks have been killed off. Because of their slow reproductive rate, it may be impossible for these numbers to get back to normal levels. Sharks are important in the oceans because they are the apex, or top, predator. Their role is to keep fish populations lower down the food chain healthy, by weeding out the old and the sick.

# SHARKS : FISHES

**WHALE SHARK**
*(Rhincodon typus)*
59 ft max. Dark gray to black body covered in white
spots and thin white lines. Three ridges along sides.

Whale Sharks are the largest fish in the sea, growing to almost 60 ft and weighing an average of 20 tons. They can live for 100-150 years. They feed by opening their wide mouths near the surface, gulping in huge amounts of water and then filtering out the plankton. They filter about 1500 gallons of water an hour.

**SCALLOPED HAMMERHEAD SHARK**
*(Sphyrna lewini)*
14 ft max. Eyes set at the edge of a wide, flattened
head with a series of rounded indentations.

**REEF SHARK**
*(Carcharhinus perezii)*
10 ft max. Darker areas under the tips of pectoral and
ventral fins. The dorsal fin starts behind the pectoral.

Sea turtles are cold-blooded reptiles, similar to land turtles, but they are unable to retract their heads into their shells. They live at sea all their lives, only coming ashore once every two to four years to lay eggs. They always return to the same spot they were hatched. They will migrate from their regular feeding sites to these nesting sites, which may be hundreds, or even up to a thousand miles away.

Green Sea Turtles eat jellyfish, algae and seagrass. Loggerheads have stronger jaws for feeding on shellfish and crustaceans. The Hawksbill feeds almost solely on sponges, and has developed a sharp beak for breaking them open.

Sea Turtles are considered endangered species. Besides losing an occasional flipper to a shark, the only real predator of turtles is man. They are hunted for their meat, and their nests are raided for their eggs. Pollution is also taking a toll. Turtles get caught up in discarded fishing nets and line, and bits of floating plastic and cigarette butts look like jellyfish and are eaten by Green Sea Turtles. Boat traffic near coral reefs can kill turtles as well, like this unlucky individual on the right. Sea Turtles only start reproducing very late in life (35 years in the case of the Loggerhead) and fewer are being given a chance to get to this age.

# SEA TURTLES

**LOGGERHEAD TURTLE**
*(Caretta caretta)*
8 ft max, up to 1000 lbs. Distinctively short neck and a rounded shell, often covered in barnacles.

**GREEN SEA TURTLE**
*(Chelonia mydas)*
5 ft max, up to 700 lbs. They have a rounded nose and a smooth shell. They can live to be 80 years old.

**HAWKSBILL TURTLE (JUVENILE)**
*(Eretmochelys imbriocota)*
Still learning to dive, they stay close to the surface. Only 1/1000 make it to adulthood and can live up to 50 years.

**HAWKSBILL TURTLE**
*(Eretmochelys imbriocota)*
3 ft max, up to 280 lbs. The most common, with a sharply pointed beak and a serrated edge to the shell.

While feeding or moving about on the reef, turtles need to surface and breathe every half hour or so. While resting or sleeping, they can hold their breath for up to 6 hours. Green Sea Turtles will often have Sharksuckers attached to their shells, feeding on the vegetable waste passed by the turtle. Although they do keep the shells clean, they are also a nuisance and slow the turtles down. A Green Turtle will try to shake the Sharksucker off, in a complicated dance as it swims to the surface.

Sea Turtles can often be seen cleaning their shells. They have favorite spots on their feeding grounds for doing this, preferring to use sponges to rub away algae and parasites from their backs. They will wear a rounded shape into the base of the Giant Barrel Sponges (p. 53).

Marine mammals are warm-blooded, with a body temperature about the same as that of humans, and have a thick layer of blubber under their skin. They breath through a single blowhole in the top of the head, about 4 times a minute in the case of dolphins. Most dolphins can dive very deep for their food and hold their breath for up to 15 minutes. Dolphins sleep for about 8 hours a day, but they still need to breathe; they will slow themselves down and let first one half of their brains sleep and then the other. Bottlenose Dolphins are the most common, and are often inquisitive, especially the younger males, who will break off from the pod to come in and investigate divers.

Dolphins are very sociable animals, normally travelling in pods of 5 to 12 individuals, but some pods can reach into the hundreds. These are often led by older females. Dolphins hunt together co-operatively, communicating with high-pitched whistles. They can each eat around 30 lbs of food a day, which is mostly fish and squid. Dolphins will have sex just for fun, females becoming sexually mature at around 12 years. Babies are born swimming, tail first, and will drink their mother's milk for their first two years and then stay with her for at least another 3 years. Unmolested, dolphins can live for up to 50 years in the wild.

# MARINE MAMMALS

### BOTTLENOSE DOLPHIN
*(Tursiops truncatus)*
12 ft max. Robust body with a short beak. The dorsal fin is curved and the flippers are pointed.

### ROUGH TOOTHED DOLPHIN
*(Steno bredanensis)*
8.5 ft max. Smaller head, with a long beak and sloping forehead. White mark above the eyes, onto the back.

### ORCA
*(Orcinus orca)*
26 ft max. Distinctive white patch behind the eye, under the chin and on the belly towards the tail. Rare, pelagic.

### SPINNER DOLPHIN
*(Stenella longirostris)*
7 ft max. Elongated body with a longer beak. Gray body with a darker streak behind the eye. White belly.

### SHORT FINNED PILOT WHALE
*(Globicephala macrorhynchus)*
24 ft max. Bulbous head with no beak. Curved dorsal fin has a distinctively long base. Thick body at the tail base.

### MANATEE
*(Trichechus manatus)*
14 ft max. Heavy body with flattened snout and short, rounded flippers. Only males are ever seen on reefs.

# SCIENTIFIC NAME INDEX

## MARINE PLANTS:

Acetabularia, calyculus, 12
   crenulata, 12
   schenckii, 12
Aglaothamnion herveyi, 27
Amphiroa, brasiliana, 29
   fragilissima, 29
   hancockii, 28
   rigida, 29
   tribulus, 28
Anadyomene stellata, 9
Avicennia germinans, 5
Avrainvillea asarifolia, 11
   longicaulis, 11
Bryopsis pennata, 9
Caulerpa, cupressoides, 15
   mexicana, 9
   nummularia, 15
   racemosa, 13
   serrulata, 13
   sertularioides, 13
   verticillata, 8
   webbiana, 13
Ceramium nitens, 25
Cladosiphon occidentalis, 19
Codium, isthmocladum, 11
   repens, 9
Conocarpus erectus, 5
Cryptonemia crenulata, 25
Danonema farinosum, 19
Dictyosphaeria cavernosa, 11
Dictyota, bartayresiana, 20
   crenulata, 19
   dichotoma, 18
   humifusa, 21
   menstrualis, 21
Dudresnaya crassa, 27
Galaxaura sp., 29
   rugosa, 26
   subverticillata, 27
Gracilaria, blodgettii, 25
   tikvahiae, 9
Halimeda, copiosa, 14
   cryptica, 14
   goreaui, 14
   incrassata, 15
   monile, 15
   opuntia, 16
   opuntia triloba, 15
   tuna, 15
Haliptilon cubense, 29
Halophila baillonis, 7
Jania adherens, 28
Laguncularia racemosa, 5
Liagora dendroidea, 24
Lobophora variegata, 20
Martensia pavonia, 25
Meristiella schrammii, 24
Microdictyon boergesenii, 9
Mucosa sp., 21
Neomeris annulata, 13
Ochtodes secundiramea, 27
Padina, boergesenii, 13
   pavonica, 21
Penicillus, capitatus, 17
   dumetosus, 17
   pyriformis, 17
Peyssonnelia sp., 23
   boergesenii, 23
   inamoena, 23
   stoechas, 23
Porolithon pachydermum, 23
Predea feldmanni, 25
Pterocladiella capillacea, 26
Rhipocephalus, brevifolius, 17
   longifolius, 17
   phoenix, 17
Rhizophora mangle, 5
Sargassum sp., 19
   fluitans, 19
   hystrix, 19
Solieria filiformis, 29
Spermothamnion gymnocarpum, 26
Stypopodium zonale, 20
Symploca sp., 27
Syringodium filiforme, 7
Taonia sp., 21
Thalassia testudinum, 7
Titanoderma sp., 23
Tricleocarpa fragilis, 24
Turbinaria tricostata, 21
Udotea sp., 11, 16
   cyathiformis, 16
   flabellum, 11
Valonia, macrophysa, 10
   utricularis, 10
Ventricaria ventricosa, 10
Wrangelia penicillata, 27
Wurdemannia miniata, 25

## SPONGES:

Aaptos pernucleata, 45
Agelas, cervicornis, 40
   citrina, 53
   clathrodes, 36
   conifera, 49
   sceptrum, 41
   sventres, 34
   wiedenmyeri, 49
Aiolochroia sp., 37
   crassa, 37
Amphimedon compressa, 41
Anthosigmella varians, 34, 45
Aplysina sp., 45

# SCIENTIFIC NAME INDEX

Aplysina archeri, 50
    bathyphila, 49
    cauliformis, 41
    fistularis, 51
    fulva, 40
    lacunosa, 51, 55
Calcarea sp., 38
Callyspongia, plicifera, 46
    vaginalis, 47
Calyx podatypa, 37
Cinachyra sp., 44
Clatharia, sp., 32
    canariensis, 38
Cliona, delitrix, 39
    langae, 35
Cribrochalina vasculum, 54
Diplastrella sp., 35
Dragmacidon reticulata, 43
Dysidea janiae, 47
Ectyoplasia ferox, 36
Geodia neptuni, 53
Halichondria lutea, 43
Halisarca sp., 35
Holopsamma helwigi, 34
Hyatella cavernosa, 49
Hyrtios sp., 49
Iotrochota birotulata, 41
Ircinia, felix, 45
    strobilina, 45
Leucandra aspera, 38
Leucetta barbata, 44
Monanchora barbadensis, 33
Mycale sp., 35
    laevis, 35
    laxissima, 47
Myrmekioderma sp., 32
    styx, 44
Neofibularia nolitangere, 55
Niphates, digitalis, 47
    erecta, 41
Oceanapia, bartschi, 53
    peltata, 43
    stalagmitica, 43
Oscarella sp., 33
Pandaros acanthifolium, 51
Phorbas amaranthus, 35
Plakinastrella onkodes, 51
Plakortis angulospiculatus, 37
Pseudoceratina crassa, 48
Ptilocaulis sp., 37
    walpersi, 42
Rhaphidophlus, juniperinus, 41
    venosus, 33
Siphonodictyon coralliphagum, 39
Smenospongia aurea, 39
Spheciospongia vesparium, 55
Spirastrella coccinea, 33
Tedania ignis, 37

Topsentia ophiraphidites, 43
Ulosa, funicularis, 43
    ruetzleri, 32
Verongula, gigantea, 53
    reiswigi, 54, 55
    rigida, 51
Xestospongia, muta, 53
    rosariensis, 55

## CORALS:

Acropora, cervicornis, 61
    palmata, 61
    prolifera, 61
Agaricia sp., 62
    agaricites, 63
    carinata, 63
    danai, 63
    fragilis, 75
    grahamae, 75
    humilis, 63
    lamarcki, 75
    purpurea, 63
    tenuifolia, 62
    undata, 75
Antipathes sp., 78, 79
    atlantica, 79
    gracilis, 79
    lenta, 79
    pennacea, 79
Briareum asbestinum, 81
Carijoa riisei, 81
Cirrhipathes leutkeni, 79
Coenocyathus caribbeana, 77
Colangia immersa, 77
Colpophyllia natans, 65
Dendrogyra cylindrus, 58
Dichocoenia stokesi, 71
Diodogorgia nodulifera, 84
Diploria, clivosa, 65
    labyrinthiformis, 65
    strigosa, 65
Ellisella, barbadensis, 88
    elongata, 89
Erythropodium caribaeorum, 81
Eunicea sp., 85
    fusca, 85
    mammosa, 85
    succinea, 86
Eusmilia, fastigiata, 67
    flabellata, 67
Favia fragum, 65
Gorgonia, flabellum, 82
    mariae, 83
    ventalina, 82
Helioceris cucullata, 63
Heterogorgia uatumani, 83
Iciligorgia schrammi, 83

# SCIENTIFIC NAME INDEX

## CORALS:

Isophyllastrea rigida, 69
Isophyllia sinuosa, 73
Madracis decactis, 69
    formosa, 59
    mirabilis, 59
    pharensis, 71
Manicina areolata, 73
Meandrina danae, 73
    meandrites, 65, 73
    brasiliensis, 65
Millepora alcicornis, 61
    complanata, 61
    squarrosa, 61
Montastraea annularis, 70
    cavernosa, 68
    faveolata, 70
    franksi, 70
Muricea elongata, 87
    laxa, 86
    muricata, 83
    pinnata, 83
Muriceopsis flavida, 87
Mussa angulosa, 67
Mycetophyllia aliciae, 73
    danaana, 70
    ferox, 70
    lamarckiana, 73
Nicella goreaui, 83
    schmitti, 88
Oculina diffusa, 69
Phacelocyathus flos, 77
Plexaurella sp., 87
    flexuosa, 87
    homomalla, 84
    nutans, 87
Porites furcata, 59
    porites, 59
    astreoides, 67
    branneri, 71
    colonensis, 75
    divaricata, 59
Pseudoplexaura sp., 85
Pseudopterogorgia sp., 89
    americana, 87
    bipinnata, 89
Pterogorgia anceps, 89
    citrina, 89
    guadalupensis, 88
Rhizopsammia goesi, 77
Rhizosmilia maculata, 76
Scolymia cubensis, 76
    lacera, 76
Siderastrea radians, 69
    siderea, 69
Solenastrea bournoni, 71
Stephanocoenia intersepta, 69

Stereotelesto corallina, 81
Stylaster roseus, 59
Swiftia exserta, 81
Thalamophyllia riisei, 77
Tubastraea coccinea, 77

## INVERTEBRATES:

Acanthopleura granulata, 155
Acanthozoon maculosum, 152
Actinaria, 105, 109
Actinopyga agassizii, 131
Aequorea aequorea, 93
Aglaja felis, 153
Aiptasia sp., 105
Agalma okeni, 97
Alicia mirabilis, 105
Alpheus sp., 183
    floridanus, 184
    peasei, 182
Analcidometra armata, 125
Anamobaea sp., 141
    orstedii, 141
Anodontia alba, 159
Anoplodactylus spp., 179
Aphelodoris antillensis, 147
Aplysia, dactylomela, 151
    juliana, 151
    parvula, 151
Arachnanthus sp., 107
    nocturnus, 106
Arenicola cristata, 137
Ascidia sydneiensis, 99
Asterina folium, 123
Astichopus multifidus, 133
Astralium phoebium, 162
Astrophyton muricatum, 124
Astropyga magnifica, 127
Aurelia aurita, 94
Austraeolis catina, 145
Axius sp., 185
Bartholomea annulata, 107
Baseodiscus sp., 136
Beroe gracilis, 95
    ovata, 95
Bispira brunnea, 140
    variegata, 141
Bornella calcarata, 144
Botrylloides sp., 101
    nigrum, 101
Botryllus sp., 101
Bracebridgia subsulcata, 119
Brachycarpus biunguiculatus, 184
Bugula minima, 119
Bunodsoma granulifera, 107
Bursa granularis, 165
Bursatella leachii, 151
Calappa angusta, 197

# SCIENTIFIC NAME INDEX

Calappa flammea, 197
    gallus, 197
    ocellata, 197
Calcinus tibicen, 189
Calliactis tricolor, 109
Callinectes sp., 195
Calliostoma javanicum, 162
Callistochiton shuttleworthianus, 155
Canda simplex, 119
Capitellidae, 137
Caribachlamys ornata, 158
Carpilius corallinus, 192
Carybdea alata, 97
    marsupialis, 97
Cassiopea frondosa, 93
    xamachana, 93
Cassis flammea., 169
    madagascariensis, 169
Caulibugula dendrograpta, 119
Ceriantharia, 106
Cerithium eburneum, 163
Cestum veneris, 97
Chaetopleura apiculata, 155
Charonia variegata, 167
Chelidonura berolina, 153
    hirundinina, 153
Chiton squamosum, 155
Chlamys imbricata, 158
Chromodoris kempfi, 149
Cinetorhynehus manningi, 180
Clavelina sp., 99
    picta, 99
Clibanarius tricolor, 189
Clypeaster rosaceus, 129
    subdepressus, 128
Cnidoscyphus marginatus, 117
Condylactis gigantea, 104
Conus cardinalis, 164
    kulkulcan, 164
    mus Hwass, 164
Corallimorpharian, 117
Cronius ruber, 195
Crassostrea gasar, 157
Cymatium sp., 169
Cymbovula acicularis, 161
Cyphoma gibbosum, 160
    mcgintyi, 161
Cypraea cervus, 167
    cinerea, 167
    zebra, 167
Cypraecassis testiculus, 167
Dardanus venosus, 188
Davidaster discoidea, 125
    rubiginosa, 125
Dendostrea frons, 157
Dendrodoris krebsii, 147
    nigrolineata, 147
Dentitheca dendritica, 117

Diadema antillarum, 127
Didemnidae, 103
Didemnum conchyliatum, 101
    vanderhorsti, 101
Diplosoma glandulosum, 103
Discodoris evelinae, 147
Discosoma carlgreni, 111
    neglectum, 111
    sanctithomae, 110
Dissodactylus mellitae, 193
    primitivus, 193
Distaplia bermudensis, 103
Domecia acanthophora, 194
    hispida, 194
Doris ilo, 147
Dromia erythropus, 196
Dromidia antillensis, 196
Echinometra lucunter, 128
    viridis, 127
Elysia crispata, 143
    ornata, 143
    tuca, 143
Enoplometopus antillensis, 199
Eostichopus arnesoni, 131
Epicystis crucifer, 105
Epizoanthus cutressi, 115
Euapta lappa, 131
Eucidaris tribuloides, 127
Eudistoma sp., 100
    obscuratum, 100
Eunice longisetis, 135
Euplakamis sp., 96
Eupolymnia crassicornis, 137
Fasciolaria tulipa, 165
Filograna huxleyi, 136
Flabellina engeli, 145
Forskalia edwardsi, 96
Glossodoris sedna, 149
Glycera dibranchiata, 137
Gnathophylloides mineri, 176
Gnathophyllum americanum, 180
    circellus, 181
Gonionemus vertens, 93
Gymnangium longicauda, 117
Halocordyle disticha, 116
Halopteris carinata, 117
Haplosyllis sp., 137
Hermodice carunculata, 134
Hexabranchus morsomus, 150
Holothuria cubana, 133
    floridana, 133
    impatiens, 133
    mexicana, 131
    thomasi, 131
Hypselodoris acriba, 149
    marci, 149
Hypsicomus sp., 141
Isaurus tuberculatus, 114

# SCIENTIFIC NAME INDEX

## INVERTEBRATES:

Isognomon alatus, 157
   radiatus, 157
Isostichopus badionotus, 132
Janicea antiguensis, 181
Justitia longimanus, 198
Latreutes parvulus, 177
Lebrunia coralligens, 105
   danae, 109
Leocothea multicornis, 95
Leodia sexiesperforata, 129
Lepas anatifera, 154
Leucozonia nassa, 161
Lima lima, 159
   pellucida, 159
   scabra, 159
Linckia guildingii, 123
Linuche unguiculata, 93
Lithopoma tectum, 162
Loimia medusa, 135
Lucida sp., 107
Lychnorhiza sp., 94
Lysiosquilla sp., 183
   scabricauda, 183
Lysmata grabhami, 175
   rathbunae, 181
   wurdemanni, 181
Lytechinus variegatus, 129
   williamsi, 128
Macrorhynchia philippina, 117
Marcocoeloma trispinosum, 187
Megalomma sp., 141
Meoma ventricosa, 129
Metapenaeopsis goodie, 185
Micropanope urinator, 194
Microphrys bicomuta, 187
Mithrax cinctimanus, 191
   coryphe, 191
   forceps, 191
   pilosus, 191
   sculptus, 191
   spinosissimus, 190
Mitra barbadensis, 163
Mnemiopsis mccraydyi, 95
Munida pusilla, 185
Muricopsis sp., 163
Mysidium spp., 185
Naticarius canrena, 165
Nemaster grandis, 125
Nemertea sp., 137
Neogonodactylus curacaoensis, 182
   oerstedii, 183
Neopontonides chacei, 178
Notaulax nudicollis, 139
   occidentalis, 139
Octopus briareus, 171
   defilippi, 171
Octopus filosus, 171
   joubini, 171
   macropus, 171
   vulgaris, 171
Ocyropsis crystallina, 95
   maculata, 95
Olindias sambaquiensis, 92
Ophidiaster guildingii, 123
Ophiocoma echinata, 121
   appressum, 121
   cinereum, 122
   guttatum, 122
Ophioderma rubicundum, 121
Ophiomyxa flaccida, 123
Ophiothrix angulata, 122
   suensonii, 120
Orchistoma pileus, 93
Oreaster reticulatus, 123
Oxynaspis gracilis, 154
Oxynoe antillarum, 143
Pachygrapsus transversus, 193
Paguristes cadenati, 189
   erythrops, 189
   punticeps, 189
   sericeus, 189
Palaemon northropi, 175
Palinurellus gundlachi, 199
Pauleo jubatus, 145
Palythoa caribaeorum, 115
   grandis, 113
Panulirus argus, 199
   guttatus, 199
Paractaea rufopunctata, 197
Parazoanthus catenularis, 115
   parasiticus, 115
   puertoricense, 115
   swiftii, 113
   tunicans, 113
Pariambus typicus, 179
Parribacus antarcticus, 199
Pelagia noctiluca, 96
Pelia mutica, 187
   rotunda, 187
Percnon gibbesi, 193
Periclimenes antillensis, 177
   antipathophilus, 176
   crinoidalis, 177
   harringtoni, 176
   longicaudatus, 177
   mclellandi, 178
   meyeri, 177
   pedersoni, 174
   rathbunae, 179
   rincewindi, 177
   yucatanicus, 174
Petalifera ramosa, 151
Petaloconchus sp., 161
Petrochirus diogenes, 188

# SCIENTIFIC NAME INDEX

Phidiana lynceus, 145
Phimochirus holthuisi, 188
Phyllidiopsis papilligera, 148
Physalia physalis, 97
Pickfordiateunthis pulchella, 173
Pilumnus floridanus, 197
Pinna carnea, 157
Plagiobrissus grandis, 129
Platydoris angustipes, 147
Platypodiella spectabilis, 193
Pleurobranchus areolatus, 146
    atlanticus, 146
    crossei, 146
Podochela sp., 186
    curvirostris, 187
Polycarpa spongiabilis, 99
Polynoide, 135
Pomatostegus stellatus, 139
Porcellana sayana, 196
Portunus sayi, 195
    sebae, 195
    spinimanus, 195
Protula sp., 139
Pseudoceros bolool, 153
    pardalis, 153
    rawlinsonae, 153
    splendidus, 152
Pseudocorynactis caribbeorum, 111
Pseudopontonides principis, 178
Pseudosquilla ciliate, 183
Pteria colymbus, 157
Ralpharia gorgoniae, 116
Renocila Spp., 185
Reteporellina evelinae, 119
Rhizophysa spp., 97
Rhopalaea abdominalis, 99
Ricordea florida, 111
Sabellastarte magnifica, 141
Salpa sp., 102
Schizoporella violacea, 118
Schizostella bifurcata, 125
Scrupocellaria sp., 119
Scyllaea pelagica, 150
Scyllarides aequinoctialis, 199
Semicassis cicatricosa, 166
Sepioteuthis sepioidea, 173
Serpulidae, 135
Sertularella speciosa, 117
Sigsbeia conifera, 125
Simnia sp., 161
Spirobranchus sp., 137
    giganteus, 138
Spondylus americanus, 156
Spurilla creutzbergi, 145
Stenocionops furcatus coelata, 187
Stenoplax purpurascens, 155
Stenopus hispidus, 175
    scutellatus, 175
Stenorhynchus seticornis, 193
Stichodactyla helianthus, 107
Stomolophus meleagris, 94
Strombus, costatus, 168
    gigas, 169
    raninus, 165, 169
Stylocheilus longicauda, 151
Symplegma viride, 103
Synalpheus sp., 182
Telmatactis americana, 109
Tellina radiata, 159
Thor amboinensis, 179
Thoracica, 154
Thysanotheuthis rhombus, 173
Thuridilla picta, 143
Tonicia schrammi, 155
Tonna pennata, 165
Tozeuma carolinense, 181
Trematooecia aviculifera, 118
Trididemum solidum, 103
Tripneustes ventricosus, 129
Tritonia bayeri, 149
    hamnerorum, 149
Tritoniopsis frydis, 148
Turbo cailletii, 163
Turbinella angulata, 169
Actinaria,, 106
Vasum muricatum, 165
Vermiliopsis n. sp., 139
Vexillum histrio, 163
    pulchellum
Viatrix globulifera, 107
Volvarina sp., 161
Zoanthidea, 113
Zoanthus pulchellus, 112
Zyzzyzus warreni, 116

## FISHES:

Abudefduf saxatilis, 242
    taurus, 243
Acanthemblemaria aspera, 215
    maria, 214
    spinosa, 215
Acanthocybium solandri, 309
Acanthostracion polygonia, 265
    quadricornis, 265
Acanthurus chirurgus, 249
    coeruleus, 248
    tractus, 249
Acentronura dendritica, 240
Achirus lineatus, 237
Aetobatus narinari, 321
Albula vulpes, 27
Alectis ciliaris, 312
Aluterus scriptus, 259
Amblycirrhitus pinos, 233
Anisotremus surinamensis, 271

# SCIENTIFIC NAME INDEX

## FISHES:

Anisotremus virginicus, 271
Aluteros monoceros, 259
Antennarius multiocellatus, 226
Apogon aurolineatus, 218
   binotatus, 219
   lachneri, 218
   maculatus, 219
   phenax, 219
   pillionatus, 219
   robinsi, 219
   townsendi, 218
Apsilus dentatus, 302
Arcos rubiginosus, 231
Ariosoma balearicum, 319
Atherinidae, 221
Aulostomus maculatus, 306
Balistes vetula, 256
Bathygobius soporator, 205
Bodianus pulchellus, 267
   rufus, 267
Bothus lunatus, 236
   maculiferus, 237
   ocellatus, 237
Calamus bajonado, 304
   calamus, 304
Cantherhines macrocerus, 258
   pullus, 259
Canthidermis maculata, 257
   sufflamen, 257
Canthigaster rostrata, 261
Caranx bartholomaei, 311
   crysos, 311
   hippos, 313
   latus, 313
   ruber, 311
Carcharhinus perezii, 323
Centropomus undecimalis, 227
Centropyge argi, 255
Cephalopholis cruentatus, 289
   fulva, 290
Chaenopsis limbaughi, 211
   ocellata, 211
Chaetodipterus faber, 312
Chaetodon aculeatus, 251
   capistratus, 251
   ocellatus, 251
   sedentarius, 251
   striatus, 250
Chilomycterus antennatus, 261
   antillarum, 260
Chromis cyanea, 245
   insolata, 247
   multilineata, 245
   scotti, 247
Clepticus parrae, 285
Conger triporiceps, 319

Coryphaena hippurus, 309
Coryphopterus alloides, 205
Coryphopterus bol, 203
   dicrus, 203
   eidolon, 201
   glaucofraenum, 203
   lipernes, 203
   personatus/hyalinus, 201
Cosmocampus albirostris, 241
   elucens, 239
Cryptotomus roseus, 279
Cyclopsetta fimbriata, 237
Dactylopterus volitans, 227
Dasyatis americana, 321
   centroura, 321
Decapterus macarellus, 313
Diodon holocanthus, 261
   hystrix, 261
Diplectrum bivittatum, 233
Diplogrammus pauciradiatus, 231
Echeneis naucrates, 315
   neucratoides, 315
Echidna catenata, 317
Elacatinus colini, 201
   lobeli, 201
   lori, 201
   louisae, 201
Elagatis bipinnulata, 311
Emblemaria hyltoni, 214
   pandionis, 212
   vitta, 213
Emblemariopsis carib sp., 210
   pricei, 215
Enchelycore carychroa, 319
   nigricans, 318
Engyophrys senta, 237
Enneanectes altivelis, 211
   atrorus, 210
   boehlkei, 211
   pectoralis, 211
Epinephelus adscensionis, 291
   guttatus, 291
   itajara, 298
   striatus, 298
Equetus lanceolatus, 225
   punctatus, 224
Eucinostomus jonesii, 305
   lefroyi, 305
   melanopterus, 305
Fistularia tabacaria, 307
Gerres cinereus, 305
Ginglymostoma cirratum, 322
Gnatholepis thompsoni, 203
Gobiosoma dilepis, 204
   pallens, 202
   saucrum, 202
Gramma linki, 286
   loreto, 286

# SCIENTIFIC NAME INDEX

Gramma melacara, 286
Grammonus claudei, 230
Gymnothorax funebris, 316
    miliaris, 317
    moringa, 317
    vicinus, 319
Haemulon album, 271
    aurolineatum, 269
    carbonarium, 270
    chrysargyreum, 271
    flavolineatum, 269
    macrostomum, 270
    melanarum, 271
    plumierii, 271
    sciurus, 269
Halicampus crinitus, 239
    forma ensenadae, 241
Halichoeres bivittatus, 285
    cyanocephalus, 283
    garnoti, 282
    maculipinna, 281
    pictus, 281
    poeyi, 283
    radiatus, 284
Hemiramphus balao, 307
Heteroconger longissimus, 319
Heteropriacanthus cruentatus, 301
Himantura schmardae, 321
Hippocampus erectus, 239
    reidi, 238
Histrio histrio, 227
Holacanthus tricolor, 255
    ciliaris, 253
Holocentrus, rufus, 220
    adscensionis, 220
Hypleurochilus pseudoaequipinnis, 207
Hypoplectrus aberrans, 295
    chlorurus, 293
    gummigutta, 293
    guttavarius, 293
    indigo, 293
    nigricans, 293
    providencianus, 295
    puella, 293
    randallorum, 295
    unicolor, 295
Inermia vittata, 307
Kryptophanaron alfredi, 230
Kyphosus sectatrix, 304
Labrisomus filamentosus, 206
    gobio, 207
    kalisherae, 207
    nuchipinnis, 207
Lachnolaimus maximus, 266
Lactophrys bicaudalis, 263
    trigonus, 265
    triqueter, 262
Liopropoma carmabi, 281

Lipoproma, mowbrayi, 281
    rubre, 281
Lipogramma trilineatum, 287
Lucayablennius zingaro, 209
Lutjanus analis, 300
    apodus, 302
    buccanella, 303
    cyanopterus, 301
    griseus, 301
    jocu, 300
    mahogani, 301
    synagris, 303
Lyhrypnus heterochroma, 205
    elasson, 205
Malacanthus plumieri, 235
Malacoctenus aurolineatus, 210
    boehlkei, 211
    macropus, 213
    triangulatus, 213
Manta birostris, 321
Megalops atlanticus, 309
Melichthys niger, 257
Microspathodon chrysurus, 244
Monacanthus tuckeri, 257
    ciliatus, 259
Mulloidichthys martinicus, 233
Mycteroperca bonaci, 297
    interstitialis, 297
    tigris, 299
    venenosa, 299
Myrichthys breviceps, 317
    ocellatus, 317
Myripristis jacobus, 221
Neoniphon marianus, 221
Nes longus, 205
Ocyurus chrysurus, 303
Odontoscion dentex, 224
Ogcocephalus nasutus, 229
Oligoplites saurus, 311
Ophidion sp., 233
Ophioblennius macclurei, 208
Opisthonema oglinum, 307
Opistognathus aurifrons, 234
    gilberti, 235
    macrognathus, 235
    whitehursti, 235
Oxyurichthys stigmalophius, 203
Paraclinus barbatus, 213
    marmoratus, 209
Paradiplogrammus bairdi, 231
Paranthias furcifer, 291
Parasphyraenops incisus, 287
Pareques acuminatus, 225
Pempheris poeyi, 305
    schomburgkii, 305
Phaeoptyx pigmentaria, 219
Platybelone argalus, 307
Plectrypops retrospinis, 221

# SCIENTIFIC NAME INDEX

## FISHES:

Pomacanthus arcuatus, 253
   paru, 255
Priacanthus arenatus, 221
Priolepis hipoliti, 202
Pseudupeneus maculatus, 233
Ptereleotris helenae, 204
Pterois volitans, 223
Quassiremus ascensionis, 317
Rhincodon typus, 323
Risor ruber, 205
Rypticus saponaceus, 288
Sanopus barbatus, 230
Sargocentron bullisi, 221
   coruscum, 221
   vexillarium, 220
Scarus coelestinus, 278
   coeruleus, 273
   guacamaia, 278
   iseri, 275
   taeniopterus, 275
   vetula, 277
Schultzea beta, 281
Scomberomorus cavalla, 309
   regalis, 309
Scorpaena grandicornis, 229
   inermis, 229
   plumieri, 229
Scorpaenodes caribbaeus, 229
Selar crumenophthalmus, 313
Seriola dumerili, 313
   riviolana, 313
Serranus annularis, 288
   baldwini, 289
   chionaraia, 288
   tabacarius, 289
   tigrinus, 289
   tortugarum, 289
Sparisoma atomarium, 277
   aurofrenatum, 273
   chrysopterum, 277
   radians, 279
   rubripinne, 279
   viride, 276
Sphoeroides spengleri, 261
   testudineus, 261
Sphyraena barracuda, 308
   picudilla, 309
Sphyrna lewini, 323
Starksia hassi, 209
   nanodes, 209
   weigti, 208
Stegastes adustus, 245
   diencaeus, 245
   leucostictus, 243
   partitus, 246
   planifrons, 243
Stegastes variabilis, 246
Stephanolepis setifer, 259
Syacium micrurum, 237
Symphurus sp., 231
Syngnathus sp., 241
   caribbaeus, 241
   pelagicus, 241
Synodus intermedius, 232
   saurus, 233
   synodus, 233
Thalassoma bifasciatum, 280
Trachinotus falcatus, 310
Tylosurus crocodilus, 307
Uraspis secunda, 311
Urolophus jamaicensis, 321
Xanthichthys ringens, 258
Xyrichtys martinicensis, 217
   novacula, 217
   splendens, 216

## TURTLES:

Caretta caretta, 325
Chelonia mydas, 325
Eretmochelys imbriocota, 325

## MAMMALS:

Globicephala macrorhynchus, 327
Orcinus orca, 327
Stenella longirostris, 327
Steno bredanensis, 327
Trichechus manatus, 327
Tursiops truncatus, 327

# COMMON NAME INDEX

## MARINE PLANTS:

Blue-Banded Alga, 21
Branching White Alga, 19
Brazilian Twig Alga, 29
Bristle Ball Brush, 17
Bulbous Alga, 25
Burgundy Crust Alga, 23
Cactus Tree Alga, 15
Cryptic Alga, 14
Cryptic Blade Alga, 25
Dead Mans Fingers, 11
Delicate Twig Alga, 29
Elongate Pinecone Alga, 17
Encrusting Fan-leaf Alga, 20
Encrusting Fuzz Alga, 26
Flat Green Feather Alga, 9
Flat Topped Bristle Brush, 17
Flat Twig Alga, 28
Fleshy Twig Alga, 9
Flower Blade Alga, 21
Fragile Branching Alga, 24
Fragile Feather Alga, 9
Fuzz Ball Alga, 27
Fuzzy Bush Alga, 27
Fuzzy Caulerpa, 8
Fuzzy Thicket Alga, 27
Fuzzy Tip Alga, 13
Golden Fuzzball Alga, 24
Grass, Manatee, 7
    Midrib Seagrass, 7
    Turtle, 7
Green Bubble Weed, 11
Green Feather Alga, 13
Green Grape Alga, 13
Green Helmet Alga, 15
Green Net Alga, 9
Hancocks Twig Alga, 28
Hanging Vine, Large Leaf, 14
    Small Leaf, 14
Jointed Stalk Alga, 15
Lavender Crust Alga, 23
Leafy Flat Blade Alga, 20
Leafy Rolled Blade Alga, 13
Mangrove, Black, 5
    Buttonwood, 5
    Red, 5
    White, 5
Maroon Hair Alga, 26
Matte Red Crust Alga, 23
Mermaids Fan, 11
Mermaids Teacup, 16
Mermaids Wineglass, Green, 12
    Pale, 12
    White, 12
Mottled Crust Alga, 23
Mucosa Pink Alga, 24
Mucosa White Alga, 21
Neptunes Shaving Brush, 17
Notched Blade Alga, 19
Paddle Blade Alga, 11
Papyrus Print Alga, 9
Peacock Alga, 25
Pinecone Algae, 17
Pink Branchlet Alga, 29
Pink Bush Alga, 27
Pink Fuzz Alga, 27
Pink Segmented Alga, 28
Pink Tangled Alga, 25
Purple Bush Alga, 27
Ragged Mermaids Teacup, 16
Ragged Pinecone Alga, 17
Red Filamant Alga, 25
Red Orange Crust Alga, 23
Reef Cement, 23
Ruffled Blade Alga, 11
Sargassum Alga, 19
Sargassum Seaweed, 19
Saucer Blade Alga, 11
Saucer Leaf Alga, 21
Sawblade Alga, 13
Sea Pearl, 10
    Creeping Bubble Alga, 10
    Elongated, 10
Serrated Alga, 13
Shiny Sea Grass, 9
Smooth Strap Alga, 18
Sprouting Blade Alga, 21
Stalked Lettuce Leaf Alga, 15
Striving Red Alga, 25
Three Finger Leaf Alga, 15
Three Lobed Alga, 15
Tubular Pink Alga, 29
Tubular Thicket Alga, 26
Watercress Alga, 16
Western Tubular Alga, 19
White Scroll Alga, 21
White Tubular Thicket Alga, 29
White Veined Sargassum, 19
Y Twig Alga, 29
Yellow Blade Alga, 20

# COMMON NAME INDEX

## SPONGES:

Ball Sponge, Black, 45
   Convoluted, 45
   Orange, 44
   Spiny, 44
Barrel Sponge, Convoluted, 55
   Giant, 53
   Leathery, 53
   Maroon, 55
   Netted, 53
   Orange, 53
   Reticulated, 54
   Yellow, 55
Boring Sponge, Red, 39
   Variable, 39
Brown Bowl Sponge, 54
Brown Octopus Sponge, 36
Brown Variable Sponge, 34, 45
Buried Sponge, 43
Calcareous Sponge, White, 38
   Yellow, 38
Circular Column Sponge, 43
Convoluted Orange Sponge, 44
Cryptic Sponge, 38
Dark Volcano Sponge, 37
Elephant Ear Sponge, 36
Encrusting Sponge, Coral, 35
   Elephant Ear, 34
   Golden, 37
   Orange, 33
   Orange Lumpy, 32
   Orange Sieve, 35
   Peach, 32
   Pink and Red, 33
   Red, 33
   Red Sieve, 35
   Star, 35
   White Veined, 33
   Yellow, 33
Fire Sponge, 37
Gray Amphora, 49
Green Finger Sponge, 41
Icing Sponge, Orange, 35
   White, 35
Loggerhead Sponge, 55
Lumpy Overgrowing Sponge, 34
Melted Sponge, 33
Netted Orange Sponge, 32
Orange Branching Sponge, 42
Pernucleata Sponge, 45

Pink Encrusting Tube Sponge, 37
Red Branching Sponge, 42
Red Encrusting Tube Sponge, 37
Red Stalagmite Sponge, 43
Rope Sponge, Erect, 41
   Horned, 40
   Lavender, 41
   Reticulated, 43
   Rounded, 41
   Row Pore, 41
   Scattered Pore, 40
   Thin, 41
   Walper's, 42
Stinker Sponge, 45
Stove Pipe Sponge, 50
Striated Sponge, 39
String Sponge, Encrusting, 43
   Yellow, 43
Touch-Me-Not Sponge, 55
Tube Sponge, Branching, 48
   Brown, 49
   Brown Clustered, 49
   Flattened, 51
   Ivory, 49
   Miniature, 49
   Pitted, 51
   Red, 51
   Rough, 53
   Yellow, 51
Vase Sponge, Azure, 46
   Branching, 47
   Pink, 47
   Rigid, 47
   Strawberry, 47
Viscous Sponge, 37

## CORALS:

Artichoke Coral, 76
Atlantic Mushroom Coral, 76
Black Coral, Bushy, 78
   Feather, 79
   Gray Sea Fan, 79
   Hairnet, 79
   Orange Seafan, 79
   Scraggly, 79
Blue Crust Coral, 71
Brain Coral, Boulder, 65
   Grooved, 65
   Knobby, 65

# COMMON NAME INDEX

Brain Coral, Symmetrical, 65
Cactus Coral, Knobby, 73
    Lowridge, 72
    Ridged, 73
    Rough, 72
    Sinuous, 73
Corky Sea Fingers, 81
Cup Coral, Baroque Cave, 76
    Button, 76
    Lesser Speckled, 76
    Orange, 76
    Orange Solitary, 76
    Speckled, 76
    Two Tone, 76
Diffuse Ivory Tree Coral, 69
Elkhorn Coral, 61
Encrusting Gorgonian, 81
Finger Coral, Branched, 59
    Club Tipped, 59
    Eight Ray, 59
    Thin, 59
Fire Coral, Blade, 61
    Box, 61
    Branching, 61
Flower Coral, Elongated, 67
    Smooth, 67
    Spiny, 67
Fragile Saucer Coral, 75
Fused Stahorn Coral, 61
Golden Sea Spray, 83
Golfball Coral, 65
Honeycomb Plate Coral, 75
Lettuce Coral, 62
    Encrusting, 63
    Keeled, 63
    Lowrelief, 63
    Purple, 63
    Scaled, 63
    Sunray, 63
    Thin Leaf, 62
Maze Coral, 65, 73
Mustard Hill Coral, 67
Pillar Coral, 58
Red Polyp Octocoral, 81
Rose Coral, 73
    Brazilian, 65
    Butterprint, 73
Rose Lace Coral, 59
Scroll Coral, 75
Sea Fan, Common, 82

Sea Fan, Deepwater, 83
    Orange Deepwater, 83
    Spiny, 83
    Venus, 82
    Wide Mesh, 83
Sea Plume, 89
    Bipinnate, 89
    Rough, 87
    Slimy, 87
Sea Rod, Bent, 87
    Black, 84
    Colorful, 84
    Delicate Spiny, 86
    Doughnut, 85
    Giant Slit Pore, 87
    Knobby, 85
    Orange Spiny, 87
    Porous, 85
    Shelf Knob, 86
    Slit-Pore, 87
Sea Whip, Angular, 89
    Bushy, 88
    Devils, 88
    Grooved Blade, 88
    Long, 89
    Yellow, 89
Sheet Coral, Grahams, 75
    Lamarcks, 75
Staghorn Coral, 61
Star Coral, Blushing, 69
    Boulder, 70
    Elliptical, 71
    Encrusting, 71
    Great, 68
    Lobed, 70
    Mountainous, 70
    Rough, 69
    Smooth, 71
    Ten Ray, 69
Starlet Coral, Lesser, 69
    Massive, 69
Swollen Knob Candelabrum, 85
Telesto, Rigid Red, 81
    White, 81
Wire Coral, 79
Yellow Pencil Coral, 59

# COMMON NAME INDEX

## INVERTEBRATES:

Amber Penshell, 157
Anemone, Beaded, 105
    Banded Tube-Dwelling, 106
    Berried, 105
    Branching, 109
    Club-Tipped, 109
    Corkscrew, 107
    Giant, 104
    Hidden, 105
    Hitchhiking, 109
    Knobby, 107
    Lavender Tube Dwelling, 106
    Lightbulb, 109
    Pale Clumping, 105
    Red Warty, 107
    Sponge, 105
    Sun, 107
    Sunburst, 109
    Transparent Tube-Dwelling, 106
    Turtle Grass, 107
    Wideband Tube-Dwelling, 107
Atlantic Tritons Trumpet, 167
Atlantic Partridge Tun, 165
Barnacles, Black Coral, 154
    Gooseneck, 154
    Sessile, 154
Basket Star, Giant, 124
    Sea Rod, 125
Box Crab, Flame, 197
    Nodose, 197
    Ocellated, 197
    Rough, 197
Brittle Star, Angular, 122
    Circle-Marked, 122
    Harlequin, 121
    Lace Coral, 125
    Ruby, 121
    Slimy, 123
    Sponge, 120
    Spotted, 122
    Blunt-Spined, 121
Bryozoan, Bleeding Teeth, 118
    Brown Fan, 119
    Purple Reef Fan, 119
    Seaweed, 119
    Tan Fan, 119
    Tubular Horn, 118
    White Fan, 119
    White Tangled, 119
Buttercup Lucine, 159
Caribbean Vase, 165
Chestnut Latirus, 161
Chocolate Lined Topsnail, 162
Chiton, Eastern Beaded, 155
    Eastern Orange, 155
    Fuzzy, 155
    Ornate, 155
    Slender, 155
    Squamose, 155
Clinging Crab, Banded, 191
    Channel, 190
    Green, 191
    Hairy, 191
    Nodose, 191
    Red Ridged, 191
Colorful Moon Snail, 165
Comb Jelly, Flattened Helmet, 95
    Sea Gooseberry
    Sea Walnut, 95
    Slender, 95
    Spotwing, 95
    Venus Sea Girdle, 97
    Warty, 95
    Winged, 95
Conch, Cameo Helmet, 169
    Flame Helmet, 169
    Hawkwing, 169
    Milk, 168
    Queen, 169
    West Indian Chank, 169
Cone, Cardinal, 164
    Kulkulcan, 164
    Mouse, 165
Corallimorph, Florida, 111
    Forked Tentacle, 111
    Orange Ball, 111
    Parachute, 111
    Umbrella, 111
    Warty, 110
Cowrie, Atlantic Deer, 167
    Atlantic Gray, 167
    Measled, 167
Crab, Batwing Coral, 192
    Cryptic Teardrop, 187
    Curved Nose Neck, 187
    Furcate Spider, 187
    Gall, 194
    Gaudy Clown, 193
    Hairy Coral, 194

# COMMON NAME INDEX

Crab, Lesser Sponge, 196
    Mottled Shore, 193
    Neck, 186
    Nimble Spray, 193
    Nodose Rubble, 197
    Plumed Hairy, 197
    Red Eye Sponge, 196
    Southern Teardrop, 187
    Speck-Claw Decorator, 187
    Spongy Decorator, 187
    Spotted Porcelain, 196
    Thorny Mud, 194
    Yellowline Arrow, 193
Crinoid, Beaded, 125
    Black and White, 125
    Golden, 125
    Swimming, 125
Doris, Antillean, 147
    Black-Lined, 147
    Brown, 147
    Ilo, 147
    Leather-Backed, 147
    Slimy, 147
Elysia, Ornate, 143
    Painted, 143
    Striped, 143
Fanworm, Blushing Star Coral, 139
    Brown, 139
    Yellow, 139
Feather Duster, Ghost, 141
    Magnificent, 141
    Ruffled, 141
    Shy, 141
    Social, 140
    Split Crown, 141
    Variegated, 141
Fileclam, Antillean, 159
    Rough, 159
    Spiny, 159
Filose Turban, 162
Flamingo Tongue, 160
Flatworm, Bolool, 153
    Leopard, 153
    Rawlinsons, 153
    Splendid, 152
    Stained, 152
Giant Atlantic Pyram, 163
Hermit Crab, Blue Legged, 189
    Blue-Eye, 189
    Giant, 188

Hermit Crab, Orange Claw, 189
    Red Banded, 189
    Red Reef, 189
    Red Stripe, 188
    Stareye, 188
    White Speckled, 189
Horseshoe Worm, Star, 139
    Red Spotted, 139
Hydroid, Branching, 117
    Christmas Tree, 116
    Feather, 117
    Feather Bush, 117
    Solitary Gorgonian, 116
    Solitary Sponge, 116
    Thread, 117
    Unbranched, 117
    White Stinger, 117
Ivory Cerith, 163
Jelly, Agua Viva, 92
    Cannonball, 94
    Clinging, 93
    Club Hydromedusa, 93
    Jelly Hydromedusa, 93
    Mangrove Upsidedown, 93
    Marble, 94
    Moon, 94
    Seawasp, 97
    Thimble, 93
    Upsidedown, 93
    Warty, 96
    Warty Seawasp, 97
Lip Triton, 165
Lobster, Burrowing, 185
    Caribbean Spiny, 199
    Common Squat, 185
    Copper, 199
    Flaming Reef, 199
    Red-Banded, 198
    Sculptured Slipper, 199
    Spanish, 199
    Spotted Spiny, 199
Mantis Shrimp, Dark, 182
    Ciliated False Squilla, 183
    Scaly-Tailed, 183
    Swollen Claw, 183
Margin Snail, 161
Miter, Barbados, 163
    Beautiful, 163
    Harlequin, 163
Murex Snail, 163

# COMMON NAME INDEX

## INVERTEBRATES:

Nudibranch, Black-Spotted, 148
   Creutzberg's Spurilla, 145
   Crisscross Tritonia, 149
   Hamner's Tritonia, 149
   Long Horn, 145
   Lynx, 145
   Purple Ring, 145
   Sargassum, 150
   Spanish Dancer, 150
   Tasseled, 144
   Tufted, 148
   White Patch Aeolid, 145
   White Speckled, 145
Octopus, Atlantic Pygmy, 171
   Caribbean Reef, 171
   Caribbean Two-Spot, 171
   Common, 171
   Long Arm, 171
   White Spotted, 171
Oyster, Atlantic Thorny, 156
   Atlantic Wing, 157
   Flat Tree, 157
   Frond, 157
   Lister Purse, 157
   Mangrove, 157
Pea Crab, Heart Urchin, 193
   Sand Dollar, 193
Reticulate Cowrie-Helmet, 167
Sand Dollar, 128
   Six Keyhole, 129
Scallop, Knobby, 158
   Ornate, 158
Sea Biscuit, Inflated, 129
   Long-Spined, 129
Sea Cucumber, Beaded, 131
   Conical, 131
   Donkey Dung, 131
   Five-Toothed, 131
   Florida, 133
   Furry, 133
   Grub, 133
   Slender, 133
   Three-Rowed, 132
   Tiger Tail, 131
Sea Goddess, Gold Crowned, 149
   Purple Crowned, 149
   Purple Spotted, 149
   Red Tipped, 149
Sea Hare, Blue Ring, 151
Sea Hare, Ragged, 151
   Ramosa, 151
   Small, 151
   Spotted, 151
   Walking, 151
Sea Slug, Berolina, 153
   Black Aglaja, 153
   Leech Headshield, 153
   Lettuce, 143
   Reticulated, 143
   Sacoglossan, 143
Sea Spider, Caribbean, 179
   Slender, 179
Sea Star, Blunt-Armed, 123
   Comet, 123
   Common Comet, 123
   Cushion, 123
Shrimp, Arrow, 180
   Banded Coral, 175
   Black Coral, 176
   Brown Featherstar, 177
   Bumble Bee, 180
   Circled Squat, 180
   Crossbanded Grass, 175
   Florida Pistol, 184
   Golden Coral, 175
   Gorgonian, 177
   Hidden Cleaner, 180
   Long-Legged, 180
   Longtail Grass, 177
   Mysid, 185
   Orange Featherstar, 177
   Pederson Cleaner, 174
   Peppermint, 180
   Possum, 185
   Red Night, 180
   Sargassum, 177
   Scarlet-Striped Cleaner, 175
   Sea Plume, 178
   Skeleton, 179
   Slimy Sea Plume, 178
   Spotted Cleaner, 175
   Squat Anemone, 179
   Squat Urchin, 176
   Sun Anemone, 179
   Swimming Crinoid, 177
   Two Claw, 184
   Velvet, 185
   White-Footed, 176
   Wire Coral, 178

# COMMON NAME INDEX

Sidegill Slug, Atlantic, 146
   Cross's, 146
   Warty, 146
Simnia, Black, 161
   Common West Indian, 161
Siphinophore, Floating, 97
   Portuguese Man-of-War, 97
   Paired Bell, 97
   Red Spotted, 96
Smooth Scotch Bonnet, 166
Snapping Shrimp, Dark, 184
   Large Claw, 182
   Orangetail, 182
   Red, 183
Soldierfish Isopod, 185
Spotted Cyphoma, 161
Squid, Caribbean Reef, 173
   Diamond Back, 173
   Grass, 173
Starsnail, Longspine, 162
   West Indian, 162
Sunrise Telluride, 159
Swimming Crab, Black Point, 195
   Blotched, 195
   Blue, 195
   Ocellate, 195
   Sargassum, 195
Triton Snail, 169
True Tulip, 165
Tunicate, Azure Overgrowing, 103
   Black Condominium, 100
   Black Overgrowing, 101
   Bulb, 99
   Encrusting Social, 103
   Flat, 101
   Geometric Encrusting, 101
   Giant, 99
   Globular Encrusting, 103
   Green Tube, 99
   Mottled Encrusting, 103
   Overgrowing, 103
   Overgrowing Mat, 103
   Painted, 99
   Pelagic, 102
   Reef, 99
   Row Encrusting, 101
   Strawberry, 100
   White Condominium, 100
   White Speck, 101
   Yellow Bulb, 99

Urchin, Jewel, 128
   Long-Spined, 127
   Magnificent, 127
   Red Heart, 129
   Reef, 127
   Rock Boring, 128
   Slate Pencil, 127
   Variegated, 129
   West Indian Sea Egg, 129
Worm, Baseodiscus, 136
   Bearded Fireworm, 134
   Bloodworm, 137
   Capitellidae, 137
   Christmas Tree, 138
   Medusa, 135
   Nemertine, 136
   Polycheate, 135
   Scaleworm, 135
   Sea Frost, 136
   Southern Lugworm, 137
   Spaghetti, 137
   Spiny Christmas Tree, 137
   Sponge, 137
   The Thing, 135
Worm Snail, 161
Zoanthid, Brown, 113
   Brown Sponge, 115
   Golden, 113
   Hydroid, 113
   Maroon Sponge, 115
   Mat, 112
   Snake Polyp, 114
   Solitary, 115
   Sponge, 115
   Sun, 113
   White Encrusting, 115
   Yellow Sponge, 115

# COMMON NAME INDEX

## FISHES:

African Pompano, 312
Angelfish, French, 255
    Gray, 253
    Queen, 253
Atlantic Flashlight Fish, 230
Atlantic Spadefish, 312
Atlantic Thread Herring, 307
Balao, 307
Balloonfish, 261
Bass, Bantam, 287
    Chalk, 289
    Harlequin, 289
    Lantern, 289
    Orangeback, 288
    Snow, 288
Basslet, Blackcap, 286
    Candy, 287
    Cave, 287
    Fairy, 286
    Peppermint, 287
    Threeline, 287
    Toothless, 287
    Yellowcheek, 286
Bearded Toadfish, 230
Bermuda Chub, 304
Bigeye, 221
Black Durgon, 257
Blenny, Arrow, 209
    Blackcheek, 208
    Diamond, 211
    Downy, 207
    Dwarf, 209
    Filament, 214
    Flagfin, 210
    Goatee, 213
    Goldline, 210
    Hairy, 207
    Marbled, 209
    Oyster, 207
    Palehead, 207
    Quillfin, 206
    Redlip, 208
    Ribbon, 213
    Ringed, 209
    Rosy, 213
    Roughhead, 215
    Saddled, 213
    Sailfin, 212
    Sea Fan, 215

Blenny, Secretary, 214
    Spinyhead, 215
Blue Tang, 248
Bluespotted Cornetfish, 307
Boga, 307
Bonefish, 227
Burrfish, Bridled, 261
    Web, 260
Butterflyfish, Banded, 250
    Foureye, 251
Butterflyfish, Longsnout, 251
    Reef, 251
    Spotfin, 251
Cardinalfish, Barred, 219
    Belted, 218
    Bridle, 218
    Broadsaddle, 219
    Dusky, 219
    Flamefish, 219
    Mimic, 219
    Roughlip, 219
    Whitestar, 218
Cero, 309
Cherubfish, 255
Chromis, Blue, 245
    Brown, 245
Common Snook, 227
Coney, 290
Cottonwick, 271
Cowfish, Honeycomb, 264
    Scrawled, 265
Creolefish, 291
Cusk Eel, 233
Damselfish, Beaugregory, 243
    Bicolor, 247
    Cocoa, 246
    Dusky, 245
    Longfin, 245
    Threespot, 243
    Yellowtail, 244
Doctorfish, 249
Dolphinfish, 309
Dragonet, Lancer, 231
    Spotted, 231
Dwarf Sand Perch, 233
Eel, Bandtooth Conger, 319
    Blackspotted, 317
    Brown Garden, 319
    Goldspotted, 317
    Manytooth Conger, 319

# COMMON NAME INDEX

Eel, Sharptail, 317
Filefish, Fringed, 259
   Orange Spotted, 259
   Pygmy, 259
   Rough, 257
   Scrawled, 259
   Slender, 257
   Unicorn, 259
   White Spotted, 258
Flounder, Channel, 237
   Eyed, 237
   Lined Sole, 237
   Maculated, 237
   Peacock, 236
   Spiny, 237
   Spotfin, 237
Flying Gunard, 227
Goatfish, Spotted, 233
   Yellow, 233
Goby, Barfin, 205
   Bridled, 203
   Caribbean Neon, 201
   Colin's Cleaning, 201
   Colon, 203
   Diphasic, 205
   Dwarf, 205
   Frillfin, 205
   Goldspot, 203
   Leopard, 202
   Linesnout, 201
   Masked/Glass, 201
   Orangesided, 204
   Orangespotted, 205
   Pallid, 201
   Peppermint, 203
   Rusty, 202
   Sand Canyon, 203
   Spotfin, 203
   Spotlight, 201
   Tusked, 205
   Wall, 202
Graysby, 289
Great Barracuda, 308
Greater Soapfish, 288
Grouper, Black, 297
   Goliath, 298
   Nassau, 298
   Tiger, 299
   Yellowfin, 299
   Yellowmouth, 297

Grunt, Bluestriped, 269
   Caesar, 270
   French, 269
   Small Mouth, 269
   Spanish, 270
   White, 269
Hamlet, Barred, 293
   Black, 293
   Butter, 293
   Golden, 293
   Indigo, 293
   Masked, 295
   Shy, 293
   Tan, 295
   Yellowbelly, 295
   Yellowtail, 293
Highhat, 225
Hind, Red, 291
   Rock, 291
Hogfish, 266
   Spanish, 267
   Spotfin, 267
Houndfish, 307
Hovering Dartfish, 204
Jack, Almaco, 313
   Bar, 311
   Cottonmouth, 311
   Crevalle, 313
   Greater Amberjack, 313
   Horse-Eye, 313
   Leatherjack, 311
   Yellow, 311
Jackknife Fish, 225
Jawfish, Banded, 235
   Dusky, 235
   Yellow, 235
   Yellowhead, 234
Keeltail Needlefish, 307
King Mackerel, 309
Lionfish, 223
Lizardfish, Bluestriped, 233
   Red, 233
   Sand Diver, 232
Longlure Frogfish, 226
Margate, Black, 271
   White, 271
Mojarra, Flagfin, 305
   Mottled, 305
   Slender, 305
   Yellowfin, 305

# COMMON NAME INDEX

## FISHES:

Moray, Chain, 317
    Chestnut, 319
    Goldentail, 317
    Green, 316
    Purplemouth, 319
    Spotted, 317
    Viper, 318
Night Sergeant, 243
Ocean Surgeonfish, 249
Parrotfish, Blue, 273
    Bluelip, 279
    Bucktooth, 279
    Greenblotch, 277
    Midnight, 278
    Princess, 275
    Queen, 277
    Rainbow, 278
    Redband, 273
    Redtail, 277
    Stoplight, 276
    Striped, 275
    Yellowtail, 279
Permit, 310
Pikeblenny, Bluethroat, 211
    Yellowface, 211
Pipefish, Banded, 239
    Caribbean, 241
    Diamond, 241
    Harlequin, 241
    Sargassum, 241
    Shortfin, 239
    Whitenose, 241
Pipehorse, 240
Porcupinefish, 261
Porgy, Jolthead, 304
    Saucer Eye, 304
Porkfish, 271
Puddingwife, 284
Puffer, Bandtail, 261
    Checkered, 261
    Sharpnose, 261
Purple Reef Fish, 247
Ray, Manta, 321
    Spotted Eagle, 321
Razorfish, Green, 216
    Pearly, 217
    Rosy, 217
Red Clingfish, 231
Red Spotted Hawkfish, 233

Reef-Cave Brotula, 230
Reef Croaker, 224
Rock Beauty, 255
Runner, Blue, 311
    Rainbow, 311
Sand Tilefish, 235
Sargassumfish, 227
Scad, Bigeye, 313
    Mackerel, 313
Schoolmaster, 302
Scorpionfish, Mushroom, 229
    Plumed, 229
    Reef, 229
    Spotted, 229
Seahorse, Lined, 239
    Longsnout, 238
Sergeant Major, 242
Shark, Nurse, 322
    Reef, 323
    Scalloped Hammerhead, 323
    Whale, 323
Sharksucker, 315
    Whitefin, 315
Shortnose Batfish, 229
Silversides, 222
Slippery Dick, 285
Snapper, Black, 302
    Blackfin, 303
    Cubera, 301
    Dog, 300
    Glasseye, 301
    Gray, 301
    Lane, 303
    Mahogany, 301
    Mutton, 300
    Yellowtail, 303
Soldierfish, Blackbar, 221
    Cardinal, 221
Southern Sennet, 309
Spotted Drum, 224
Squirrelfish, 220
    Deepwater, 221
    Dusky, 220
    Longjaw, 221
    Longspine, 220
    Reef, 221
Stingray, Caribbean Whiptail, 321
    Roughtail, 321
    Southern, 321
    Yellow, 321

# COMMON NAME INDEX

Sweeper, Glassy, 305
    Shortfin, 305
Sunshine Fish, 247
Tarpon, 309
Tobaccofish, 289
Tomtate, 271
Tonguefish, 231
Triggerfish, Ocean, 257
    Queen, 256
    Sargassum, 258
Triplefin, Blackedge, 211
    Lofty, 210
    Redeye, 211
    Roughhead, 211
Trumpetfish, 306
Trunkfish, Buffalo, 265
    Smooth, 262
    Spotted, 263
Wahoo, 309
Wrasse, Blackear, 283
    Bluehead, 280
    Clown, 281
    Creole, 285
    Rainbow, 281
    Yellowcheek, 283
    Yellowhead, 282

## TURTLES:

Green Sea Turtle, 325
Hawksbill Turtle, 325
Loggerhead Turtle, 325

## MAMMALS:

Bottlenose Dolphin, 327
Manatee, 327
Orca, 327
Rough Toothed Dolphin, 327
Short Finned Pilot Whale, 327
Spinner Dolphin, 327

## OTHER SPECIES: